Middle School 2-2

기말고사 완벽대비

KB084525

적중 100

영어 기출 문제집

중 **2**

미래 | 최연희

Best Collection

구성과 특징

교과서의 주요 학습 내용을 중심으로 학습 영역별 특성에 맞춰 단계별로 다양한 학습 기회를 제공하여 단원별 학습능력 평가는 물론 중간 및 기말고사 시험 등에 완벽하게 대비할 수 있도록 내용을 구성

Words & Expressions

Step1 Key Words 단원별 핵심 단어 설명 및 풀이
Key Expression 단원별 핵심 숙어 및 관용어 설명
Word Power 반대 또는 비슷한 뜻 단어 배우기
English Dictionary 영어로 배우는 영어 단어

Step2 실력평가 단원별 수시평가 대비 주관식, 객관식 문제풀이

Step3 서술형 대비 학업성취도 및 수행능력평가 대비 서술형 문제풀이

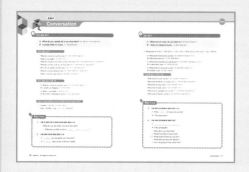

Conversation

Step1 핵심 의사소통 의사소통에 필요한 주요 표현 방법 요약
핵심 Check 기본적인 표현 방법 및 활용능력 확인

Step2 대화문 익히기 상황에 따른 대화문 활용 및 연습

Step3 기본평가 시험대비 기초 학습 능력 평가

Step4 실력평가 단원별 수시평가 대비 주관식, 객관식 문제풀이

Step5 서술형 대비 학업성취도 및 수행능력평가 대비 서술형 문제풀이

Grammar

Step1 주요 문법 단원별 주요 문법 사항과 예문을 알기 쉽게 설명
핵심 Check 기본 문법사항에 대한 이해 여부 확인

Step2 기본평가 시험대비 기초 학습 능력 평가

Step3 실력평가 단원별 수시평가 대비 주관식, 객관식 문제풀이

Step4 서술형 대비 학업성취도 및 수행능력평가 대비 서술형 문제풀이

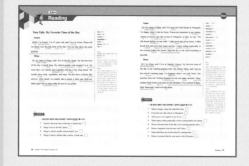

Reading

Step1 구문 분석 단원별로 제시된 문장에 대한 구문별 분석과 내용 설명
확인문제 문장에 대한 기본적인 이해와 인지능력 확인

Step2 확인학습A 빈칸 채우기를 통한 문장 완성 능력 확인

Step3 확인학습B 제시된 우리말을 영어로 완성하여 작문 능력 키우기

Step4 실력평가 단원별 수시평가 대비 주관식, 객관식 문제풀이

Step5 서술형 대비 학업성취도 및 수행능력평가 대비 서술형 문제풀이
교과서 구석구석 교과서에 나오는 기타 문장까지 완벽 학습

Composition

|영역별 핵심문제|
단어 및 어휘, 대화문, 문법, 독해 등 각 영역별 기출문제의 출제 유형을 분석하여 실전에 대비하고 연습할 수 있도록 문제를 배열

|서술형 실전 및 창의사고력 문제|
학교 시험에서 점차 늘어나는 서술형 시험에 집중 대비하고 고득점을 취득하는데 만전을 기하기 위한 학습 코너

|단원별 예상문제|
기출문제를 분석한 후 새로운 시험 출제 경향을 더하여 새롭게 출제될 수 있는 문제를 포함하여 시험에 완벽하게 대비할 수 있도록 준비

|단원별 모의고사|
영역별, 단계별 학습을 모두 마친 후 실전 연습을 위한 모의고사

on the textbook .... 교과서 파헤치기

- 단어Test1~2 영어 단어 우리말 쓰기와 우리말을 영어 단어로 쓰기
- 대화문Test1~2 대화문 빈칸 완성 및 전체 대화문 쓰기
- 본문Test1~5 빈칸 완성, 우리말 쓰기, 문장 배열연습, 영어 작문하기 복습 등 단계별 반복 학습을 통해 교과서 지문에 대한 완벽한 습득
- 구석구석지문Test1~2 지문 빈칸 완성 및 전문 영어로 쓰기

Contents

Lesson 7

Think Big, Start Small

🎤 의사소통 기능

- 알고 있음 표현하기
  I've heard our music teacher is getting married.

- 상기시켜 주기
  A: I'm going to go hiking.
  B: Don't forget to take a bottle of water.

🎤 언어 형식

- 5형식 동사+목적어+형용사
  Add some bleach to **keep the water clear**.

- 사역동사
  Let me just **put** your phone in a glass.

Words & Expressions

Key Words

- **actress** [ǽktris] 명 여배우
- **amazing** [əméiziŋ] 형 놀라운
- **amusement park** 놀이공원
- **bend(–bent–bent)** [bend] 동 구부리다, 휘다
- **blackout** [blǽkaut] 명 대규모 정전 사태
- **bleach** [bli:tʃ] 명 표백제
- **bottle** [bɑ́tl] 명 병
- **ceiling** [sí:liŋ] 명 천장
- **charity** [tʃǽrəti] 명 자선단체
- **chief** [tʃi:f] 형 주요한 명 우두머리, 부장
- **darkness** [dɑ́:rknis] 명 어둠, 암흑
- **difficult** [dífikʌlt] 형 어려운
- **dim sum** 딤섬(중국식 작은 만두 요리)
- **electricity** [ilektrísəti] 명 전기
- **enough** [inʌ́f] 형 충분한
- **exciting** [iksáitiŋ] 형 흥미로운
- **favorite** [féivərit] 형 가장 좋아하는
- **foundation** [faundéiʃən] 명 재단
- **impossible** [impɑ́səbl] 형 불가능한
- **install** [instɔ́:l] 동 설치하다
- **interesting** [íntərəstiŋ] 형 흥미로운
- **invent** [invént] 동 발명하다
- **last** [læst] 동 지속되다
- **leave(–left–left)** [li:v] 동 떠나다

- **leftover** [léftouvər] 명 남은 음식
- **less** [les] 형 더 적은
- **magic** [mǽdʒik] 형 마법의, 신기한
- **meal** [mi:l] 명 식사
- **packed** [pækt] 형 꽉 들어찬
- **popular** [pɑ́pjulər] 형 인기 있는
- **remain** [riméin] 동 남아 있다
- **roof** [ru:f] 명 지붕
- **safe** [seif] 형 안전한
- **save** [seiv] 동 구하다
- **shake(–shook–shaken)** [ʃeik] 동 흔들다, 털다
- **shelter** [ʃéltər] 명 주거지, 쉼터
- **shout** [ʃaut] 동 외치다
- **single** [síŋgl] 형 단 하나의
- **spread(–spread–spread)** [spred] 동 퍼지다
- **surprisingly** [sərpráiziŋli] 부 놀랍게도
- **teach(–taught–taught)** [ti:tʃ] 동 가르치다
- **thing** [θiŋ] 명 (복수형으로) 상황
- **times** [taimz] 명 (반복되는 행위의) ~번
- **village** [vílidʒ] 명 마을
- **whole** [houl] 형 전체의
- **widely** [wáidli] 부 널리, 폭넓게
- **winter break** 겨울 방학
- **work** [wə:rk] 동 작동하다

Key Expressions

- **at least** 최소한, 적어도
- **because of+명사** ~ 때문에
- **be going to부정사** ~할 예정이다
- **not ~ anymore** 더 이상 ~ 않다
- **dry off** ~을 말리다
- **get married** 결혼하다
- **I can't wait to부정사** 빨리 ~하고 싶다
- **just like** ~와 꼭 마찬가지로
- **forget to부정사** ~할 것을 잊다
- **how to부정사** ~하는 방법

- **fill A with B** A를 B로 채우다
- **come up with** ~을 생각해 내다, ~을 만들어 내다
- **have to+동사원형** ~해야 한다
- **light up** ~을 환하게 밝히다
- **pay for** 지불하다
- **thanks to** ~ 덕분에
- **thousands of** 수천의
- **too+형용사+to부정사** 너무 ~해서 …할 수 없다
- **turn off** ~을 끄다
- **turn up** (소리 등을) 높이다

Word Power

※ 서로 반대되는 뜻을 가진 어휘

- □ **difficult** (어려운) ↔ **easy** (쉬운)
- □ **popular** (인기 있는) ↔ **unpopular** (인기 없는)
- □ **possible** (가능한) ↔ **impossible** (불가능한)

- □ **exciting** (흥미로운) ↔ **boring** (지루한)
- □ **safe** (안전한) ↔ **dangerous** (위험한)
- □ **whole** (전체의) ↔ **partial** (일부분의)

※ 서로 비슷한 뜻을 가진 단어

- □ **shout** : **yell** (외치다)
- □ **save** : **rescue** (구하다)
- □ **last** : **continue** (지속하다)

- □ **install** : **set up** (설치하다)
- □ **work** : **operate** (작동하다)
- □ **chief** : **main** (주요한)

English Dictionary

- □ **blackout** 정전
  → a time when there is no light or power because of an electricity failure
  전기 시스템의 고장으로 빛이나 전력이 없는 때

- □ **bleach** 표백제
  → a strong chemical used for cleaning things or removing colour from things
  물건을 청소하거나 사물에서 색을 제거하기 위해 사용되는 강한 화학물질

- □ **charity** 자선, 자선단체
  → a system of giving money, food, or help free to those who are in need because they are ill, poor, or have no home, or any organization that has the purpose of providing money or helping in this way
  병들거나 가난하거나 집이 없기 때문에 어려움에 처한 사람들에게 무료로 돈, 음식 또는 도움을 주는 시스템, 또는 이런 식으로 돈과 도움을 제공할 목적을 가지고 있는 단체

- □ **ceiling** 천장
  → the inside surface of a room that you can see when you look above you
  위쪽을 바라볼 때 볼 수 있는 방의 안쪽 표면

- □ **daytime** 낮
  → the period between the time when the sun rises and the time it goes down, or the part of the day that is neither evening nor night
  해가 뜨는 시간과 지는 시간 사이의 기간이나 저녁도 밤도 아닌 하루의 부분

- □ **electricity** 전기
  → a form of energy that can be produced in several ways and that provides power to devices that create light, heat, etc
  여러 가지 방법으로 생산될 수 있고 빛, 열 등을 만드는 장치에 동력을 제공하는 에너지의 형태

- □ **install** 설치하다
  → to put furniture, a machine, or a piece of equipment into position and make it ready to use
  가구, 기계 또는 장비를 제 위치에 놓고 사용할 준비가 되게 하다

- □ **invent** 발명하다
  → to design and/or create something that has never been made before
  이전에 만들어진 적이 없는 어떤 것을 디자인하거나 만들다

- □ **lamp** 램프, 등
  → a device for giving light, especially one that has a covering
  특히 덮개가 있는 빛을 제공하는 장치

- □ **last** 지속되다
  → to continue to exist
  계속해서 존재하다

- □ **roof** 지붕
  → the covering that forms the top of a building, vehicle, etc
  건물이나 차량의 상부를 형성하는 덮개

- □ **spread** 퍼지다
  → to cover, reach, or have an effect on a wider or increasing area
  더 넓은 또는 증가하는 영역을 덮거나, 도달하거나, 영향을 미치다

서답형

01 다음 짝지어진 두 단어의 관계가 같도록 빈칸에 알맞은 단어를 쓰시오.

> difficult : easy = partial : _____

[02~03] 다음 빈칸에 들어갈 말로 가장 적절한 것은?

02

> "I can't read a book in my room!" shouted Marco, a boy in a village in the Philippines. His house has no _____ just like all the other houses in the village.

① sunlight　　② roof
③ tradition　　④ electricity
⑤ ceiling

03

> This amazing plastic bottle is called a Moser lamp because it was _____ by Alfredo Moser.

① invited　　② saved
③ taught　　④ interested
⑤ invented

[04~05] 다음 영영풀이에 해당하는 단어를 고르시오.

04

> a device for giving light, especially one that has a covering

① lamp　　② wheel
③ ceiling　　④ roof
⑤ bottle

05

> a form of energy that can be produced in several ways and that provides power to devices that create light, heat, etc

① device　　② daytime
③ electricity　　④ bleach
⑤ charity

06 밑줄 친 부분의 의미가 잘못된 것은?

① Bend the straw to use it easily. (굽히다)
② Strong lightning can cause a blackout.(정전)
③ Use bleach to make your clothes clean. (표백제)
④ His father is the chief of police. (주요한)
⑤ The daytime gets longer in the summer. (낮)

서답형

[07~08] 우리말 해석에 맞게 주어진 문장의 빈칸에 세 단어의 영어를 쓰시오.

07

> 이 정전들은 그가 집을 밝히는 새로운 방법을 생각해 내도록 만들었다.
> ➡ These blackouts made him _____ a new way to light his house.

08

> 병의 3분의 1은 지붕 위에 남아 있도록 한다.
> ➡ Let _____ the bottle remain above the roof.

01 영영풀이에 해당하는 단어를 〈보기〉에서 찾아 첫 번째 칸에 쓰고, 두 번째 칸에는 우리말 뜻을 쓰시오.

> ┌ 보기 ┐
> ceiling / roof / daytime / blackout / bleach

(1) _____: the period between the time when the sun rises and the time it goes down, or the part of the day that is neither evening nor night: _____

(2) _____: the inside surface of a room that you can see when you look above you: _____

(3) _____: a time when there is no light or power because of an electricity failure: _____

02 다음 주어진 우리말에 맞게 빈칸을 채우시오. (필요하면 변형하여 쓰시오.)

(1) Moser 램프는 앞으로 오랫동안 많은 사람들의 삶을 밝혀 줄 것이다.
   ➡ Moser lamps will _____ the lives of many people for many years to come. (두 단어로 쓰시오)

(2) 햇빛이 병 속의 물에 의해 굴절되어 방에 퍼진다.
   ➡ Sunlight is _____ by the water in the bottle and _____ around the room.

03 우리말 해석을 읽고, 주어진 철자를 알맞은 순서로 배열하여 빈칸을 채우시오.

(1) 남은 음식을 집에 가져가시겠어요?
   ➡ Do you want to take the _____ home? (e, o, t, e, l, f, r, v)

(2) 필리핀에서 Moser 램프는 My Shelter 재단에 의해 널리 사용된다.
   ➡ In the Philippines, Moser lamps are widely used by the My Shelter _____. (t, d, o, a, f, i, u, n, n, o)

04 다음 빈칸에 알맞은 단어를 〈보기〉에서 골라 쓰시오. (형태 변화 가능)

> ┌ 보기 ┐
> wide / chief / bleach / whole

(1) She played the _____ scientist in the movie *Jupiter*.

(2) Add some _____ to keep the water clear.

(3) Today, gas is _____ used for cooking.

05 영어 설명을 읽고, 문장의 빈칸에 들어갈 알맞은 단어를 쓰시오.

> an empty space in an object, usually with an opening to the object's surface, or an opening that goes completely through an object

(1) Make a _____ in the roof, and push the bottle into the _____.

> with special powers or happening in an unusual or unexpected way, or easily or quickly

(2) Surprisingly, it is very easy to make this _____ lamp.

Conversation

1 알고 있음 표현하기

> • I've heard our music teacher is getting married. 우리 음악 선생님께서 결혼하신다고 들었어.

■ 어떤 사실을 들어서 알고 있음을 말할 때 'I've heard (that) ~.' 표현을 쓴다.

알고 있는지 묻기

• Do you know about ~? / You know ~, don't you?
"~에 관해 알고 있니?" / "너는 ~을 알고 있지, 그렇지 않니?"

• Are you aware of ~? / Have you heard ~? "~을 알고 있니? / ~을 들었니?"

알고 있음 표현하기

• I've heard that ~. / I heard ~. / I know ~. "나는 ~라고 들었어 / 나는 알고 있어"

• A: Are you aware of today's lunch menu? 오늘의 점심 메뉴가 뭔지 알고 있니?
B: I've heard that today's lunch menu is Kimchi fried rice.
나는 오늘 점심이 김치 볶음밥이라고 들었어.

• I heard you didn't come to school yesterday. 나는 네가 어제 학교에 오지 않았다고 들었어.

핵심 Check

1. 다음 대화의 빈칸에 들어갈 알맞은 것은?

A: Do you know why Ted was absent from school yesterday?

B: _____

① I know he is very healthy.
② I've heard he was sick.
③ He likes to study in his room.
④ I wanted to go to school.
⑤ He feels good today.

2 상기시켜 주기

A I'm going to go hiking. 나는 하이킹을 하러 갈 거야.

B Don't forget to take a bottle of water. 물 한 병 챙기는 것을 잊지 마.

■ '~하는 것을 잊지 마'라는 뜻으로 상대방에게 해야 할 일을 상기시켜 줄 때 'Don't forget to부정사'나 'Remember to부정사'를 사용한다.

- A: Are you ready for your trip to Jejudo? 너는 제주도로 여행 갈 준비되었니?

  B: Not yet. What should I bring? 아직. 내가 무엇을 가져가야만 하니?

  A: Don't forget to bring a camera and a map of Jejudo.

    = Remember to bring a camera and a map of Jejudo.
    카메라와 제주도 지도를 가져가야 할 것을 잊지 마[기억해라].

- A: Don't forget to be quiet in the library. 도서관에서 조용히 하는 것 잊지 마.

  B: I won't forget. 잊지 않을게요.

- A: What will you take with you to a deserted island? 너는 무인도에 무엇을 가져갈 것이니?

  B: I will take a pen and some paper to write a diary. 나는 일기를 쓸 펜과 종이를 가져갈 거야.

  A: Don't forget to take some matches. 성냥을 가져가야 할 것도 잊지 마.

핵심 Check

2. 다음 빈칸에 들어갈 말로 알맞은 것은?

    A: I'm going bike riding.

    B: Have fun and _____ .

    A: Okay, I won't.

    ① it's fine today
    ② I think we should not make fun of others
    ③ don't forget to wear a helmet
    ④ I'm interested in baseball
    ⑤ I'm going to go on a trip to Jejudo

Listen & Speak 1-A-1

G: ❶Can you turn up the volume on your phone? I like this song.

B: ❷I can't turn it up anymore. It's the highest volume.

G: ❸Let me just put your phone in a glass. ❹I've heard a glass works like a speaker.

B: ❺What an interesting idea! Let's try it now.

G: 네 휴대폰 소리를 키워줄 수 있겠니? 이 노래가 좋아.
B: 소리를 더는 키울 수 없어. 음량이 이미 가장 높은데.
G: 그냥 네 휴대폰을 유리잔 안에 넣게 해 줘. 유리잔이 스피커처럼 쓰인다고 들었어.
B: 재미있는 생각이야! 지금 해 보자.

❶ 상대방에게 요청할 때 사용하는 표현으로 '~해 줄 수 있니?'의 의미다.
❷ 'turn up'은 '볼륨을 높이다'는 의미로 목적어가 대명사(it)일 때 '동사+대명사+부사'의 어순을 취한다. not ~ anymore는 '더 이상 ~ 않다'는 의미다.
❸ 'Let+목적어+동사원형'은 '…가 ~하게 하다'는 의미다.
❹ 어떤 사실을 들어서 알고 있음을 말할 때 'I've heard (that) ~.' 표현을 쓴다. 'work'는 '작동하다'는 의미다.
❺ 감탄문으로 'What+a(n)+형용사+명사+주어+동사 ~!'의 어순을 취한다.

Check(√) True or False

(1) G likes the song in B's phone.　　　　　　　　T ☐ F ☐

(2) G suggests that B should use a speaker to listen to the song.　　T ☐ F ☐

Listen & Speak 1-A-2

B: ❶I've heard that a movie star is coming to our school.

G: That's right. She's my favorite actress.

B: Oh, who is she?

G: Miranda Kim. She played the chief scientist in the movie *Jupiter*.

B: Wow, ❷I can't wait to see her!

B: 우리 학교에 영화 배우가 온다고 들었어.
G: 맞아. 내가 가장 좋아하는 여배우야.
B: 오, 누군데?
G: Miranda Kim이야. 영화 《주피터》에서 책임 과학자를 연기했어.
B: 우와, 빨리 만나보고 싶은데!

❶ 어떤 사실을 들어서 알고 있음을 말할 때 사용하는 표현으로 '~을 들었다'는 뜻이다. 'is coming'은 현재진행형으로 미래의 일을 나타낸다.
❷ 'I can't wait to부정사'는 '빨리 ~하고 싶어'라는 뜻이다.

Check(√) True or False

(3) B knows a movie star is coming to his school.　　　　T ☐ F ☐

(4) B saw the movie in which Miranda Kim played the chief scientist the actress coming to his school.
　　　　　　　　　　　　　　　　　　　　　　　　　T ☐ F ☐

Listen & Speak 2-A-1

W: Excuse me, ❶are you finished with your meal?

M: Yes, it was really good.

W: Do you want to take the leftovers home?

M: Yes, please.

W: ❷Don't forget to eat the leftovers by tomorrow.

❶ 'be finished with'는 '~을 마치다, ~을 끝내다'는 의미다.

❷ '~하는 것을 잊지 마'라는 뜻으로 상대방에게 해야 할 일을 상기시켜 줄 때 사용하는 표현이다. 이때 'forget to부정사'는 '~할 것을 잊다'는 미래의 일을 나타낸다.

Listen & Speak 2-A-2

B: ❶What's your plan for this winter break?

G: ❷I'm going to visit Hong Kong with my parents.

B: That sounds exciting. What are you going to do there?

G: I'm going to go to an amusement park. I'm also going to try all kinds of food.

B: Good. ❸Don't forget to try some dim sum.

❶ 미래의 계획을 물어볼 때 사용하는 표현이다.

❷ 'be going to부정사'는 '~할 예정이다'는 뜻으로 미래 계획을 말할 때 사용한다.

❸ '~하는 것을 잊지 마'라는 뜻으로 상대방에게 해야 할 일을 상기시켜 줄 때 사용하는 표현이다.

Communicate A

Yuri: What's wrong, Jaden?

Jaden: My science homework is too difficult.

Yuri: ❶What do you have to do?

Jaden: I need to find a way ❷to save trees.

Yuri: That's easy. ❸I've heard that we can save trees ❹by using less paper.

Jaden: Oh, I think I've heard that, too. Then, I can just ❺stop using paper cups.

Yuri: Yes! You can also use just one paper towel to dry off your hands.

Jaden: That's impossible. I need at least two or three paper towels.

Yuri: Just shake your hands before you use a paper towel. Then, one will be ❻more than enough.

Jaden: Oh, that's a good idea, Yuri! I'll try that next time.

Yuri: Good! Just ❼don't forget to shake your hands at least 10 times.

❶ 'have to부정사'는 '~해야 한다'는 의미다.

❷ 'to save'는 명사 'a way'를 꾸며주는 형용사 용법이다.

❸ 어떤 사실을 들어서 알고 있음을 말할 때 사용하는 표현으로 '~을 들었다'는 뜻이다.

❹ 'by -ing'는 '~함으로써'의 뜻이다.

❺ 'stop -ing'는 '~하는 것을 멈추다'라는 뜻이다.

❻ 'more than enough'는 '충분하고도 남을 거야'라는 뜻이다.

❼ '~하는 것을 잊지 마'라는 뜻으로 상대방에게 해야 할 일을 상기시켜 줄 때 사용하는 표현이다.

Communicate B

A: ❶I've heard that saving electricity is the best way to save the Earth.

B: I've heard that, too. What can we do to save electricity?

A: ❷Why don't we turn off the light when we're not using it?

B: That's a good idea. ❸Don't forget to turn off the light when you leave your room.

❶ 어떤 사실을 들어서 알고 있음을 말할 때 사용하는 표현으로 '~을 들었다'라는 뜻이다.

❷ '~하는 게 어때?'라는 뜻으로 상대방에게 제안할 때 사용한다.

❸ '~하는 것을 잊지 마'라는 뜻으로 상대방에게 해야 할 일을 상기시켜 줄 때 사용하는 표현이다.

Progress Check

1. B: ❶I've heard that a famous baseball player is coming to our school.

   G: That's right. He's my favorite player.

   B: Oh, who is he?

   G: I'm not going to tell you. It's a surprise!

2. B: What's your plan for this winter break?

   G: I'm going to visit Vietnam with my parents.

   B: That sounds exciting. What are you going to do there?

   G: I'm going to spend some time on the beach and eat lots of seafood.

   B: Good. ❷Don't forget to try the fruit there, too.

   G: O.K., I won't forget.

❶ 어떤 사실을 들어서 알고 있음을 말할 때 사용하는 표현이다.

❷ '~하는 것을 잊지 마'라는 뜻으로 상대방에게 해야 할 일을 상기시켜 줄 때 사용하는 표현이다.

● 다음 우리말과 일치하도록 빈칸에 알맞은 말을 쓰시오.

Listen & Speak 1-A

1. **G:** Can you _____ _____ the volume on your phone? I like this song.

   B: I can't _____ _____ _____ _____ . It's the _____ volume.

   G: _____ me just _____ your phone in a glass. _____ _____ a glass _____ _____ a speaker.

   B: _____ _____ _____ _____ ! _____ try it now.

2. **B:** _____ _____ that a movie star _____ _____ to our school.

   G: That's right. She's my _____ _____ .

   B: Oh, who is she?

   G: Miranda Kim. She _____ the _____ scientist in the movie *Jupiter*.

   B: Wow, I _____ _____ _____ see her!

1. G: 네 휴대폰 소리를 키워줄 수 있겠니? 이 노래가 좋아.
   B: 소리를 더는 키울 수 없어. 음량이 이미 가장 높은데.
   G: 그냥 네 휴대폰을 유리잔 안에 넣게 해 줘. 유리잔이 스피커처럼 쓰인다고 들었어.
   B: 재미있는 생각이야! 지금 해 보자.

2. B: 우리 학교에 영화 배우가 온다고 들었어.
   G: 맞아. 내가 가장 좋아하는 여배우야.
   B: 오, 누군데?
   G: Miranda Kim이야. 영화 《주피터》에서 책임 과학자를 연기했어.
   B: 우와, 빨리 만나보고 싶은데!

Listen & Speak 2-A

1. **W:** Excuse me, are you _____ with your meal?

   M: Yes, it was really _____ .

   W: Do you _____ _____ _____ the _____ home?

   M: Yes, please.

   W: _____ _____ _____ _____ the leftovers by tomorrow.

2. **B:** What's _____ _____ _____ this _____ _____ ?

   G: _____ _____ _____ visit Hong Kong with my parents.

   B: That sounds _____ . What are you _____ _____ there?

   G: I'm _____ _____ _____ to an _____ park. I'm also going to try _____ _____ of food.

   B: Good. _____ _____ _____ _____ some dim sum.

1. W: 실례합니다, 식사를 마치셨나요?
   M: 네, 정말 좋았어요.
   W: 남은 음식을 집에 가져가시겠어요?
   M: 네, 부탁합니다.
   W: 내일까지는 남은 음식을 다 드시는 걸 잊지 마세요.

2. B: 이번 겨울 방학에는 뭘 할 거야?
   G: 부모님과 홍콩에 갈 거야.
   B: 신나겠는걸. 거기서 뭘 할 거니?
   G: 놀이공원에 갈 거야. 그리고 온갖 음식들을 먹어 볼 거야.
   B: 좋은데. 딤섬을 먹어 보는 걸 잊지 마.

Communicate A

Yuri: What's _____, Jaden?

Jaden: My science homework is too _____.

Yuri: What do you _____ _____ do?

Jaden: I need to find a way _____ _____ trees.

Yuri: That's easy. _____ _____ _____ we can save trees _____ _____ _____ paper.

Jaden: Oh, I think _____ _____ _____, _____. Then, I can just _____ _____ paper cups.

Yuri: Yes! You can also use just one paper towel _____ _____ _____ your hands.

Jaden: That's _____. I need _____ _____ two or three paper towels.

Yuri: Just _____ your hands _____ you use a paper towel. Then, one will be _____ _____ _____.

Jaden: Oh, that's a good idea, Yuri! I'll _____ that _____ _____.

Yuri: Good! Just _____ _____ _____ _____ your hands _____ _____ 10 _____.

Communicate B

A: _____ _____ that _____ _____ is the best way _____ _____ the Earth.

B: I've _____ _____, _____. What can we do to _____ electricity?

A: Why don't we _____ _____ the light _____ we're not using it?

B: That's a good idea. _____ _____ to _____ _____ the light _____ you _____ your room.

Progress Check

1. **B:** _____ _____ _____ a famous baseball player _____ _____ to our school.

   G: That's right. He's my _____ player.

   B: Oh, who is he?

   G: I'm not going to tell you. It's a _____!

2. **B:** What's your _____ _____ this winter break?

   G: I'm going _____ _____ Vietnam with my parents.

   B: That _____ _____. What are you going to do there?

   G: I'm going to _____ some time on the _____ and eat lots of _____.

   B: Good. _____ _____ _____ _____ the fruit there, too.

   G: O.K., I _____ _____.

해석

유리: 무슨 일 있니, Jaden?
Jaden: 과학 숙제가 너무 어려워.
유리: 뭘 해야 하는데?
Jaden: 나무들을 살리는 방법을 찾아야 해.
유리: 그건 쉬워. 나는 종이를 덜 사용함으로써 나무들을 살릴 수 있다고 들었어.
Jaden: 아, 나도 들어 본 것 같아. 그럼, 종이컵 쓰는 걸 멈추면 되겠네.
유리: 맞아! 그리고 손을 말리는 데 종이 수건을 한 장만 쓸 수도 있지.
Jaden: 그건 불가능해. 나는 종이 수건이 적어도 두세 장은 필요해.
유리: 종이 수건을 쓰기 전에 손을 털어봐. 그럼, 한 장으로 충분하고도 남을 거야.
Jaden: 오, 좋은 생각이야, 유리야! 다음에 해 봐야겠어.
유리: 좋아! 손을 적어도 열 번은 털어야 한다는 걸 잊지 마.

A: 전기를 절약하는 게 지구를 살리는 데 가장 좋은 방법이라고 들었어.
B: 나도 들었어. 전기를 절약하기 위해 무엇을 할 수 있을까?
A: 사용하지 않을 때는 전기를 끄는 게 어때?
B: 좋은 생각이야. 방을 나갈 때 불 끄는 것을 잊지 마.

1. B: 유명한 야구 선수가 우리 학교로 온다고 들었어.
   G: 맞아. 그는 내가 가장 좋아하는 선수야.
   B: 오, 누군데?
   G: 말해주지 않을 거야. 놀라게 할 거야!

2. B: 이번 겨울 방학에 무슨 계획이 있니?
   G: 부모님과 함께 베트남에 갈 거야.
   B: 재미있겠다. 거기서 뭘 할 거야?
   G: 바닷가에서 시간을 좀 보내고 해산물을 많이 먹을 거야.
   B: 좋아. 거기 과일을 먹어 보는 것도 잊지 마.
   G: 알겠어, 잊지 않을게.

01 다음 대화의 빈칸에 들어갈 말로 알맞은 것은?

> B: _____
>
> G: That's right. He's my favorite player.
>
> B: Oh, who is he?
>
> G: I'm not going to tell you. It's a surprise!

① I heard you didn't come to school yesterday.

② I've heard the car was invented earlier than the bicycle.

③ I've heard that a famous baseball player is coming to our school.

④ I heard chocolate isn't good for dogs.

⑤ Ted, I've been told Mr. Brown is going back to Canada.

[02~03] 다음 대화를 읽고, 물음에 답하시오.

> W: Excuse me, (A)식사를 마치셨나요?
>
> M: Yes, it was really good.
>
> W: Do you want to take the leftovers home?
>
> M: Yes, please.
>
> W: _____ (B)

02 (A)의 우리말에 맞게 주어진 단어를 알맞은 순서로 배열하시오.

> (finished / you / with / are / your / meal / ?)

➡ _____

03 빈칸 (B)에 들어갈 말로 알맞은 것은?

① Don't remember to eat the leftovers by tomorrow.

② Don't forget eating the leftovers by tomorrow.

③ Remember eating the leftovers by tomorrow.

④ Don't forget to come home until 7.

⑤ Don't forget to eat the leftovers by tomorrow.

01 다음 중 짝지어진 대화가 어색한 것은?

① A: What's your plan for this winter break?

　B: I'm going to visit Hong Kong with my parents.

② A: What's wrong, Jaden?

　B: Don't forget to bring my science homework tomorrow.

③ A: You can also use just one paper towel to dry off your hands.

　B: That's impossible.

④ A: What can we do to save electricity?

　B: Why don't we turn off the light when we're not using it?

⑤ A: Don't forget to try the fruit there, too.

　B: O.K., I won't forget.

[02~03] 다음 대화를 읽고 물음에 답하시오.

G: _____ (A) _____ I like this song.

B: I can't turn it up anymore. It's the highest volume.

G: Let me just put your phone in a glass. _____ (B) _____

B: What an interesting idea! Let's try it now.

02 빈칸 (A)에 알맞은 말을 고르시오.

① Can I play soccer with my friends after school?

② Would you turn down the volume on your phone?

③ I think the volume of your phone is high.

④ Can you turn up the volume on your phone?

⑤ What are you interested in?

03 빈칸 (B)에 들어갈 알맞은 말은?

① Be carful to put your phone in a glass

② Do you know about my latest cell phone?

③ I've heard a glass works like a speaker.

④ I've heard you have a nice speaker.

⑤ I use a phone to take pictures.

[04~05] 다음 대화를 읽고 물음에 답하시오.

B: What's your plan for this winter break?

G: _____ (A) _____ visit Hong Kong with my parents.

B: That sounds exciting. What are you going to do there?

G: I'm going to go to an amusement park. I'm also going to try all kinds of food.

B: Good. _____ (B) _____ some dim sum.

04 빈칸 (A), (B)에 들어갈 말로 알맞은 것은?

① I'm going to – Don't remember to try

② I was going to – Don't forget trying

③ I'm going to – Don't forget trying

④ I was going to – Remember trying

⑤ I'm going to – Don't forget to try

서답형

05 다음 영영풀이에 해당하는 단어를 대화에서 찾아 쓰시오.

> a Chinese meal or snack of small dishes including different foods fried or cooked in steam

➡ _____

[06~07] 다음 대화를 읽고 물음에 답하시오.

Yuri: What's wrong, Jaden?

Jaden: My science homework is too difficult.

Yuri: What do you have to do? (①)

Jaden: I need to find a way to save trees.

Yuri: That's easy. I've heard that we can save trees by using less paper. (②)

Jaden: Oh, I think I've heard that, too. Then, I can just stop using paper cups. (③)

Yuri: Yes! You can also use just one paper towel to dry off your hands.

Jaden: That's impossible. (④)

Yuri: Just shake your hands before you use a paper towel. Then, one will be more than enough. (⑤)

Jaden: Oh, that's a good idea, Yuri! I'll try that next time.

Yuri: Good! Just don't forget to shake your hands at least 10 times.

06 위 대화의 (①)~(⑤) 중 다음 주어진 말이 들어갈 알맞은 곳은?

> I need at least two or three paper towels.

①   ②   ③   ④   ⑤

07 위 대화의 내용과 일치하지 않는 것은?

① They are talking about an easy way to save trees.

② Jaden thinks that his science homework is difficult.

③ Jaden has to find a way to save trees.

④ Yuri suggests that Jaden should stop using paper cups and use just one paper towel to dry off his hands.

⑤ Yuri suggests to Jaden that he should shake his hands at least 10 times before he uses a paper towel.

[08~09] 다음 대화를 읽고 물음에 답하시오.

A: I've heard that _____(A)_____ is the best way to save the Earth.

B: I've heard that, too. What can we do to save electricity?

A: _____(B)_____ when we're not using it?

B: That's a good idea. Don't forget to turn off the light when you leave your room.

08 위 대화의 빈칸 (A)에 들어갈 말로 알맞은 것은?

① saving electricity

② saving water

③ using less paper

④ washing hands

⑤ using paper towels

09 빈칸 (B)에 들어갈 말로 알맞은 것은?

① Why did you turn off the light

② Are you planning to turn off the light

③ Why don't we turn off the light

④ Shall I turn off the light

⑤ Don't forget turning off the light

[01~02] 다음 대화를 읽고 물음에 답하시오.

Boy: What's your plan for this winter break?

Girl: I'm going to visit Vietnam with my parents.

Boy: That sounds exciting. What are you going to do there?

Girl: I'm going to spend some time on the beach and eat lots of seafood.

Boy: Good. Don't forget to try the fruit there, too.

Girl: O.K., (A)잊지 않을게(forget).

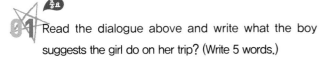

01 Read the dialogue above and write what the boy suggests the girl do on her trip? (Write 5 words.)

➡ He suggests that _____.

02 밑줄 친 (A)의 우리말에 맞게 주어진 단어를 이용하여 영작하시오. (3단어로 쓸 것)

➡ _____

[03~04] 다음 대화를 읽고 물음에 답하시오.

Yuri: What's wrong, Jaden?

Jaden: My science homework is too difficult.

Yuri: What do you have to do?

Jaden: I need to find a way to save trees.

Yuri: That's easy. (A)나는 종이를 덜 사용함으로써 나무들을 살릴 수 있다고 들었어.

Jaden: Oh, I think I've heard that, too. Then, I can just stop using paper cups.

Yuri: Yes! You can also use just one paper towel to dry off your hands.

Jaden: That's impossible. I need at least two or three paper towels.

Yuri: Just shake your hands before you use a paper towel. Then, one will be more than enough.

Jaden: Oh, that's a good idea, Yuri! I'll try that next time.

Yuri: Good! Just _____ (B)

03 밑줄 친 (A)의 우리말에 맞게 주어진 단어를 이용하여 영어로 쓰시오.

I've / that / can / by / use / little

➡ _____

04 대화의 빈칸 (B)에 주어진 조건과 우리말 해석에 맞게 한 문장을 쓰시오.

┤ 조건 ├
'forget'을 이용하여 상기시켜 주는 표현을 쓸 것.

┤ 해석 ├
'손을 적어도 열 번은 털어야 한다는 걸 잊지 마'

➡ _____

05 Read the sentence below and fill in the blank to complete the advice that the boy gives to the girl.

Girl: I'm going to go hiking tomorrow, but I'm worried about bad weather.

➡ Boy: _____ take an umbrella with you.

06 다음 우리말에 맞게 주어진 어휘를 바르게 배열하시오.

우리 학교에 영화배우가 온다고 들었어.
(I've / a movie / heard / star / that / is / to / our school / coming)

➡ _____

Grammar

1 5형식 동사+목적어+형용사

- Add some bleach to **keep** the water **clear**. 물을 깨끗이 유지하기 위해 표백제를 조금 넣어라.
- You'll **find** it **interesting**. 너는 그게 재미있다는 걸 알 거야.

■ '주어+동사+목적어+목적격보어'의 어순으로 이루어진 문장을 5형식 문장이라고 하며, 목적격보어 자리에는 명사, 형용사, to부정사, 현재분사, 과거분사, 동사원형 등 다양한 형태가 올 수 있다. 이때, 목적격보어는 목적어의 특징이나 상태 등을 설명하는 역할을 한다. 형용사를 목적격보어로 취하는 동사에는 find, get, keep, leave, make, paint, think 등이 있다.

- He **made** his daughter a **teacher**. 〈명사〉 그는 그의 딸을 교사로 만들었다.
- She **makes** me **happy**. 〈형용사〉 그녀는 나를 행복하게 해.

■ 목적격 보어를 형용사가 아닌 부사로 쓰지 않도록 주의해야 한다.

- Do you **think** him **honest**? 너는 그가 정직하다고 생각하니?
- This jacket will **keep** you **warm**. 이 재킷이 너를 따뜻하게 해 줄 거야.

■ **5형식 문장과 4형식 문장 비교**

5형식 문장: 주어+동사+목적어+목적격보어

- He **kept** his room **clean**. (his room = clean) 그는 그의 방을 깨끗하게 유지했다.

4형식 문장: 주어+동사+간접목적어+직접목적어

- Her mom **made** her a **dress**. (her ≠ a dress) 그녀의 엄마는 그녀에게 옷을 만들어 주었다.

핵심 Check

1. 다음 우리말에 맞게 빈칸에 알맞은 말을 쓰시오.

   (1) 그는 그녀가 유명하게 만들었다.

   ➡ He made her _____.

   (2) 아름다운 꽃들은 그녀를 행복하게 만든다.

   ➡ Beautiful flowers make her _____.

② 사역동사

• **Let** me just **put** your phone in a glass. 그냥 네 휴대폰을 유리잔 안에 넣게 해 줘.

■ 사역동사

  • 의미: (목적어)가 ~하게 하다/~하도록 시키다

  • 형태: 사역동사(let/make/have)+목적어+동사원형

■ 사역동사는 '사역동사+목적어+목적격보어'의 형태로 '(목적어)가 ~하게 하다/~하도록 시키다'의 뜻을 가지며 사역동사에는 make, have, let이 있다.

  • Mom **made** me **do** the dishes. 엄마는 내게 설거지를 하도록 시켰다.

  • She **let** me **go** home early. 그녀는 내가 집에 일찍 가도록 해 주었다.

■ 목적격보어로 동사원형이 오면 능동의 의미로 '~(목적어)가 …(목적격보어)을 하게 하다'의 뜻을 가지며, 과거분사가 오면 수동의 의미로 '~(목적어)가 …(목적격보어)을 당하게[되게] 하다'의 뜻을 갖는다.

  • I **had** him **call** her. 〈능동〉 나는 그가 그녀에게 전화하도록 했다. (그가 전화하는 것으로 능동)

  • He **had** his computer **repaired**. 〈수동〉 그는 그의 컴퓨터가 수리되도록 했다. (컴퓨터가 수리되는 것으로 수동)

■ 'help'와 'get'

  • help는 목적격보어로 동사원형이나 to부정사가 나오며 뜻의 차이는 없다.

  • It **helped** her **forget** life on the streets.
    = It **helped** her **to forget** life on the streets. 그것은 그녀로 하여금 거리에서의 삶을 잊는 데 도움이 되었다.

  • get이 '~하게 하다'라는 사역동사의 뜻으로 쓰일 때 목적격보어로 능동의 의미일 때는 to부정사를, 수동의 의미일 때는 과거분사를 쓴다.

  • He **got** her **to finish** her homework. 〈능동〉 그는 그녀가 숙제를 끝내도록 시켰다.
    = He **had** her **finish** her homework.

  • He **got** his computer **repaired**. 〈수동〉 그는 그의 컴퓨터가 수리되도록 했다.
    = He **had** his computer **repaired**.

핵심 Check

2. 다음 괄호 안에서 알맞은 것을 고르시오.

  (1) Dad had me (wash / to wash) his car.

  (2) Carol got her house (paint / painted).

  (3) Minhee helped me (to do / doing) my homework.

  (4) They got him (sign / to sign) the contract.

01 다음 문장에서 어법상 <u>어색한</u> 부분을 바르게 고쳐 쓰시오.

(1) The funny movie made me to laugh.

_____ ➡ _____

(2) I let him finishing cleaning his room.

_____ ➡ _____

(3) The song made me sadly.

_____ ➡ _____

(4) Too much homework makes me tiring.

_____ ➡ _____

02 주어진 단어를 어법에 맞게 빈칸에 쓰시오.

(1) She had her son _____ the trash away. (throw)

(2) She had the trash _____ away. (throw)

(3) She got him _____ her at the station. (meet)

(4) He helped his sister _____ her homework. (do)

03 다음 우리말을 영어로 바르게 옮긴 것은?

> 그 소설은 그녀를 유명하게 만들었다.

① The novel made her famously.
② The novel made her famous.
③ The novel had her famous.
④ She made the novel famous.
⑤ She made the novel famously.

04 주어진 단어를 바르게 배열하여 다음 우리말을 영어로 쓰시오.

> • 제게 그녀의 이름을 알게 해 주세요.
> (me / name / know / let / her)

➡ _____

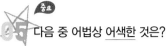
01 다음 빈칸에 알맞은 말이 순서대로 바르게 짝지어진 것은?

• His parents let him _____ a pet.
• We had a math test yesterday and found it _____.

① to have – difficultly
② having – difficultly
③ having – difficult
④ have – difficultly
⑤ have – difficult

02 다음 빈칸에 들어갈 말로 적절한 것을 모두 고르시오.

His neighbor helped him _____ his roof.

① fix   ② fixes   ③ fixed
④ fixing   ⑤ to fix

03 중요

다음 빈칸에 알맞은 말을 고르시오.

Merriam _____ the garden in the backyard very beautiful.

① found   ② called   ③ asked
④ ordered   ⑤ begged

04 서답형

주어진 어구를 이용하여 다음 우리말을 영어로 쓰시오. (7 단어)

그 항아리는 과일을 차갑게 유지할 수 있다. (the pot, keep, the fruit)

➡ _____

05 중요

다음 중 어법상 어색한 것은?

① Could you let Cindy know that I'll call her later?
② Finally we got the little child to sit still long enough for photo.
③ Her wish was to have her son's name mention at graduation.
④ It helped him to forget other things.
⑤ I'll make my robot clean my room.

06 서답형

괄호 안에서 알맞은 것을 고르시오.

(1) Catherine wanted to have her son (learn / to learn) Chinese.
(2) Let me (see / seeing) if I can get there on time.
(3) Amy got her room (to clean / cleaned).
(4) Did the coach (make / help) the team to win the soccer match?
(5) The teacher gets us (read / to read) many books.
(6) I found the movie (interesting / interestingly).
(7) I tried to do exercise (regular / regularly) and it made me (health / healthy).

07 다음 중 어법상 올바른 문장을 고르시오.

① Add some bleach to keep the water clearly.
② This food will make me healthily.
③ What made you so angry last Saturday?
④ Reading a lot of books will make me well at English.
⑤ This heater will make us stay warmly in winter.

08 다음 중 어법상 바르지 <u>않은</u> 것은?

> I ①had the beef ②cook and ③put ④it ⑤into sandwiches.

①　　②　　③　　④　　⑤

09 다음 문장에서 어법상 틀린 부분을 찾아 바르게 고쳐 쓰시오.

> When I arrived at home, I found my wallet steal.

_____ ➡ _____

[10~11] 다음 우리말을 영어로 바르게 옮긴 것을 고르시오.

10 (2개)

> Ben은 Marie가 의자에 앉도록 도와주었다.

① Ben helped Marie sits on the chair.
② Ben helped Marie sat on the chair.
③ Ben helped Marie sit on the chair.
④ Ben helped Marie to sit on the chair.
⑤ Ben helped Marie sitting on the chair.

11

> 내가 아기를 안전하게 지킬 것이다.

① The baby will keep me safe.
② The baby will keep me safely.
③ The baby will keep I safe.
④ I'll keep the baby safe.
⑤ I'll keep the baby safely.

12 다음 문장의 빈칸에 알맞지 <u>않은</u> 것은?

> Venus _____ her daughter be on a healthy diet.

① made　　② had　　③ let
④ helped　　⑤ got

13 밑줄 친 부분과 용법이 <u>다른</u> 것은?

> Eating vegetables every day will <u>make</u> me healthy.

① She always <u>makes</u> me happy.
② His lie <u>made</u> her angry.
③ She <u>made</u> her son sad.
④ My dad <u>made</u> me a model train.
⑤ The comedy <u>made</u> them laugh.

14 다음 중 어법상 <u>어색한</u> 문장을 <u>모두</u> 고르시오.

① He helped her to carry her cases up the stairs.
② Elizabeth had the meat roast in the garden.
③ Morris got the girl stand up in front of students.
④ Alicia had her daughter take care of her cats.
⑤ Playing soccer always makes Beckham feel excited.

15 다음 중 (A)~(C)에서 어법상 옳은 것끼리 바르게 짝지은 것은?

> • Charlotte made Tom (A)(bake / baking) some cookies for her.
> • Angelina got him (B)(take / to take) some photos of her.
> • Richard had his bike (C)(fix / fixed).

	(A)	(B)	(C)
①	baking	take	fixed
②	baking	to take	fix
③	bake	to take	fix
④	bake	take	fix
⑤	bake	to take	fixed

서답형

16 두 문장의 뜻이 같도록 빈칸에 알맞은 말을 쓰시오.

(1) Kirk found the test difficult.
= Kirk found that _____ _____ _____ difficult.

(2) I think him silly.
= I think that _____ _____ _____.

서답형

17 다음 문장에서 어법상 어색한 부분을 바르게 고치시오.

(1) The police made the thief to wear handcuffs.
_____ ➡ _____

(2) Julie got the man write down 25 things he wanted to do.
_____ ➡ _____

(3) The girl had her purse steal on the train.
_____ ➡ _____

서답형

18 다음 괄호 안에 주어진 어구를 이용하여 우리말을 영어로 옮기시오.

(1) 우리 아버지는 차를 깨끗이 유지하신다. (my father, keep, clean)
➡ _____

(2) 비 오는 날은 나를 슬프게 한다. (rainy days, sad, make)
➡ _____

(3) 그녀의 새 책은 그녀를 유명하게 만들었다. (make, famous)
➡ _____

(4) 나는 내 아이들이 TV를 보게 하지 않을 것이다. (let, watch, TV)
➡ _____

(5) 재미있는 이야기가 나를 웃게 했다. (the funny story, make)
➡ _____

(6) 나는 그 남자에게 내 컴퓨터를 고치도록 했다. (have, the man, fix)
➡ _____

[19~20] 다음 빈칸에 알맞은 말을 고르시오.

19
> My brother _____ my room dirty.

① made   ② ordered   ③ did
④ asked   ⑤ have

20
> My boss _____ a meeting.

① got me arrange
② made me arranged
③ got me arranged
④ made me arrange
⑤ makes I arranged

01 다음 중 어법상 <u>어색한</u> 부분을 찾아 바르게 고쳐 다시 쓰시오.

(1) She made him to finish his work by the next day.

➡ _____

_____

(2) She doesn't let her children playing online games.

➡ _____

_____

(3) I must go to the dry cleaner's to have my suit clean.

➡ _____

_____

(4) Mom got me help my sister with her homework.

➡ _____

_____

(5) I helped him calming down before playing the guitar on the stage.

➡ _____

_____

02 다음 문장의 빈칸에 한 단어씩을 채워 비슷한 뜻을 갖는 문장으로 바꿔 쓰시오.

(1) As I read the book, I felt sad.
= The book made _____ _____.

(2) When he did exercise regularly, he became healthy.
= Regular exercise _____ _____

_____.

03 다음 두 문장을 주어진 〈조건〉에 맞춰 〈보기〉와 같이 한 문장으로 완성하시오.

┌─ 보기 ├─
• My mom was busy today.
• So, she asked me to prepare dinner tonight.
→ My mom had me prepare dinner tonight.
└─

┌─ 조건 ├─
1. 동사 have와 repair를 이용할 것.
2. 5 단어로 쓸 것.
└─

• Eric had a broken camera.
• So, he brought it to a repair shop and asked a repairman to repair it.

➡ _____

04 다음 중 어법상 <u>어색한</u> 부분을 찾아 바르게 고쳐 다시 쓰시오.

(1) A strange man broke into my house, but he stole nothing and left it cleanly.

➡ _____

_____

(2) They made Stacy happiness by saying white lies.

➡ _____

(3) He found his new smartphone broke.

➡ _____

(4) At first, Samanda thought William honestly.

➡ _____

(5) This thick blanket will keep you warmly.

➡ _____

05 다음 그림을 참고하여 단어 turn의 알맞은 형태를 빈칸에 채우시오.

➡ I made him _____ up the volume of his smartphone.

06 〈보기〉에서 의미상 적절한 단어를 골라 빈칸에 알맞은 형태로 쓰시오.

┌─ 보기 ├─
be   watch   carry   find   clean
└──────────────────────────────────┘

(1) The teacher made the students _____ their desks yesterday.

(2) Mom had the heavy box _____ upstairs.

(3) They got him _____ in the prison for a while.

(4) Yesterday I helped Jaden _____ his lost keys.

(5) His parents let him _____ TV after he finishes his homework.

07 그림을 보고 괄호 안에 주어진 단어들을 바르게 배열하여 문장을 완성하시오.

(holidays, year, her, lots, next, makes, having, excited, of)

➡ _____

_____

08 다음 문장을 〈보기〉와 같이 사역동사를 이용하여 바꿔 쓰시오.

┌─ 보기 ├─
Mr. Kim got Jack to open the window.
= Mr. Kim had Jack open the window.
└──────────────────────────────────┘

(1) Eve allowed Adam to use her pen.

➡ _____

(2) She forced Dan to follow her advice.

➡ _____

09 다음 괄호 안에 주어진 단어를 이용하여 우리말을 영어로 옮기시오.

(1) 그는 어제 그의 차가 닦여지게 했다. (have, wash)

➡ _____

(2) 우리는 램프를 더 밝게 만들 수 있었다. (the lamp, make, bright.)

➡ _____

One-Dollar Magic Lamps

"Wow, I can read a book in my room now!" shouted Marco, a boy in a village in the Philippines. His house has no electricity just like all the other houses in the village. People in the village are too poor to pay for electricity. Even during the daytime, they live in darkness because the houses are packed close together. Now things are changing because of a single plastic bottle. One plastic bottle in the ceiling can light up a whole room without using any electricity.

This amazing plastic bottle is called a Moser lamp because it was invented by Alfredo Moser. In 2002, there were many blackouts in his town in Brazil. These blackouts made him come up with a new way to light his house.

A Moser lamp can be made for about one dollar and lasts for about 10 years. It is also very safe. It can never start a house fire. Surprisingly, it is very easy to make this magic lamp.

---

magic: 마법의, 신기한
lamp: 램프, 등
shout: 외치다
electricity: 전기
village 마을
daytime: 낮, 주간
packed 꽉 들어찬
ceiling: 천장
whole 전체의
blackout 정전 사태
last 지속되다

 확인문제

● 다음 문장이 본문의 내용과 일치하면 T, 일치하지 않으면 F를 쓰시오.

1 Marco's house has no electricity just like all the other houses in the village. ☐

2 During the daytime, they live in the bright room. ☐

3 A Moser lamp can be made for about one dollar and lasts for about 10 years. ☐

4 It is not easy to make this magic lamp. ☐

How to make a Moser lamp from a bottle
how to+동사원형: ~하는 방법

1. Fill a clear plastic bottle with water.
~으로

2. Add some bleach to keep the water clear.
keep+목적어+목적격 보어(5형식): 목적격 보어의 자리에 형용사를 씀. to keep: 부사적 용법

3. Make a hole in the roof, and push the bottle into the hole.

4. Let a third of the bottle remain above the roof.
사역동사 let+목적어+목적격 보어(동사원형): ~이 …하게 하다

5. Sunlight is bent by the water in the bottle and spreads around the
and로 연결된 병렬 구조. spreads 앞에 주어 sunlight가 생략됨.

room.

In the Philippines, Moser lamps are widely used by the My Shelter
수동태

Foundation. The charity also teaches local people how to make and

install the lamps. Thanks to the charity, thousands of homes in the
thousands of+명사: 수천의 ~. cf. hundred. thousand. million 등의 단어가
숫자 뒤에서 단위로 사용될 때: 단수형으로만 사용 e.g. two hundred. three million

Philippines now have Moser lamps. It has also made Moser lamps
= The charity   현재완료 계속 용법   5형식 동사+목적어+목적격보어(형용사)

popular in other countries, such as Argentina, India, and Fiji. Moser
~와 같은

lamps will light up the lives of many people for many years to come.
life의 복수형   앞으로 오랫동안

bleach: 표백제

hole: 구멍

bend: 구부러지다, 휘다 (bend–bent–bent)

spread: 펼치다, (여러 장소로) 퍼뜨리다

thanks to: ~ 덕분에

charity: 자선 단체

install: 설치하다

life: 삶, 생활

확인문제

● 다음 문장이 본문의 내용과 일치하면 T, 일치하지 않으면 F를 쓰시오.

1 To make a Moser lamp from a bottle, you must fill a clear plastic bottle with water. ☐

2 You need to add some bleach to keep the water cool. ☐

3 You must let two thirds of the bottle remain above the roof. ☐

4 Sunlight is bent by the water in the bottle and spreads around the room. ☐

5 The My Shelter Foundation teaches local people how to make and install Moser lamps. ☐

6 Thanks to the My Shelter Foundation, thousands of homes in the Philippines now have Moser lamps. ☐

● 우리말을 참고하여 빈칸에 알맞은 말을 쓰시오.

1 _____ Magic Lamps

2 "Wow, I can read a book in my room now!" shouted Marco, a boy in a village _____ _____ _____.

3 His house _____ _____ _____ just like _____ _____ _____ _____ in the village.

4 People in the village are _____ poor _____ pay for electricity.

5 Even during the daytime, they live in darkness because the houses _____ _____ _____ _____.

6 Now things are changing _____ _____ a single plastic bottle.

7 One plastic bottle in the ceiling can _____ _____ a whole room _____ _____ any electricity.

8 This amazing plastic bottle _____ _____ a Moser lamp _____ it _____ _____ _____ Alfredo Moser.

9 In 2002, there were _____ _____ in his town in Brazil.

10 These blackouts made him _____ _____ _____ a new way to light his house.

11 A Moser lamp can _____ _____ _____ about one dollar and _____ _____ about 10 years.

12 It is also _____ _____.

---

1 1달러짜리 마법의 전구

2 "우와, 이젠 제 방에서 책을 읽을 수 있어요!" 필리핀의 한 마을에 사는 소년인 Marco가 외쳤다.

3 그의 집은 마을의 다른 모든 집들과 마찬가지로 전기가 없다.

4 마을 사람들은 너무나 가난해서 전기세를 낼 수가 없다.

5 심지어 낮 동안에도, 집들이 빽빽하게 들어차 있어서 그들은 어둠 속에 살아간다.

6 이제 플라스틱병 하나 때문에 상황이 바뀌고 있다.

7 천장에 있는 플라스틱병 하나는 전기를 쓰지 않고 방 전체를 밝힐 수 있다.

8 이 놀라운 플라스틱병은 Moser 램프라고 불리는데, 그것이 Alfredo Moser에 의해 발명되었기 때문이다.

9 2002년, 브라질에 있는 그의 마을에는 정전이 잦았다.

10 이 정전들은 그가 집을 밝히는 새로운 방법을 생각해 내도록 만들었다.

11 Moser 램프는 1달러 정도로 만들 수 있고 10년 정도 지속된다.

12 그것은 또한 매우 안전하다.

13 It can _____ _____ a house fire.

14 Surprisingly, it is very easy _____ _____ this magic lamp.

15 _____ _____ _____ a Moser lamp from a bottle

16 1. _____ a clear plastic bottle _____ water.

17 2. _____ some bleach _____ _____ the water _____.

18 3. Make a hole in the roof, and _____ the bottle _____ the hole.

19 4. Let _____ _____ of the bottle _____ above the roof.

20 5. Sunlight _____ _____ by the water in the bottle and _____ around the room.

21 In the Philippines, Moser lamps _____ _____ _____ by the My Shelter Foundation.

22 _____ _____ also teaches local people _____ _____ _____ and _____ the lamps.

23 _____ _____ the charity, _____ _____ homes in the Philippines now have Moser lamps.

24 It _____ also _____ Moser lamps popular in other countries, _____ _____ Argentina, India, and Fiji.

25 Moser lamps will light up the lives of many people _____ _____ _____ _____ _____.

13 그것은 절대 집에 불을 낼 수 없다.

14 놀랍게도, 이 신기한 램프를 만드는 것은 매우 쉽다.

15 병으로 Moser 램프를 만드는 법

16 1. 투명한 플라스틱병에 물을 채운다.

17 2. 물을 깨끗이 유지하기 위해 표백제를 조금 넣는다.

18 3. 지붕에 구멍을 내고, 병을 구멍 안으로 넣는다.

19 4. 병의 3분의 1은 지붕 위에 남아 있도록 한다.

20 5. 햇빛이 병 속의 물에 의해 굴절되어 방에 퍼진다.

21 필리핀에서 Moser 램프는 My Shelter 재단에 의해 널리 사용된다.

22 또한 그 자선단체는 지역 사람들에게 램프를 만들고 설치하는 법을 가르친다.

23 이 자선단체 덕분에, 필리핀의 수천 가구가 이제 Moser 램프를 갖고 있다.

24 그 단체는 아르헨티나, 인도, 피지와 같은 다른 나라들에서도 Moser 램프가 유명해 지도록 만들었다.

25 Moser 램프는 앞으로 오랫동안 많은 사람들의 삶을 밝혀 줄 것이다.

● 우리말을 참고하여 본문을 영작하시오.

1 1달러짜리 마법의 전구

➡ _____

2 "우와, 이젠 제 방에서 책을 읽을 수 있어요!" 필리핀의 한 마을에 사는 소년인 Marco가 외쳤다.

➡ _____

3 그의 집은 마을의 다른 모든 집들과 마찬가지로 전기가 없다.

➡ _____

4 마을 사람들은 너무나 가난해서 전기세를 낼 수가 없다.

➡ _____

5 심지어 낮 동안에도, 집들이 빽빽하게 들어차 있어서 그들은 어둠 속에 살아간다.

➡ _____

6 이제 플라스틱병 하나 때문에 상황이 바뀌고 있다.

➡ _____

7 천장에 있는 플라스틱병 하나는 전기를 쓰지 않고 방 전체를 밝힐 수 있다.

➡ _____

8 이 놀라운 플라스틱병은 Moser 램프라고 불리는데, 그것이 Alfredo Moser에 의해 발명되었기 때문이다.

➡ _____

9 2002년, 브라질에 있는 그의 마을에는 정전이 잦았다.

➡ _____

10 이 정전들은 그가 집을 밝히는 새로운 방법을 생각해 내도록 만들었다.

➡ _____

11 Moser 램프는 1달러 정도로 만들 수 있고 10년 정도 지속된다.

➡ _____

12 그것은 또한 매우 안전하다.

➡ _____

13 그것은 절대 집에 불을 낼 수 없다.

➡ _____

14 놀랍게도, 이 신기한 램프를 만드는 것은 매우 쉽다.

➡ _____

15 병으로 Moser 램프를 만드는 법

➡ _____

16 1. 투명한 플라스틱병에 물을 채운다.

➡ _____

17 2. 물을 깨끗이 유지하기 위해 표백제를 조금 넣는다.

➡ _____

18 3. 지붕에 구멍을 내고, 병을 구멍 안으로 넣는다.

➡ _____

19 4. 병의 3분의 1은 지붕 위에 남아 있도록 한다.

➡ _____

20 5. 햇빛이 병 속의 물에 의해 굴절되어 방에 퍼진다.

➡ _____

21 필리핀에서 Moser 램프는 My Shelter 재단에 의해 널리 사용된다.

➡ _____

22 또한 그 자선단체는 지역 사람들에게 램프를 만들고 설치하는 법을 가르친다.

➡ _____

23 이 자선단체 덕분에, 필리핀의 수천 가구가 이제 Moser 램프를 갖고 있다.

➡ _____

24 그 단체는 아르헨티나, 인도, 피지와 같은 다른 나라들에서도 Moser 램프가 유명해 지도록 만들었다.

➡ _____

25 Moser 램프는 앞으로 오랫동안 많은 사람들의 삶을 밝혀 줄 것이다.

➡ _____

[01~04] 다음 글을 읽고 물음에 답하시오.

"Wow, I can read a book in my room now!" shouted Marco, a boy in a village in the Philippines. (①) His house has no electricity just like all the other houses in the village. (②) People in the village are too poor to pay ___ⓐ___ electricity. (③) Even during the daytime, they live ___ⓑ___ darkness because the houses are packed close together. (④) One plastic bottle in the ceiling can light up a whole room without using any ___ⓒ___. (⑤)

01 위 글의 빈칸 ⓐ와 ⓑ에 들어갈 전치사가 바르게 짝지어진 것은?

① for – on
② to – in
③ in – from
④ for – in
⑤ to – from

중요

02 위 글의 빈칸 ⓒ에 들어갈 말로 가장 옳은 것을 고르시오.

① source
② electricity
③ chemicals
④ gas
⑤ resource

03 위 글의 흐름으로 보아, 주어진 문장이 들어가기에 가장 적절한 곳은?

> Now things are changing because of a single plastic bottle.

①   ②   ③   ④   ⑤

중요

04 위 글의 내용과 일치하지 않는 것은?

① Marco의 집은 마을의 다른 모든 집들과 마찬가지로 전기가 없다.

② Marco의 마을 사람들은 너무나 가난해서 전기세를 낼 수가 없다.

③ 낮 동안에는 대부분의 마을 사람들의 집안에 햇빛이 들어온다.

④ 이제 플라스틱병 하나 때문에 어둠 속에서 살아가던 상황이 바뀌고 있다.

⑤ 천장에 있는 플라스틱병 하나로 방 전체를 밝힐 수 있다.

[05~07] 다음 글을 읽고 물음에 답하시오.

How to make a Moser lamp from a bottle
1. ___ⓐ___ a clear plastic bottle with water.
2. ___ⓑ___ some bleach to ___ⓒ___ the water clear.
3. ___ⓓ___ a hole in the roof, and ___ⓔ___ the bottle into the hole.
4. (A)Let a third of the bottle remain above the roof.
5. (B)Sunlight is bent by the water in the bottle and spreads around the room.

05 위 글의 빈칸 ⓐ~ⓔ에 들어갈 수 없는 단어를 고르시오. (대·소문자 무시)

① push
② make
③ give
④ fill
⑤ add

서답형

06 위 글의 밑줄 친 (A)를 다음과 같이 바꿔 쓸 때 빈칸에 들어갈 알맞은 말을 쓰시오.

➡ Let _____ of the bottle remain below the roof.

서답형

07 위 글의 밑줄 친 (B)를 능동태로 고치시오.

➡ _____

[08~10] 다음 글을 읽고 물음에 답하시오.

This amazing plastic bottle is called a Moser lamp because it was invented by Alfredo Moser. In 2002, there were many blackouts in his town in Brazil. These blackouts made him come up with a new way ⓐto light his house.

A Moser lamp can be made for about one dollar and ___(A)___ for about 10 years. It is also very safe. It can never start a house fire. Surprisingly, it is very easy to make this magic lamp.

서답형

08 주어진 영영풀이를 참고하여 빈칸 (A)에 철자 l로 시작하는 단어를 알맞은 형태로 쓰시오.

to continue to be able to be used for a particular length of time

➡ _____

09 위 글의 밑줄 친 ⓐto light와 to부정사의 용법이 다른 것을 모두 고르시오.

① To take a walk is good for the health.
② John needed someone to help him.
③ He stopped his car to check the engine.
④ She was sad to hear the news.
⑤ I have much homework to finish by tomorrow.

중요

10 위 글의 제목으로 알맞은 것을 고르시오.

① Various Uses of a Plastic Bottle
② Alfredo Moser, the Inventor of the Moser Lamp
③ The Cheap and Safe Magic Lamp
④ Blackouts Caused the Invention of a Lamp
⑤ The Amazing Effect of a Creative Idea

[11~14] 다음 글을 읽고 물음에 답하시오.

In the Philippines, Moser lamps are widely used by the My Shelter Foundation. The charity also teaches local people how to make and install the lamps. ___ⓐ___ the charity, ⓑ 필리핀의 수천 가구 now have Moser lamps. It has also made Moser lamps popular in other countries, ⓒsuch as Argentina, India, and Fiji. Moser lamps will light ___ⓓ___ the lives of many people for many years to come.

중요

11 위 글의 빈칸 ⓐ에 들어갈 알맞은 말을 고르시오.

① Instead of   ② Without
③ In place of   ④ Thanks to
⑤ Unlike

서답형

12 위 글의 밑줄 친 ⓑ의 우리말을 다음 주어진 단어를 이용하여 여섯 단어로 쓰시오.

of, home

➡ _____

서답형

13 위 글의 밑줄 친 ⓒsuch as와 바꿔 쓸 수 있는 단어를 쓰시오.

➡ _____

14 위 글의 빈칸 ⓓ에 들어갈 알맞은 말을 고르시오.

① up   ② to
③ for   ④ from
⑤ with

[15~18] 다음 글을 읽고 물음에 답하시오.

How to make a Moser lamp from a bottle
1. Fill a clear plastic bottle ___ⓐ___ water.
2. Add some bleach ⓑto keep the water clear.
3. Make a hole in the roof, and push the bottle ___ⓒ___ the hole.
4. ⓓLet a third of the bottle to remain above the roof.
5. Sunlight is bent by the water in the bottle and spreads around the room.

🌟 중요
15 위 글의 빈칸 ⓐ와 ⓒ에 들어갈 전치사가 바르게 짝지어진 것은?

① in – from
② with – from
③ in – into
④ to – by
⑤ with – into

16 아래 보기에서 위 글의 밑줄 친 ⓑto keep과 to부정사의 용법이 다른 것의 개수를 고르시오.

─┤ 보기 ├─
① Give me something to write on.
② I went to London to meet my uncle.
③ She worked hard to be a professor.
④ She is planning to visit her uncle.
⑤ You had better come early to get seats.

① 1개 ② 2개 ③ 3개 ④ 4개 ⑤ 5개

서답형
17 위 글의 밑줄 친 ⓓ에서 어법상 틀린 부분을 찾아 고치시오.

_____ ➡ _____

🌟 중요
18 다음 중 '플라스틱병으로 Moser 램프를 만드는 법'을 올바르게 이해하지 못한 사람을 고르시오.

① 성민: 불투명한 플라스틱병에 물을 채워 넣어야 한다.

② 재희: 표백제를 조금 넣는 이유는 물을 깨끗이 유지하기 위해서이다.
③ 보람: 지붕에 구멍을 내고, 병을 구멍 안으로 넣어야 한다.
④ 형규: 병의 3분의 1은 지붕 위에 남아 있도록 해야 한다.
⑤ 민수: 햇빛이 병 속의 물에 의해 굴절되어 방에 퍼지게 된다.

[19~21] 다음 글을 읽고 물음에 답하시오.

In the Philippines, Moser lamps are widely used by the My Shelter Foundation. The charity also teaches local people how to make and ⓐinstall the lamps. Thanks to the charity, thousands of homes in the Philippines now have Moser lamps. It has also made Moser lamps popular in other countries, such as Argentina, India, and Fiji. Moser lamps will light up the lives of many people for many years ⓑto come.

서답형
19 위 글의 밑줄 친 ⓐinstall 앞에 생략된 말을 쓰시오.

➡ _____

20 아래 〈보기〉에서 위 글의 밑줄 친 ⓑto come과 문법적 쓰임이 다른 것의 개수를 고르시오.

─┤ 보기 ├─
① I think it necessary to do the work now.
② Sujin is happy to meet her old friends.
③ We are ready to leave for London.
④ He promised me to send a postcard to me from Paris.
⑤ This apron has no pocket to put things in.

① 1개 ② 2개 ③ 3개 ④ 4개 ⑤ 5개

21 위 글의 주제로 알맞은 것을 고르시오.

① the strong points of the Moser lamps
② people who work for the My Shelter Foundation
③ the remarkable activities of the My Shelter Foundation
④ the popularity of the Moser lamps
⑤ the long-lasting power of the Moser lamps

[22~24] 다음 글을 읽고 물음에 답하시오.

This amazing plastic bottle is called a Moser lamp because it was invented by Alfredo Moser. In 2002, there were many blackouts in his town in Brazil. These blackouts made him come up with a new way to light his house.

A Moser lamp can be made for ⓐabout one dollar and lasts for about 10 years. It is also very safe. ⓑIt can never start a house fire. Surprisingly, it is very easy to make this magic lamp.

22 위 글의 밑줄 친 ⓐabout과 같은 의미로 쓰인 것을 고르시오.

① Tell me all about it.
② It costs about $10.
③ The film is about poor boys.
④ There is nobody about.
⑤ What is he about?

서답형

23 위 글의 밑줄 친 ⓑIt이 가리키는 것을 본문에서 찾아 쓰시오.

➡ _____

24 위 글을 읽고 대답할 수 없는 질문은?

① What's the name of the amazing plastic bottle?
② Why did Alfredo Moser come up with a new way to light his house?
③ Is it expensive to make a Moser lamp?
④ How long does a Moser lamp last?
⑤ How long does it take to make a Moser lamp?

[25~27] 다음 글을 읽고 물음에 답하시오.

You can make ⓐa lot of things with a CD case. You can even make a grass container. First, fill half of the CD case with soil and water, and put grass seeds into the soil. Second, close the case and tape all of the sides. Finally, leave it in the sun (A)[during / for] about ten days. Now, your grass container is ready. It will make you (B)[happy / happily] when the grass (C)[grows / will grow].

서답형

25 위 글의 괄호 (A)~(C)에서 어법상 알맞은 낱말을 골라 쓰시오.

➡ (A) _____ (B) _____ (C) _____

26 위 글의 밑줄 친 ⓐa lot of와 바꿔 쓸 수 없는 말을 고르시오.

① lots of   ② many
③ plenty of   ④ a number of
⑤ much

서답형

27 CD 케이스로 잔디를 기르는 용기를 만드는 법을 우리말로 설명하시오.

➡ (1) _____
(2) _____
(3) _____

[01~03] 다음 글을 읽고 물음에 답하시오.

"Wow, I can read a book in my room now!" shouted Marco, a boy in a village in the Philippines. His house has no electricity just like all the other houses in the village. ⓐ People in the village are too poor to pay for electricity. Even during the daytime, they live in darkness ⓑ집들이 빽빽하게 들어차 있어서. Now things are changing because of a single plastic bottle. One plastic bottle in the ceiling can light up a whole room without using any electricity.

01 위 글의 밑줄 친 ⓐ를 다음과 같이 바꿔 쓸 때 빈칸에 들어갈 알맞은 말을 쓰시오.

➡ People in the village are _____ poor _____ they _____ pay for electricity.

02 위 글의 밑줄 친 ⓑ의 우리말에 맞게 한 단어를 보충하여, 주어진 어휘를 알맞게 배열하시오.

together / packed / the houses / close / because

➡ _____

03 다음 문장에서 위 글의 내용과 다른 부분을 찾아서 고치시오.

Now people in Marco's village can light up a whole room with using some electricity by installing one plastic bottle in the ceiling.

_____ ➡ _____

[04~06] 다음 글을 읽고 물음에 답하시오.

This amazing plastic bottle is called a Moser lamp because it was invented by Alfredo Moser. In ⓐ2002, there were many blackouts in his town in Brazil. These blackouts made him come up with ⓑa new way to light his house.

A Moser lamp can be made for about one dollar and lasts for about 10 years. It is also very safe. It can never start a house fire. Surprisingly, ⓒit is very easy to make this magic lamp.

04 위 글의 밑줄 친 ⓐ2002를 영어로 읽는 법을 쓰시오.

➡ _____

05 위 글의 밑줄 친 ⓑa new way to light his house가 가리키는 것을 본문에서 찾아 쓰시오.

➡ _____

06 위 글의 밑줄 친 ⓒ를 다음과 같이 바꿔 쓸 때 빈칸에 들어갈 알맞은 말을 쓰시오.

➡ (1) _____ _____ this magic lamp is very easy

(2) _____ this magic lamp is very easy

(3) _____ _____ _____ is very easy to make

[07~08] 다음 글을 읽고 물음에 답하시오.

In the Philippines, ⓐMoser lamps are widely used by the My Shelter Foundation. The charity also teaches local people how to make and install the lamps. Thanks to the charity, thousands of homes in the Philippines now have Moser lamps. ⓑIt has also made Moser lamps popularly in other countries, such as Argentina, India, and Fiji. Moser lamps will light up the lives of many people for many years to come.

07 위 글의 밑줄 친 ⓐ를 능동태로 고치시오.

➡ _____

또는 _____

08 위 글의 밑줄 친 ⓑ에서 어법상 틀린 부분을 찾아 고치시오.

_____ ➡ _____

[09~11] 다음 글을 읽고 물음에 답하시오.

This amazing plastic bottle is called a Moser lamp because it was invented by Alfredo Moser. In 2002, there were many blackouts in his town in Brazil. ⓐThese blackouts made him come up with a new way to light his house.
ⓑMoser 램프는 1달러 정도로 만들 수 있고 10년 정도 지속된다. It is also very safe. It can never start a house fire. Surprisingly, it is very easy to make this magic lamp.

09 위 글의 밑줄 친 ⓐ를 다음과 같이 바꿔 쓸 때 빈칸에 들어갈 알맞은 말을 쓰시오.

➡ _____ these blackouts, he came up with a new way to light his house.

10 위 글의 밑줄 친 ⓑ의 우리말에 맞게 한 단어를 보충하여, 주어진 어휘를 알맞게 배열하시오.

> lasts / a Moser lamp / for about 10 years / about one dollar / can be made / and

➡ _____
_____

11 위 글에 나타난 Moser lamp의 장점 네 가지를 우리말로 쓰시오.

➡ (1) _____ (2) _____
(3) _____ (4) _____

[12~13] 다음 글을 읽고 물음에 답하시오.

In the Philippines, Moser lamps are (A)[wide / widely] used by the My Shelter Foundation. The charity also teaches local people (B)[how / what] to make and install the lamps. ⓐThanks to the charity, thousands of homes in the Philippines now have Moser lamps. It has also made Moser lamps popular in other countries, such as Argentina, India, and Fiji. Moser lamps will (C)[light up / lighten up] the lives of many people for many years to come.

12 위 글의 괄호 (A)~(C)에서 문맥이나 어법상 알맞은 낱말을 골라 쓰시오.

➡ (A) _____ (B) _____ (C) _____

13 위 글의 밑줄 친 ⓐ를 다음과 같이 바꿔 쓸 때 빈칸에 들어갈 알맞은 말을 쓰시오.

➡ The charity makes it possible for thousands of homes in the Philippines _____ now.

해석

Link - Share

We thought we could make the lamp brighter with a glass bottle. We made one
we 앞에 접속사 that 생략   [도구·수단] ~으로, ~을 사용하여

lamp out of a plastic bottle and another lamp out of a glass bottle. All the other
~으로 (= from)   another+단수 명사   다른 모든 단계들(복수에 주의)

steps were the same. We learned that the glass bottle lamp was brighter than
알았다   비교급

the plastic bottle lamp.

구문해설 • make A out of B: B로 A를 만들다

우리는 우리가 램프를 유리병으로 더 밝게 만들 수 있다고 생각했다. 우리는 플라스틱병으로 램프를 하나 만들고 유리병으로 또 다른 하나를 만들었다. 다른 모든 단계는 똑같았다. 우리는 유리병 램프가 플라스틱병 램프보다 더 밝다는 것을 알았다.

Write

You can make a lot of things with a CD case. You can even make a grass
= many

container. First, fill half of the CD case with soil and water, and put grass
fill A with B: A를 B로 채우다

seeds into the soil. Second, close the case and tape all of the sides. Finally,
(동사) 닫다   = Lastly

leave it in the sun for about ten days. Now, your grass container is ready.
= the case   약

It will make you happy when the grass grows.
5형식 구문으로, 목적격보어의 자리에 형용사 happy를 쓰는 것이 적절하다.

구문해설 • container: 그릇, 용기 • seed: 씨, 씨앗 • tape: (테이프로) 붙이다; 테이프

당신은 CD 케이스로 많은 것들을 만들 수 있다. 당신은 심지어 잔디를 기르는 용기를 만들 수도 있다. 먼저 CD 케이스의 절반을 흙과 물로 채우고, 잔디 씨앗을 흙 안에 넣어라. 두 번째. 케이스를 닫고 모든 옆면에 테이프를 붙여라. 마지막으로, 햇빛이 비치는 곳에 약 10일 동안 놓아 두어라. 이제, 당신의 잔디를 기르는 용기가 준비되었다. 잔디가 자랄 때 그것은 당신을 행복하게 만들어 줄 것이다.

Culture Project - Share

We'd like to talk about a pot-in-pot cooler. It keeps food fresh without
~하고 싶다(= want to)   keep+목적어+목적격보어(형용사)

electricity. It's very easy to make one. First, put a pot inside a larger pot. Then,
가주어   진주어

pour sand and water between these pots. Just let the water dry off, and it'll
let(사역동사)+목적어+동사원형

cool the food.

구문해설 • cooler 냉장고 • fresh 신선한 • electricity 전기 • pot 항아리 • inside ~ 안에
• pour 붓다 • dry off 마르다

우리는 pot-in-pot cooler (항아리 냉장고)에 대해 이야기하고 싶다. 그것은 전기 없이 식품을 신선하게 유지할 수 있다. 그것을 만드는 것은 매우 쉽다. 우선, 항아리 하나를 더 큰 항아리에 넣는다. 그리고 항아리들 사이에 모래와 물을 넣는다. 물이 그저 마르게 두면, 그것이 음식을 시원하게 할 것이다.

Words & Expressions

01 다음 주어진 두 단어의 관계가 같도록 빈칸에 주어진 철자로 단어를 쓰시오.

shout : yell = set up : i_____

02 우리말에 맞게 밑줄 친 'hang'을 이용하여 빈칸을 완성하시오.

옷걸이에 옷을 거는 것을 잊지 마.
Don't forget to hang your clothes on the
_____.

03 다음 〈보기〉의 단어를 사용하여 자연스러운 문장을 만들 수 없는 것은?

─┤ 보기 ├─
volume / install / leftovers / lamp / forward

① Can you turn down the _____, please?
② Don't _____ rumors about other people.
③ It is good to take the _____ home to avoid waste.
④ Turn on the _____ when it gets dark.
⑤ Let's step _____ to take a closer look.

04 다음 빈칸에 어울리는 단어를 고르시오.

His house has no electricity just like all the other houses in the village. People in the village are too poor to _____ electricity.

① save   ② invent
③ turn off   ④ dry off
⑤ pay for

05 다음 우리말에 해당하는 단어를 주어진 철자로 시작하여 쓰시오.

이제 플라스틱병 하나 때문에 상황이 바뀌고 있다.
Now t_____ are changing because of a single plastic bottle.

Conversation

[06~07] 다음 대화를 읽고 물음에 답하시오.

W: Excuse me, ⓐare you finished with your meal?
M: Yes, it was ⓑreally good.
W: Do you want to ⓒtake the leftovers home?
M: Yes, please.
W: ⓓDon't forget eating the leftovers ⓔby tomorrow.

06 위 대화의 ⓐ~ⓔ 중 어법상 어색한 것은?
① ⓐ   ② ⓑ   ③ ⓒ   ④ ⓓ   ⑤ ⓔ

07 다음에 주어진 영어 설명에 해당하는 단어를 위 대화에서 찾아 그 단어와 뜻을 쓰시오.

<영어 설명> food remaining after a meal

➡ _____

[08~09] 다음 대화를 읽고 물음에 답하시오.

> B: What's your plan for this winter break? (①)
> G: I'm going to visit Hong Kong with my parents. (②)
> B: That sounds exciting. (③)
> G: I'm going to go to an amusement park. (④) I'm also going to try all kinds of food. (⑤)
> B: Good. _____(A)_____

08 위 대화의 (①)~(⑤) 중 주어진 문장이 들어갈 위치로 알맞은 것은?

> What are you going to do there?

①   ②   ③   ④   ⑤

09 빈칸 (A)에 들어갈 말로 알맞은 것은?

① Don't forget to bring your lunch.
② Don't forget to return those books.
③ Don't forget to try some dim sum.
④ Don't forget to visit my grandma.
⑤ Don't forget to go hiking.

10 다음 중 두 사람의 대화가 <u>어색한</u> 것은?

① A: Excuse me, are you finished with your meal?
   B: Yes, it was really good.
② A: I've heard that a movie star is coming to our school.
   B: That's right. She's my favorite actress.
③ A: Don't forget to recycle the cans and bottles.
   B: Sure, I will.
④ A: I've heard you didn't come to school yesterday.
   B: I got a bad cold.
⑤ A: I've heard the car was invented earlier than the bicycle.
   B: Really? That's interesting.

[11~12] 다음 대화를 읽고 물음에 답하시오.

> Yuri: What's wrong, Jaden?
> Jaden: My science homework is too difficult.
> Yuri: What do you have to do?
> Jaden: I need to find a way to save trees.
> Yuri: That's easy. I've heard that we can save trees by using less paper.
> Jaden: Oh, I think I've heard that, too. Then, I can just stop using paper cups.
> Yuri: Yes! You can also use just one paper towel to dry off your hands.
> Jaden: That's impossible. I need at least two or three paper towels.
> Yuri: Just shake your hands before you use a paper towel. Then, one will be more than enough.
> Jaden: Oh, that's a good idea, Yuri! I'll try that next time.
> Yuri: Good! Just don't forget to shake your hands at least 10 times.

11 다음 물음에 대한 답을 대화에서 찾아 9단어의 영어로 답하시오.

> Q: What does Yuri suggest to Jaden?

➡ _____

12 위 대화를 읽고 답할 수 <u>없는</u> 질문은?

① What are the speakers talking about?
② What does Jaden have to do for his science homework?
③ How can we use only one paper towel to dry off our hands?
④ According to Yuri, how can we save trees?
⑤ How many paper towels does Yuri use a day?

13 다음 중 어법상 바르지 <u>않은</u> 것은?

① Please let me go.

② I had my hair cut at a famous salon last week.

③ I saw him getting on a bus.

④ Mom made me wash the dishes after dinner.

⑤ He got his car wash yesterday.

14 다음 그림을 보고 괄호 안에 주어진 어휘를 이용하여 빈칸에 알맞은 말을 쓰시오.

My father made me _____ the tree.
(plant)

15 주어진 어휘를 알맞게 배열하여 다음 우리말을 영어로 옮기시오.

그녀는 텔레비전이 시간 낭비라고 생각해서 그녀의 아이들이 TV를 보게 하지 않는다.
(she, she, her children, a waste, television, TV, time, is, watch, doesn't, thinks, let, so, of)

➡ _____

_____

16 다음 문장을 주어진 어휘로 시작하는 문장으로 바꿔 쓰시오.

(1) When my daughter was born, I was really happy.

➡ My daughter's birth made _____. (2단어)

(2) When she heard about the accident, she got nervous.

➡ Hearing about the accident made _____. (2단어)

17 다음 빈칸에 공통으로 들어갈 말로 가장 알맞은 것은?

• She couldn't _____ them silent.
• Mike, _____ your room clean.

① ask   ② find   ③ keep
④ take   ⑤ tell

18 다음 중 어법상 바른 문장의 개수는?

ⓐ My brother got his robot to do his homework.

ⓑ I heard my name called.

ⓒ My parents won't let me to go out late at night.

ⓓ It will help me improving my English.

ⓔ I'll make my robot tell funny stories.

ⓕ Being sick makes me sad.

ⓖ Eating an apple a day can make us healthily.

ⓗ My father always keeps his car clean and shiny.

ⓘ I like the music because it always makes me relaxed.

① 2개   ② 3개   ③ 4개   ④ 5개   ⑤ 6개

19 다음 빈칸에 공통으로 들어갈 말은?

> • Sunny days _____ me happy.
> • I'll _____ my robot cook for me.

① have   ② find   ③ let
④ make   ⑤ take

[20~21] 다음 빈칸에 알맞은 것은?

20

> Eddie's room is not tidy. I'll make him keep it _____.

① clean   ② cleans   ③ cleaned
④ cleaning   ⑤ to clean

21

> Emily had her boy friend _____ some games with her sisters.

① play   ② plays   ③ played
④ playing   ⑤ to play

22 다음 밑줄 친 단어의 쓰임이 주어진 문장과 같은 것은?

> He made me wash his car yesterday.

① Harry wanted to make me a bowl of spaghetti.
② The heavy snowstorm made us stay at home.
③ They wonder if taking a foot bath can make us relaxed.
④ We made him captain.
⑤ Do you know what made her upset?

Reading

[23~24] 다음 글을 읽고 물음에 답하시오.

> "Wow, I can read a book in my room now!" shouted Marco, a boy in a village in the Philippines. His house has no electricity just ⓐlike all the other houses in the village. People in the village are too poor to pay for electricity. Even during the daytime, they live in darkness because the houses are packed close together. Now things are changing because of a single plastic bottle. One plastic bottle in the ceiling can light up a whole room without __(A)__ any electricity.

23 위 글의 빈칸 (A)에 use를 알맞은 형태로 쓰시오.

➡ _____

24 위 글의 밑줄 친 ⓐlike와 같은 의미로 쓰인 것을 모두 고르시오.

① He ran like the wind.
② They responded in like manner.
③ I like to paint in my spare time.
④ What do you like about him?
⑤ She acts like a fool.

[25~27] 다음 글을 읽고 물음에 답하시오.

> This amazing plastic bottle is called a Moser lamp because it was invented by Alfredo Moser. In 2002, there were many blackouts in his town in Brazil. These blackouts made him come up with a new way to light his house.
> A Moser lamp can be made for about one dollar and lasts for about 10 years. It is also very safe. It can never start a house fire. Surprisingly, it is very easy ⓐto make this magic lamp.

25 What made Alfredo Moser come up with a new way to light his house? Fill in the blanks with suitable words.

➡ _____ in his town in Brazil in 2002 made him do so.

26 위 글의 밑줄 친 @to make와 to부정사의 용법이 다른 것을 <u>모두</u> 고르시오.

① He decided <u>to sell</u> his car.

② He is looking for friends <u>to go</u> camping with.

③ My dream is <u>to become</u> a famous actor.

④ That club is not easy <u>to join</u>.

⑤ I found it useless <u>to teach</u> him math.

27 위 글의 내용과 일치하지 <u>않는</u> 것은?

① 이 놀라운 플라스틱병은 발명가의 이름을 따서 Moser 램프라고 불린다.

② 2002년, 브라질에 있는 Alfredo Moser의 마을에는 정전이 잦았다.

③ Moser 램프는 1달러 정도로 만들 수 있고 10년 정도 지속된다.

④ Moser 램프는 매우 안전해서 절대 집에 불을 낼 수 없다.

⑤ 이 신기한 램프를 만드는 것은 다소 어렵다.

[28~30] 다음 글을 읽고 물음에 답하시오.

1. Fill a clear plastic bottle with water.
2. Add some ___@___ to keep the water (A) [clear / clearly].
3. Make a hole in the roof, and push the bottle into the hole.
4. Let (B)[a third / a thirds] of the bottle remain above the roof.
5. Sunlight (C)[bends / is bent] by the water in the bottle and spreads around the room.

28 주어진 영영풀이를 참고하여 빈칸 @에 철자 b로 시작하는 단어를 쓰시오.

> a chemical that is used to make cloth white

➡ _____

29 위 글의 괄호 (A)~(C)에서 어법상 알맞은 낱말을 골라 쓰시오.

➡ (A) _____ (B) _____ (C) _____

30 위 글의 제목으로 가장 알맞은 것을 고르시오.

① How to Use a Clear Plastic Bottle

② Are There Any Ways to Use Natural Resources?

③ Is It Easy to Make a Hole in the Roof?

④ How to Make a Moser Lamp from a Bottle

⑤ We Must Use Sunlight Effectively!

[31~32] 다음 글을 읽고 물음에 답하시오.

You can make a lot of things with a wire hanger. You can even make a book holder. First, bend a wire hanger in the middle. Second, bend both ends up and forward. ___@___ , bend down the top part of the hanger. Now, your book holder is ready. ⓑIt will keep your hands free.

31 위 글의 빈칸 @에 들어갈 알맞은 말을 <u>모두</u> 고르시오.

① Lastly   ② At last

③ In the end   ④ Finally

⑤ As a result

32 위 글의 밑줄 친 ⓑIt이 가리키는 것을 본문에서 찾아 쓰시오.

➡ _____

01 다음 두 단어의 관계가 같도록 빈칸에 알맞은 말을 쓰시오. 출제율 85%

popular : unpopular = dangerous : _____

02 우리말에 맞게 빈칸 (A), (B)에 알맞은 단어를 쓰시오. 출제율 95%

- 심지어 낮 동안에도, 집들이 빽빽하게 들어차 있어서 그들은 어둠 속에 살아간다.
  Even during the daytime, they live in darkness because the houses are (A)_____ close together.
- 이 자선단체 덕분에, 필리핀의 수천 가구가 이제 Moser 램프를 갖고 있다.
  (B)_____ the charity, thousands of homes in the Philippines now have Moser lamps.

[03~04] 다음 영영풀이에 해당하는 단어를 찾으시오.

03 출제율 90%

a strong chemical used for cleaning things or removing colour from things

① lamp   ② thing
③ bleach   ④ magic
⑤ paint

04 출제율 90%

to cover, reach, or have an effect on a wider or increasing area

① cross   ② last
③ shout   ④ spend
⑤ spread

[05~06] 다음 대화를 읽고 물음에 답하시오.

G: Can you ①turn up the volume on your phone? I like this song.
B: I can't ②turn up it anymore. It's ③the highest volume.
G: Let me just put your phone in a glass. ④I've heard a glass works like a speaker.
B: ⑤What an interesting idea! Let's (A)try it now.

05 위 대화의 ①~⑤ 중 어법상 어색한 것은? 출제율 100%

①   ②   ③   ④   ⑤

06 위 대화의 밑줄 친 (A)try it이 의미하는 것을 본문에서 찾아 6단어로 쓰시오. 출제율 90%

➡ _____

07 다음 대화의 빈칸에 들어갈 말로 알맞은 것은? 출제율 95%

B: I've heard that a movie star is coming to our school.
G: That's right. She's my favorite actress.
B: Oh, who is she?
G: Miranda Kim. She played the chief scientist in the movie *Jupiter*.
B: Wow, _____

① I can't wait to see her!
② don't forget to take something to eat.
③ don't forget to take lots of rest.
④ I know that.
⑤ how wonderful you are!

08 다음 대화의 밑줄 친 우리말에 맞게 주어진 단어를 알맞은 순서로 배열하시오.

A: I've heard that saving electricity is the best way to save the Earth.
B: I've heard that, too. What can we do to save electricity?
A: Why don't we turn off the light when we're not using it?
B: That's a good idea. <u>방을 나갈 때 불 끄는 것을 잊지 마.</u> (turn off / when / don't / to / you / leave / forget / the light / your room)

➡️ _____

_____

[09~10] 다음 대화를 읽고 물음에 답하시오.

Yuri: What's wrong, Jaden?
Jaden: My science homework is too difficult.
Yuri: What do you have to do?
Jaden: I need to find a way to ⓐsave trees.
Yuri: That's easy. I've heard that we can save trees by using ⓑless paper.
Jaden: Oh, I think I've heard that, too. Then, I can just ⓒstop using paper cups.
Yuri: Yes! You can also use just one paper towel to dry off your hands.
Jaden: That's ⓓpossible. I need at least two or three paper towels.
Yuri: Just shake your hands before you use a paper towel. Then, _____(A)_____.
Jaden: Oh, that's a good idea, Yuri! I'll try that next time.
Yuri: Good! Just ⓔdon't forget to shake your hands at least 10 times.

09 위 대화의 빈칸 (A)에 들어갈 말로 알맞은 것은?

① you will have to save trees
② you will need more paper towels
③ you will stop using paper cups
④ your hands will be dried up faster
⑤ one will be more than enough

10 위 대화의 밑줄 친 ⓐ~ⓔ 중, 어휘의 쓰임이 <u>어색한</u> 것은?

① ⓐ　　② ⓑ　　③ ⓒ　　④ ⓓ　　⑤ ⓔ

[11~12] 어법상 바른 문장을 <u>모두</u> 고르시오.

11 ① You'd better have the tooth pulled out.
② Let him joining your club.
③ He made me to introduce myself.
④ She had Mike called me.
⑤ She got me to walk her dog.

12 ① We found the window break.
② I saw him sang in front of students.
③ She left him alone.
④ The novel made her famous.
⑤ Let's keep the room clean.

13 다음 우리말을 주어진 어휘를 이용하여 영작하시오.

(1) 이 영화는 그 배우들을 유명하게 만들었다.
(make, famous)

➡️ _____

(2) 내 부모님은 내가 열심히 공부하도록 시키신다.
(make, hard)

➡️ _____

출제율 90%

14 다음 문장에서 어법상 틀린 부분을 찾아 바르게 고치시오.

> He got me wash the dishes.

_____ ➡ _____

[15~16] 다음 글을 읽고 물음에 답하시오.

"Wow, I can read a book in my room now!" shouted Marco, a boy in a village in the Philippines. His house has no electricity just like all the other houses in the village. ⓐ마을 사람들은 너무나 가난해서 전기세를 낼 수가 없다. Even (A)[during / while] the daytime, they live in darkness because the houses are (B)[packing / packed] close together. Now things are changing because of a single plastic bottle. One plastic bottle in the ceiling can light up a whole room without using (C)[any / no] electricity.

출제율 90%

15 위 글의 밑줄 친 ⓐ의 우리말에 맞게 주어진 어휘를 이용하여 11단어로 영작하시오.

> people, too, pay for

➡ _____

출제율 95%

16 위 글의 괄호 (A)~(C)에서 어법상 알맞은 낱말을 골라 쓰시오.

➡ (A) _____ (B) _____ (C) _____

[17~19] 다음 글을 읽고 물음에 답하시오.

(A)This amazing plastic bottle is called a Moser lamp because it was invented ① by Alfredo Moser. ②In 2002, there were many blackouts in his town in Brazil. These blackouts made him come up ③with a new way to light his house.

A Moser lamp can be made ④by about one dollar and lasts ⑤for about 10 years. It is also very safe. It can never start a house fire. Surprisingly, ⓐit is very easy to make this magic lamp.

출제율 85%

17 위 글의 밑줄 친 ①~⑤ 중 전치사의 쓰임이 어색한 것을 찾아 고치시오.

_____ 번 ➡ _____

출제율 90%

18 위 글의 밑줄 친 ⓐit과 문법적 쓰임이 다른 것을 모두 고르시오.

① I gave it to her.

② It is impossible to master English in a month or two.

③ They considered it impossible for us to climb the mountain.

④ How far is it from here to the station?

⑤ It is strange that he says so.

출제율 100%

19 위 글을 읽고 밑줄 친 (A)This amazing plastic bottle에 대해 알 수 없는 것을 고르시오.

① 이름 ② 발명가 ③ 발명 동기
④ 제작비 ⑤ 제작 방법

[20~21] 다음 글을 읽고 물음에 답하시오.

How to make a Moser lamp from a bottle
1. Fill a clear plastic bottle with water.
2. Add some bleach @물을 깨끗이 유지하기 위해.
3. Make a hole in the roof, and push the bottle into the hole.
4. Let a third of the bottle remain above the roof.
5. Sunlight is bent by the water in the bottle and spreads around the room.

출제율 90%

20 위 글의 밑줄 친 @의 우리말을 다섯 단어로 쓰시오.

➡ _____

출제율 100%

21 위 글을 읽고 대답할 수 <u>없는</u> 질문은?

① What do you need to make a Moser lamp?
② Why do you need to add some bleach?
③ Where do you install a Moser lamp?
④ How long does it take to install a Moser lamp?
⑤ How does a Moser lamp operate?

[22~24] 다음 글을 읽고 물음에 답하시오.

In the Philippines, Moser lamps are widely used by the My Shelter @Foundation. ⓑ또한 그 자선단체는 지역 사람들에게 램프를 만들고 설치하는 법을 가르친다. Thanks to the charity, thousands of homes in the Philippines now have Moser lamps. It has also made Moser lamps popular in other countries, such as Argentina, India, and Fiji. Moser lamps will light up the lives of many people for many years to come.

출제율 85%

22 위 글의 밑줄 친 @Foundation과 같은 의미로 쓰인 것을 고르시오.

① These stories have no <u>foundation</u>.
② They are getting enough financial support from a religious <u>foundation</u>.
③ The organization has grown enormously since its <u>foundation</u> in 1955.
④ The rumour is totally without <u>foundation</u>.
⑤ The holiday is also called the National <u>Foundation</u> Day of Korea.

출제율 95%

23 위 글의 밑줄 친 ⓑ의 우리말에 맞게 한 단어를 보충하여, 주어진 어휘를 알맞게 배열하시오.

to make / also / the lamps / local people / teaches / and / the charity / install

➡ _____

_____

출제율 100%

24 다음 중 'My Shelter Foundation'의 활동에 대한 설명으로 옳지 <u>않은</u> 것을 고르시오.

① 필리핀에서 My Shelter Foundation에 의해 Moser 램프가 널리 사용된다.
② 지역 사람들에게 램프를 만드는 법을 가르친다.
③ 지역 사람들에게 램프를 설치하는 법을 가르친다.
④ 필리핀의 수만 가구가 이제 Moser 램프를 갖게 해주었다.
⑤ 아르헨티나, 인도, 피지와 같은 다른 나라들에서도 Moser 램프가 유명해지도록 만들었다.

[01~02] 다음 대화를 읽고 물음에 답하시오.

Yuri: What's wrong, Jaden?

Jaden: My science homework is too difficult.

Yuri: What do you have to do?

Jaden: I need to find a way to save trees.

Yuri: That's easy. _____(A)_____

Jaden: Oh, I think I've heard that, too. Then, I can just stop using paper cups.

Yuri: Yes! You can also use just one paper towel to dry off your hands.

Jaden: That's impossible. I need at least two or three paper towels.

Yuri: (B)종이 수건을 쓰기 전에 손을 털어 봐. Then, one will be more than enough.

Jaden: Oh, that's a good idea, Yuri! I'll try that next time.

Yuri: Good! Just don't forget to shake your hands at least 10 times.

01 위 대화의 빈칸 (A)에 들어갈 표현을 주어진 〈조건〉에 맞게 영어로 쓰시오.

┤ 조건 ├
• 어떤 사실을 들어서 알고 있음을 말할 때 사용하는 표현을 쓸 것
• 'hear'를 이용하여 현재완료로 표현할 것
• 'that'절에 'save trees', 'by', 'less'를 이용하여 '우리가 종이를 덜 사용함으로써 나무들을 살릴 수 있다'는 우리말에 맞게 쓸 것

➡ _____

02 위 대화의 밑줄 친 우리말에 맞게 주어진 단어를 알맞은 순서로 배열하시오.

hands / before / shake / just / your / you / a / use / paper / towel

➡ _____

03 다음 문장의 빈칸에 들어갈 말을 주어진 〈조건〉에 맞게 영어로 쓰시오.

B: What's your plan for this winter break?

G: I'm going to visit Vietnam with my parents.

B: That sounds exciting. What are you going to do there?

G: I'm going to spend some time on the beach and eat lots of seafood.

B: Good. _____, too.

G: O.K., I won't forget.

┤ 조건 ├
• 상대방에게 상기시키는 표현을 쓸 것
• '~할 것을 잊지 마'라는 뜻으로 쓸 것
• 'try the fruit there'라는 표현을 사용할 것

➡ _____

04 다음 우리말을 주어진 어휘를 이용하여 영작하시오.

(1) 나는 사촌의 생일잔치에 가고 싶지 않았으나 엄마가 나를 가도록 하셨다. (my cousin, my mom, make)

➡ _____
_____

(2) 그들은 그들의 집이 칠해지도록 시켰다. (have, their house, paint)

➡ _____

(3) 그 선물은 그 아이들을 종일 행복하게 해 주었다. (present, make, all day long)

➡ _____

05 다음 문장에서 어법상 어색한 것을 고쳐 다시 쓰시오.

(1) The noise kept me wake.

➡ _____

(2) He found the exam difficultly.

➡ _____

(3) These blackouts made him to come up with a new way to light his house.

➡ _____

_____

(4) He had his computer repair yesterday.

➡ _____

(5) Help me taking some pictures of them.

➡ _____

07 주어진 영영풀이에 해당하는 단어를 위 글에서 찾아 쓰시오.

> periods of time during which the electricity supply to a place is temporarily cut off

➡ _____

08 본문의 내용과 일치하도록 다음 빈칸에 알맞은 단어를 쓰시오.

> We can say that a Moser lamp is _____ _____ because it can never start a house fire.

[06~08] 다음 글을 읽고 물음에 답하시오.

ⓐThis amazing plastic bottle is called a Moser lamp because it was invented by Alfredo Moser. In 2002, there were many blackouts in his town in Brazil. These blackouts made him come up with a new way to light his house.

A Moser lamp can be made for about one dollar and lasts for about 10 years. It is also very safe. It can never start a house fire. Surprisingly, it is very easy to make this magic lamp.

[09~10] 다음 글을 읽고 물음에 답하시오.

In the Philippines, Moser lamps are widely used by the My Shelter Foundation. ⓐThe charity also teaches local people how to make and install the lamps. ⓑThanks to the charity, thousand of homes in the Philippines now have Moser lamps. It has also made Moser lamps popular in other countries, such as Argentina, India, and Fiji. Moser lamps will light up the lives of many people for many years to come.

06 위 글의 밑줄 친 ⓐ를 능동태로 고치시오.

➡ _____

_____

09 위 글의 밑줄 친 ⓐThe charity가 가리키는 것을 본문에서 찾아 쓰시오.

➡ _____

10 위 글의 밑줄 친 ⓑ에서 어법상 틀린 부분을 찾아 고치시오.

_____ ➡ _____

01 상자 안의 Plan과 Advice를 읽고 어울리는 것끼리 연결하여, 계획과 조언을 말하는 대화를 〈보기〉와 같이 작성하시오.

Plan	Advice
go to Gyeongju go on a field trip	visit the National Museum take something to eat

┌─ 보기 ─────────────────────────────────────┐

• Plan: go hiking   • Advice: take a bottle of water

A: I'm going to go hiking.

B: Don't forget to take a bottle of water.

A: O.K., I won't forget.

└──┘

02 다음 문장을 make를 이용하여 비슷한 의미의 문장으로 바꿔 쓰시오.

(1) Mom told me to do the dishes this morning.

(2) The doctor ordered him to stop smoking.

(3) Miranda asked her husband to buy some fruit.

(1) _____

(2) _____

(3) _____

03 다음 내용을 바탕으로 자신이 만들고 싶은 물건에 관한 글을 쓰시오.

a book holder

1. Bend a wire hanger in the middle.

2. Bend both ends up and forward.

3. Bend down the top part of the hanger.

4. Put your book on the book holder.

You can make a lot of things with a (A)_____. You can even make a book holder. First, (B)_____ a wire hanger in the middle. Second, bend (C)_____ up and forward. Finally, bend down the (D)_____ of the hanger. Now, your book holder is ready. It will keep your hands (E)_____.

단원별 모의고사

01 다음 단어에 대한 영어 설명이 <u>어색한</u> 것은?

① roof: the covering that forms the top of a building, vehicle, etc
② last: to continue to exist
③ invent: to design and/or create something that has never been made before
④ install: to put furniture, a machine, or a piece of equipment into position and make it ready to use
⑤ surprisingly: including a lot of different places, people, subjects, etc

02 다음 우리말에 맞게 빈칸에 알맞은 단어를 쓰시오.

(1) 나는 나무를 심기 위해 구멍을 파고 있다.
➡ I am digging a _____ to plant a tree.

(2) 전선을 구부릴 때 적절한 도구를 사용해라.
➡ Use the right tools when you bend a _____.

03 다음 영영풀이에 해당하는 단어를 고르시오.

a system of giving money, food, or help free to those who are in need because they are ill, poor, or have no home, or any organization that has the purpose of providing money or helping in this way

① company   ② charity
③ kingdom   ④ government
⑤ foundation

04 빈칸에 들어갈 단어를 영어 설명을 보고 주어진 철자로 시작하여 쓰시오.

This a_____ plastic bottle is called a Moser lamp because it was invented by Alfredo Moser.
<영어 설명>
extremely surprising

05 대화의 빈칸에 들어갈 말은?

B: I've heard that a famous baseball player is coming to our school.
G: That's right. He's my favorite player.
B: Oh, who is he?
G: I'm not going to tell you. _____

① I won't forget.
② I've heard that, too.
③ Sorry to hear that.
④ It's a surprise!
⑤ I had a great time there.

06 주어진 문장에 이어질 글의 순서로 알맞은 것은?

W: Excuse me, are you finished with your meal?

(A) Yes, please.
(B) Do you want to take the leftovers home?
(C) Yes, it was really good.
(D) Don't forget to eat the leftovers by tomorrow.

① (A) – (B) – (C) – (D)
② (B) – (C) – (A) – (D)
③ (C) – (A) – (D) – (B)
④ (C) – (B) – (A) – (D)
⑤ (D) – (B) – (C) – (A)

07 대화의 밑줄 친 ①~⑤ 중 어휘의 쓰임이 <u>어색한</u> 것은?

> A: I've heard that ①<u>saving</u> electricity is the best way to ②<u>save</u> the Earth.
>
> B: I've heard that, too. What can we do to save electricity?
>
> A: Why don't we ③<u>turn off</u> the light when we're not using it?
>
> B: That's a good idea. Don't ④<u>forget to</u> <u>turn off</u> the light when you ⑤<u>enter</u> your room.

①   ②   ③   ④   ⑤

08 다음 중 짝지어진 대화가 <u>어색한</u> 것은?

① A: I'm going to the supermarket.

    B: Don't forget to buy some toilet paper. We're running out of it.

② A: Tom, are you finished with your art homework?

    B: Yes, I'm almost done.

③ A: I've heard the school soccer team won the soccer match.

    B: Really? That's nice.

④ A: I've heard the school gym is going to open next month.

    B: I will, thanks.

⑤ A: You know what? I've heard the car was invented earlier than the bicycle.

    B: Really? That's interesting.

[09~10] 다음 대화를 읽고 요약문의 빈칸을 완성하시오.

09

> B: What's your plan for this winter break?
>
> G: I'm going to visit Hong Kong with my parents.
>
> B: That sounds exciting. What are you going to do there?

> G: I'm going to go to an amusement park. I'm also going to try all kinds of food.
>
> B: Good. Don't forget to try some dim sum.

⬇

> The girl is going to visit Hong Kong with _____ during this _____. She is going to go to an _____, and she will also try all kinds of _____. And the boy suggests that she try some _____.

10

> B: I've heard that a movie star is coming to our school.
>
> G: That's right. She's my favorite actress.
>
> B: Oh, who is she?
>
> G: Miranda Kim. She played the chief scientist in the movie *Jupiter*.
>
> B: Wow, I can't wait to see her!

⬇

> The boy has _____ that a _____ is coming to their school. Actually, the movie star is the girl's _____ _____. Her name is Miranda Kim, and she _____ the _____ scientist in the movie *Jupiter*.

[11~12] 다음 대화를 읽고 물음에 답하시오.

> Yuri: What's wrong, Jaden?
>
> Jaden: My science homework is too difficult.
>
> Yuri: What do you have to do?
>
> Jaden: I need to find a way to save trees.
>
> Yuri: That's easy. _____ (A)
>
> Jaden: Oh, I think I've heard that, too. Then, I can just stop using paper cups.
>
> Yuri: Yes! You can also use just one paper towel to dry off your hands.

Jaden: That's impossible. I need at least two or three paper towels.

Yuri: Just shake your hands before you use a paper towel. Then, one will be more than enough.

Jaden: Oh, that's a good idea, Yuri! I'll try that next time.

Yuri: Good! Just don't forget to shake your hands at least 10 times.

11 빈칸 (A)에 알맞은 말은?

① I've heard that drinking coffee very often isn't good for our health.

② I've never been to the Chinese restaurant.

③ I've heard that we can save trees by using less paper.

④ I've heard that we have to plant as many trees as possible.

⑤ I've heard that using paper cups is a way to save the earth.

12 위 대화를 읽고 다음 질문에 대해 영어로 답하시오.

> Q: How can we use only one paper towel to dry off our hands?

➡ We can _____

_____.

13 다음 그림을 보고 괄호 안에 주어진 어휘를 이용하여 주어진 대화의 빈칸을 한 단어씩 알맞게 채우시오.

A: Did you like the sandwich?

B: Yes, I did. Having delicious sandwiches always makes _____ _____. (happy)

14 다음 중 어법상 바르지 <u>않은</u> 것은?

① I don't want to have my picture take by a stranger.

② Don't make me say that again.

③ I won't let the cake be touched.

④ Let's keep the classroom clean.

⑤ The song has made him popular.

15 다음 중 어법상 <u>어색한</u> 부분을 바르게 고치시오.

(1) They took care of the apartment and kept it tidily.

_____ ➡ _____

(2) Dad had the tree plant.

_____ ➡ _____

16 주어진 문장의 밑줄 친 부분과 용법이 <u>다른</u> 하나는?

> My brother always <u>makes</u> me clean the room.

① It <u>makes</u> me pleased.

② Playing the game <u>made</u> me excited.

③ Her mom <u>made</u> her a dress.

④ I will <u>make</u> her call you tomorrow.

⑤ He <u>made</u> me buy the book.

17 다음 글에서 어법상 틀린 부분을 찾아 바르게 고쳐 쓰시오.

> Sam really wanted a dog, but his parents didn't let him to have a pet.

_____ ➡ _____

[18~20] 다음 글을 읽고 물음에 답하시오.

"Wow, I can read a book in my room now!" shouted Marco, a boy in a village in (A) [Philippines / the Philippines]. His house has no electricity just like all the other houses in the village. People in the village are _____ⓐ_____ poor _____ⓑ_____ pay for electricity. Even during the daytime, they live in darkness (B) [because / because of] the houses are packed close together. Now things are changing (C) [because / because of] a single plastic bottle. One plastic bottle in the ceiling can light up a whole room without using any electricity.

18 위 글의 빈칸 ⓐ와 ⓑ에 들어갈 알맞은 말을 고르시오.

① so – that   ② too – to
③ such – that   ④ so – as to
⑤ enough – to

19 위 글의 괄호 (A)~(C)에서 어법상 알맞은 낱말을 골라 쓰시오.

➡ (A) _____   (B) _____
(C) _____

20 Does a plastic bottle in the ceiling need any electricity to light up a whole room? Answer in English in a full sentence. (3 words)

➡ _____

[21~22] 다음 글을 읽고 물음에 답하시오.

This amazing plastic bottle is called a Moser lamp ⓐbecause it was invented by Alfredo Moser. In 2002, there were many blackouts in his town in Brazil. ⓑThese blackouts made him to come up with a new way to light his house.
A Moser lamp can be made for about one dollar and lasts for about 10 years. It is also very safe. It can never start a house fire. Surprisingly, it is very easy to make this magic lamp.

21 위 글의 밑줄 친 ⓐ를 능동태로 고치시오.

➡ _____

22 위 글의 밑줄 친 ⓑ에서 어법상 틀린 부분을 찾아 고치시오.

_____ ➡ _____

[23~24] 다음 글을 읽고 물음에 답하시오.

In the Philippines, Moser lamps are widely used by the My Shelter Foundation. The charity also teaches local people how to make and install the lamps. Thanks to the charity, thousands of homes in the Philippines now have Moser lamps. It has also made Moser lamps popular in other countries, such as Argentina, India, and Fiji. Moser lamps will light up the lives of many people for many years to come.

23 What enables thousands of homes in the Philippines to have Moser lamps now? Answer in English. (5 words)

➡ _____

24 위 글의 내용과 일치하지 <u>않는</u> 것은?

① In the Philippines, the My Shelter Foundation widely uses Moser lamps.
② The My Shelter Foundation teaches local people how to make the lamps.
③ The My Shelter Foundation teaches local people how to install the lamps.
④ Thousands of homes in the Philippines now have Moser lamps by the help of the My Shelter Foundation.
⑤ Many people of the Philippines have made Moser lamps popular in other countries.

Lesson 8

Have Fun This Winter!

 ## 의사소통 기능

- 관심 있는 것 말하기
  I'm interested in reading history books.

- 빈도 묻고 답하기
  A: How often do you clean your room?
  B: I clean my room once a week.

 ## 언어 형식

- 지각동사
  Gunnar **saw the river ice cracking**.

- tell/want/ask+목적어+to부정사
  Gunnar **told Balto to continue** on.

Words & Expressions

Key Words

- **around** [əráund] 부 대략
- **arrive** [əráiv] 동 도착하다
- **awesome** [ɔ́:səm] 형 굉장한, 엄청난
- **bark** [bɑ:rk] 동 (개가) 짖다
- **broadcast** [brɔ́:dkæst] 명 방송
- **cage** [keidʒ] 명 우리
- **celebrate** [séləbrèit] 동 기념하다, 축하하다
- **climb** [klaim] 동 오르다, 올라가다
- **cover** [kʌ́vər] 동 가다, 이동하다
- **crack** [kræk] 동 갈라지다, 금이 가다
- **disease** [dizí:z] 명 질병, 병, 질환
- **favorite** [féivərit] 형 가장 좋아하는
- **frozen** [fróuzn] 형 얼어붙은
- **gorilla** [gərílə] 명 고릴라
- **granddaughter** [grǽnddɔ̀:tər] 명 손녀, 외손녀
- **grandparent** [grǽndpɛ̀ərənt] 명 조부모
- **grandparents' place** 조부모님 댁
- **happen** [hǽpən] 동 발생하다, 일어나다
- **heart-warming** 가슴 따뜻한
- **heavy snow** 폭설
- **highlight** [háilait] 명 하이라이트, 가장 흥미로운 부분
- **hockey** [háki] 명 하키
- **interesting** [íntərəstiŋ] 형 흥미로운
- **language** [lǽŋgwidʒ] 명 언어
- **lead dog** 선두 개, 우두머리 개
- **live** [laiv] 형 생방송의, 생중계의
- **medicine** [médsn] 명 약
- **neck** [nek] 명 목
- **outdoor** [áutdɔr] 형 실외의
- **popular** [pápjulər] 형 인기 있는
- **race** [reis] 동 경주하다, 달리다 명 경주, 질주
- **reach** [ri:tʃ] 동 도달하다, 닿다
- **rescue** [réskju:] 동 구하다, 구조하다
- **relay** [rí:lei] 명 릴레이 경주, 계주
- **save** [seiv] 동 구하다
- **shout** [ʃaut] 동 외치다
- **sled** [sled] 명 썰매
- **slip** [slip] 동 미끄러지다
- **snowstorm** [snóustɔ̀:rm] 명 눈보라
- **special** [spéʃəl] 형 특별한
- **spread** [spred] 동 (사람들 사이로) 퍼지다
- **table tennis** 탁구
- **terrible** [térəbl] 형 끔찍한
- **trail** [treil] 명 코스, 흔적
- **the Winter Olympics** 동계올림픽
- **weekend** [wí:kend] 명 주말
- **winter break** 겨울 방학

Key Expressions

- **at least** 적어도
- **be good at** ~을 잘하다
- **be interested in** ~에 관심이 있다
- **be sure to**부정사 반드시 ~하다
- **continue on** 계속하다
- **get[become]+형용사** ~가 되다
- **Good for you!** 잘됐다!
- **go on a trip** 여행을 가다
- **go skating** 스케이트 타러 가다
- **go sledding** 썰매 타러 가다
- **go swimming** 수영하러 가다
- **I can't wait to**부정사 빨리 ~하고 싶다
- **in memory of** ~을 기념[추모]하여
- **just in time** 제때
- **keep -ing** 계속 ~하다
- **once a month** 한 달에 한 번
- **on the trail** 루트[코스]를 따라가는
- **right away** 곧바로, 즉시
- **take part in** ~에 참여[참가]하다
- **take place** 개최되다, 일어나다

Word Power

※ 서로 반대되는 뜻을 가진 어휘

□ **climb** (올라가다) ↔ **descend** (내려오다)

□ **popular** (인기 있는) ↔ **unpopular** (인기 없는)

□ **special** (특별한) ↔ **general** (일반적인)

□ **reach** (도달하다) ↔ **leave** (떠나다)

□ **terrible** (끔찍한) ↔ **awesome** (굉장한)

□ **continue** (계속하다) ↔ **stop** (멈추다)

※ 서로 비슷한 뜻을 가진 단어

□ **shout** : **yell** (외치다)

□ **save** : **rescue** (구하다)

□ **arrive in**[at] : **reach** (도착하다)

□ **crack** : **break**, **split** (갈라지다)

□ **slip** : **slide** (미끄러지다)

□ **happen** : **take place** (일어나다, 발생하다)

English Dictionary

□ **continue** 계속하다
→ to keep happening, existing, or doing something, or to cause something or someone to do this
계속 일어나거나, 존재하거나, 무언가를 하거나, 혹은 무언가나 누군가가 이런 일을 하게 하다

□ **crack** 금이 가다, 갈라지다
→ to break or to make something break, either so that it gets lines on its surface, or so that it breaks into pieces
표면에 금이 가게 하거나 조각으로 부수기 위해 무언가를 깨다

□ **disease** 질병
→ illness of people, animals, plants, etc., caused by infection or a failure of health rather than by an accident
사고에 의해서라기보다는 감염이나 건강 쇠약으로 야기되는 사람, 동물, 식물 등이 아픈 것

□ **medicine** 약
→ a substance, especially in the form of a liquid or a pill, that is a treatment for illness or injury
특히 액체 또는 알약의 형태로, 질병 또는 부상의 치료제인 물질

□ **race** 경주
→ a competition in which all the competitors try to be the fastest and to finish first
모든 경쟁자들이 가장 빠르게 먼저 끝내려고 하는 시합

□ **reach** 도달하다
→ to arrive at a place, especially after spending a long time or a lot of effort travelling
특히 이동하면서 많은 시간이나 많은 노력을 소모한 후에 어떤 장소에 도착하다

□ **relay** 릴레이 경주, 계주
→ a running or swimming race between two or more teams in which each person in the team runs or swims part of the race
팀 내의 각 사람이 경주의 일부를 달리거나 수영하는 두 개 이상의 팀 간의 달리기 또는 수영 경주

□ **rescue** 구하다
→ to help someone or something out of a dangerous, harmful, or unpleasant situation
위험하거나, 해롭거나, 불쾌한 상황에서 나오도록 누군가나 어떤 것을 돕다

□ **sled** 썰매
→ an object used for travelling over snow and ice with long, narrow strips of wood or metal
길고 좁은 나무 조각이나 금속 조각으로 눈과 얼음 위를 여행하는 데 사용되는 물체

□ **snowstorm** 눈보라
→ a heavy fall of snow that is blown by strong winds
강한 바람에 의해 날리는 폭설

□ **spread** 퍼지다
→ to cover, reach, or have an effect on a wider or increasing area
더 넓은 또는 증가하는 영역을 덮거나, 도달하거나, 영향을 미치다

□ **take place** 개최되다, 일어나다
→ to happen, especially after being planned or arranged
특히 계획되거나 준비된 후에 발생하다

□ **terrible** 끔찍한
→ extremely severe in a way that causes harm or damage
해나 손상을 야기하는 식으로 극도로 심각한

□ **trail** 흔적, 코스
→ a long line or a series of marks that have been left by someone or something
긴 줄 또는 누군가 혹은 무언가에 의해 남겨진 일련의 표시

서답형

01 다음 짝지어진 두 단어의 관계가 같도록 빈칸에 알맞은 단어를 쓰시오.

> crack : split = save : _____

[02~03] 다음 빈칸에 들어갈 말로 가장 적절한 것은?

02

> In early March every year, the world's biggest sled dog race _____ in Alaska.

① slips ② spreads
③ takes part ④ rescues
⑤ takes place

중요

03

> One cold winter day in 1925, a terrible thing happened in Nome. Some children got very sick, and the _____ kept spreading.

① cage ② disease
③ sled ④ medicine
⑤ race

[04~05] 다음 영영 풀이에 해당하는 단어를 고르시오.

04

> to help someone or something out of a dangerous, harmful, or unpleasant situation

① crack ② reach
③ continue ④ rescue
⑤ shout

05

> a competition in which all the competitors try to be the fastest and to finish first

① device ② history
③ race ④ team
⑤ snowstorm

중요

06 밑줄 친 부분의 의미가 잘못된 것은?

① Be sure to watch MBS Sports to enjoy our live broadcasts. (생중계)
② A terrible snowstorm hit us, but we continued on our way. (계속했다)
③ The old wall has started to crack. (갈라지다)
④ Go straight until you reach the main street. (도달하다)
⑤ This trail will lead us to the top of this mountain. (계단)

07 밑줄 친 단어와 가장 가까운 의미를 가진 것은?

> Each team has to cover about 1,800 km from Anchorage to Nome.

① hide ② reveal
③ travel ④ envelop
⑤ wrap

서답형

08 우리말 해석에 맞게 빈칸에 알맞은 말을 세 단어로 쓰시오.

> 21개의 개 팀이 릴레이에 참여했다.
> ➡ Twenty-one dog teams were _____.

01 영영풀이에 해당하는 단어를 〈보기〉에서 찾아 첫 번째 칸에 쓰고, 두 번째 칸에는 우리말 뜻을 쓰시오.

┌─ 보기 ─┐
climb / continue / language / sled / disease

(1) _____ : to keep happening, existing, or doing something, or to cause something or someone to do this : _____

(2) _____ : illness of people, animals, plants, etc., caused by infection or a failure of health rather than by an accident: _____

(3) _____ : an object used for travelling over snow and ice with long, narrow strips of wood or metal: _____

02 다음 우리말 해석에 맞게 주어진 단어를 활용하여 빈칸을 채우시오. (두 단어로 쓰시오)

(1) 몇몇 아이들이 매우 아팠고 병이 계속 퍼졌다.
➡ Some children got very sick, and the disease _____. (spread)

(2) 놈의 사람들은 당장 약이 필요했지만 마을에는 약이 하나도 없었다.
➡ The people of Nome needed medicine _____, but the town did not have any. (away)

03 우리말 해석에 맞게 주어진 철자를 알맞은 순서로 배열하여 빈칸을 채우시오.

(1) 수영을 얼마나 자주 하러 가는데?
➡ How _____ do you go swimming? (t, n, o, f, e)

(2) 아이디타로드 경주는 Nome을 구한 개들을 기념하여 1973년에 시작되었다.
➡ The Iditarod Race began in 1973 in _____ of the dogs that saved Nome. (m, m, o, y, e, r)

04 다음 빈칸에 알맞은 단어를 〈보기〉에서 골라 쓰시오. (형태 변화 가능)

┌─ 보기 ─┐
illness / medicine / outdoor / sled / reach

(1) My little brother likes to ride his _____.

(2) Go straight until you _____ the main street.

(3) Take this _____, and you will get better soon.

05 영어 설명을 읽고 빈칸에 들어갈 알맞은 단어를 쓰시오.

┌────────────────────────────────┐
(1) a program on the radio or on television
(2) the best or most exciting, entertaining, or interesting part of something
└────────────────────────────────┘

Be sure to watch MBS Sports to enjoy our live (1)_____ from 6 p.m. to 11 p.m. At 11 p.m. every night, you can also enjoy our (2)_____ of the most interesting games of the day.

교과서
Conversation

① 관심있는 것 말하기

> • **I'm interested in reading history books.** 나는 역사책들을 읽는 것에 관심이 있다.

■ 자신이 관심 있는 것에 대해 말할 때는 'I'm interested in ~.' 표현을 쓴다. in 뒤에는 명사구를 사용한다.

관심을 표현할 때

- I'm into sports. 나는 정말 스포츠에 흥미가 있어.
- I'm interested in languages. 나는 언어에 관심이 있어.
- My main interest is cars. 나의 주요 관심사는 자동차야.
- I enjoy cooking. 나는 요리하는 것을 즐겨.
- I like[love] taking pictures. 나는 사진 찍는 것을 좋아해.
- I am interested in K-pop. = I have an interest in K-pop. = I am fascinated by K-pop.
  저는 K-pop에 관심이 있습니다.

관심에 대해 물을 때

- Are you interested in science? 너는 과학에 관심이 있니?
- Are you interested in taking pictures? 너는 사진을 찍는 데 관심이 있니?
- What are you interested in? = What are you into? = What are your main interests?
  너는 무엇에 관심이 있니?

핵심 Check

1. 다음 대화의 빈칸에 들어갈 말로 알맞지 <u>않은</u> 것은?

A: What are you interested in?

B: _____

① I have an interest in cooking.
② I enjoy listening to music.
③ I want to be a singer.
④ I'm interested in baseball.
⑤ I'm into cooking.

② 빈도 묻고 답하기

A How often do you clean your room? 너는 얼마나 자주 네 방을 청소하니?

B I clean my room once a week. 일주일에 한 번 청소해.

■ '얼마나 자주 ~을 하니?'를 물을 때는 'How often do you ~?' 표현을 쓰고, 답할 때는 always, usually, sometimes, often, never 등의 빈도부사를 이용하거나, every day[weekend], once[twice / three times] a week[month] 등의 표현으로 빈도를 나타낸다.

- A: How often do you exercise? 너는 얼마나 자주 운동하니?

  B: I exercise almost every day. How about you? 나는 거의 매일 운동해. 너는?

  A: I never exercise. 나는 절대로 운동하지 않아.

- A: How often do you eat fast food? 너는 얼마나 자주 패스트푸드를 먹니?

  B: Every Saturday. 매주 토요일마다.

- A: How often do you brush your teeth? 너는 얼마나 자주 양치질을 하니?

  B: Three times a day. 하루에 3번.

핵심 Check

2. 다음 빈칸에 들어갈 말로 알맞은 것은?

A: How often do you exercise?

B: _____

① It takes two hours to run around the village.
② I think exercise is good for your health.
③ Four times a week.
④ It's too far away from here.
⑤ I'm going to go to the gym.

3. 다음 주어진 우리말 해석에 맞게 빈칸에 알맞은 말을 쓰시오.

A: How often do you get a haircut?

B: 한 달에 한 번.

➡ _____

Listen & Speak 1-A-1

B: What are you doing?

G: ❶I'm listening to old pop songs.

B: Oh, do you like old pop songs?

G: No, ❷I'm not interested in them. I just want to sing my grandma's favorite songs at her birthday party next week.

B: Wow, ❸what a nice granddaughter!

B: 뭐 하고 있어?
G: 오래된 팝송들을 듣고 있어.
B: 오, 오래된 팝송들을 좋아하니?
G: 아니, 거기에 관심이 있지는 않아. 그냥 다음 주 할머니 생신에 할머니께서 가장 좋아하시는 노래들을 불러 드리고 싶어.
B: 우와, 정말 착한 손녀구나!

❶ 현재진행형으로 '~하고 있는 중이다'라는 뜻이다.
❷ be not interested in ~'은 관심이 없음을 나타내는 표현이다. 전치사 in 다음에는 대명사나 명사가 온다.
❸ 'What a+형용사+명사!' 형태로 감탄문을 나타낸다.

Check(√) True or False

(1) G doesn't like old pop songs.　　　　　　　　　　　　　　T ☐ F ☐

(2) G wants to sing her grandma the songs which her grandma likes most.　T ☐ F ☐

Listen & Speak 1-A-2

M: ❶Are you interested in watching the Winter Olympics? Then, ❷ be sure to watch MBS Sports to enjoy our live broadcasts from 6 p.m. to 11 p.m. At 11 p.m. every night, you can also enjoy our highlights of ❸the most interesting games of the day.

M: 동계 올림픽을 보는 것에 관심이 있나요? 그럼, 오후 6시에서 11시까지 하는 MBS Sports의 경기 생중계를 꼭 보세요. 또한 매일 밤 11시에, 여러분은 그날 가장 흥미진진했던 경기의 하이라이트를 즐길 수 있습니다.

❶ 관심에 대해 물어보는 표현으로 'Are you interested in ~?'을 사용한다. 전치사 in 다음에는 동사 'watch'를 동명사 'watching'으로 바꾸어 준다.
❷ be sure to부정사'는 '반드시 ~하다'라는 뜻이다.
❸ 형용사 'interesting'의 최상급은 the most interesting이다.

Check(√) True or False

(3) The speaker may be an announcer working for MBS.　　　　　T ☐ F ☐

(4) You can enjoy the highlights of the most interesting games all day long.　T ☐ F ☐

Listen & Speak 2-A-1

G: ❶What's your favorite sport, James?

B: I don't like sports much, but I sometimes go swimming.

G: ❷How often do you go swimming?

B: ❸Not very often. I only go swimming once a month.

❶ 상대방의 관심사를 묻는 표현이다.
❷ '얼마나 자주 ~을 하니?'의 뜻으로 빈도를 묻는 표현이다.
❸ 빈도를 묻는 말에 대한 답으로 '그렇게 자주는 아니야.'의 뜻으로, 빈도부사를 이용하여 답할 수 있다.

Listen & Speak 2-A-2

B: ❶Do you have any special plans for this weekend, Hana?

G: Well, I'm going to play table tennis with my dad and brother.

B: ❸How often do you play?

G: Every weekend. I love playing table tennis. How about you?

B: I like playing soccer. I enjoy outdoor sports.

❶ 미래의 계획을 물어볼 때 사용하는 표현이다.
❷ 'be going to부정사'는 '~할 예정이다'는 뜻으로 미래 계획을 말할 때 사용한다.
❸ '얼마나 자주 ~을 하니?'를 묻는 말로 빈도를 나타낸다.

Communicate A

Anna: Do you have any special plans for the winter break?

Suho: I'm going to go to my grandparents' place in Pyeongchang. ❶I'll go skating and sledding there. I love winter sports.

Anna: Good for you! I love winter sports, too. My favorite is ice hockey.

Suho: Oh, ❷I've never played ice hockey, but ❸I'm interested in learning how to play it.

Anna: Really? I can teach you ❹how to play.

Suho: That's awesome. Is ice hockey the most popular sport in Canada?

Anna: Yes, it is. ❺Everyone I know loves watching it and playing it.

Suho: ❻How often did you play ice hockey when you were in Canada?

Anna: I played at least two or three times a week in the winter.

Suho: Wow, I'm sure you're really good at ice hockey. ❼I can't wait to learn from you.

❶ 'go -ing' 형태로 '~하러 가다'라는 뜻이다.
❷ 현재완료 형태로 '~해 본 적이 없어'라는 과거 경험을 말하는 표현이다.
❸ 자신이 관심 있는 것에 대해 말할 때 사용하는 표현으로 'be interested in+명사/동명사'를 사용한다.
❹ 'how(의문사)+to부정사'는 '~하는 방법'이란 뜻이다.
❺ everyone은 단수 취급하므로 단수 동사 loves를 사용한다. I know는 목적격 관계대명사절로 주어 Everyone를 수식한다.
❻ 빈도를 묻는 표현으로 '얼마나 자주 ~을 하니?'의 뜻이다.
❼ 'I can't wait to부정사'는 '빨리 ~하고 싶어'의 뜻이다.

Communicate B

A: ❶What winter sport are you interested in?

B: ❷I'm interested in ice skating.

A: How often do you go ice skating?

B: I go ❸once or twice a month.

❶ 상대방에게 무엇에 관심이 있는지 묻는 표현이다.
❷ 자신이 관심 있는 것에 대해 말할 때 사용하는 표현이다.
❸ 빈도를 묻는 말에 대한 답으로 '한 달에 한두 번'의 뜻이다.

Progress Check

1. B: What are you doing?
   G: I'm practicing badminton.
   B: ❶Do you like playing badminton?
   G: No, ❷I'm not interested in it. I just want to pass the badminton test next week.
   B: O.K. Good luck!

2. G: ❶What's your favorite TV show, Jason?
   B: I don't watch TV, but I listen to the radio.
   G: How often do you listen to the radio?
   B: Almost every day.

3. M: ❸It's important to show your love for the people around you. How often do you tell everyone in your family ❹that you love them?

❶ 상대방의 관심사를 묻는 표현이다.
❷ '~에 관심이 없다'는 뜻이다.
❸ 가주어(It) ~ 진주어(to부정사) 구문이다.
❹ tell의 직접목적어로 사용된 that절이다.

• 다음 우리말과 일치하도록 빈칸에 알맞은 말을 쓰시오.

Listen & Speak 1-A

1. B: _____ are you _____?

   G: I'm _____ _____ old pop songs.

   B: Oh, _____ _____ _____ old pop songs?

   G: No, _____ _____ _____ _____ them. I just want _____ _____ my grandma's _____ songs at her birthday party next week.

   B: Wow, _____ _____ _____ granddaughter!

2. M: _____ _____ _____ _____ _____ the Winter Olympics? Then, _____ _____ _____ _____ MBS Sports to enjoy our live broadcasts from 6 p.m. to 11 p.m. At 11 p.m. _____ _____, you can also _____ our _____ of _____ _____ _____ games of the day.

Listen & Speak 2-A

1. W: What's your _____ sport, James?

   B: I don't like sports much, but I sometimes _____ _____.

   G: _____ _____ do you _____ _____?

   B: _____ _____ _____ _____. I only _____ _____ _____ _____ _____ _____.

2. B: Do you have _____ _____ _____ for this weekend, Hana?

   G: Well, I'm going _____ _____ table tennis with my dad and brother.

   B: _____ _____ do you play?

   G: _____ _____. I love playing table tennis. _____ _____ you?

   B: I _____ _____ soccer. I enjoy _____ sports.

해석

1. B: 뭐 하고 있어?
   G: 오래된 팝송들을 듣고 있어.
   B: 오, 오래된 팝송들을 좋아하니?
   G: 아니, 거기에 관심이 있지는 않아. 그냥 다음 주 할머니 생신에 할머니께서 가장 좋아하시는 노래들을 불러 드리고 싶어.
   B: 우와, 정말 착한 손녀구나!

2. M: 동계 올림픽을 보는 것에 관심이 있나요? 그럼, 오후 6시에서 11시까지 하는 MBS Sports의 경기 생중계를 꼭 보세요. 또한 매일 밤 11시에, 여러분은 그날 가장 흥미진진했던 경기의 하이라이트를 즐길 수 있습니다.

1. G: James, 가장 좋아하는 스포츠가 뭐야?
   B: 스포츠를 많이 좋아하지는 않지만, 가끔 수영하러 가.
   G: 수영을 얼마나 자주 하러 가는데?
   B: 그렇게 자주는 아니야. 한 달에 한 번만 가.

2. B: 하나야, 이번 주말에 특별한 계획 있어?
   G: 음, 우리 아빠와 남동생하고 탁구를 할 거야.
   B: 얼마나 자주 하는데?
   G: 매주 주말. 탁구 하는 걸 정말 좋아하거든. 너는 어때?
   B: 나는 축구 하는 걸 좋아해. 야외 스포츠가 좋아.

Communicate A

Anna: Do you have any _____ _____ for the _____ _____?

Suho: I'm going _____ _____ to my grandparents' _____ in Pyeongchang. I'll _____ _____ and _____ there. I love winter sports.

Anna: _____ for you! I love winter sports, too. My _____ is ice hockey.

Suho: Oh, I've _____ _____ ice hockey, but _____ _____ _____ _____ how _____ _____ it.

Anna: Really? I can teach you _____ _____ _____.

Suho: That's _____. Is ice hockey _____ _____ _____ sport in Canada?

Anna: Yes, it is. _____ I know _____ watching it and _____ it.

Suho: _____ _____ did you play ice hockey _____ you were in Canada?

Anna: I played _____ _____ two or _____ _____ a week in the winter.

Suho: Wow, _____ _____ you're really _____ _____ ice hockey. I _____ _____ _____ learn from you.

Communicate B

A: _____ _____ _____ are you _____ _____?

B: I'm _____ _____ ice skating.

A: _____ _____ _____ you go ice skating?

B: I go _____ or twice _____ _____.

Progress Check

1. **B:** What are you doing?
   G: I'm practicing badminton.
   B: Do you like _____ badminton?
   G: No, I'm _____ _____ _____ it. I just want _____ _____ the badminton test next week.
   B: O.K. _____ _____!

2. **G:** What's your _____ TV show, Jason?
   B: I don't watch TV, but I _____ _____ the radio.
   G: _____ _____ do you listen to the radio?
   B: _____ every day.

3. **M:** _____ important _____ _____ your love for the people around you. _____ _____ do you _____ everyone in your family _____ you love them?

해석

Anna: 너는 겨울 방학 때 특별한 계획이 있니?

수호: 나는 평창에 계신 할머니 할아버지 댁에 갈 거야. 거기서 스케이트와 썰매를 타러 갈 거야. 난 겨울 스포츠를 정말 좋아하거든.

Anna: 잘됐다! 나도 겨울 스포츠를 정말 좋아해. 내가 제일 좋아하는 것은 아이스하키야.

수호: 오, 나는 아이스하키를 해 본 적은 없지만, 하는 법을 배우는 데에는 관심이 있어.

Anna: 정말? 내가 어떻게 하는지 가르쳐 줄 수 있어.

수호: 정말 잘 됐다. 캐나다에서는 아이스하키가 가장 인기 있는 스포츠니?

Anna: 응, 맞아. 내가 아는 모든 사람들은 아이스하키를 보는 것과 직접 하는 것을 정말 좋아해.

수호: 너는 캐나다에 있을 때 아이스하키를 얼마나 자주 했니?

Anna: 겨울에는 일주일에 적어도 두세 번은 했어.

수호: 우와, 네가 아이스하키를 정말 잘 할 거라고 확신해. 너한테 빨리 배우고 싶다.

A: 어떤 겨울 스포츠에 관심이 있니?
B: 스케이트 타기에 관심이 있어.
A: 얼마나 자주 스케이트 타러 가?
B: 한 달에 한두 번 가.

1. B: 뭐 하고 있어?
   G: 배드민턴을 연습하고 있어.
   B: 배드민턴 하는 걸 좋아해?
   G: 아니, 관심이 있지는 않아. 그냥 다음주에 있는 배드민턴 시험에 통과하고 싶어.
   B: 그렇구나. 행운을 빌어!

2. G: Jason, 네가 가장 좋아하는 TV 쇼는 뭐니?
   B: TV를 보지는 않지만, 라디오는 들어.
   G: 얼마나 자주 라디오를 들어?
   B: 거의 매일.

3. M: 당신의 사랑을 주변 사람들에게 보여주는 것은 중요합니다. 당신은 얼마나 자주 가족 모두에게 사랑한다고 말해 주나요?

01 다음 대화의 빈칸에 들어갈 말로 알맞은 것은?

> G: What's your favorite sport, James?
>
> B: I don't like sports much, but I sometimes go swimming.
>
> G: _____
>
> B: Not very often. I only go swimming once a month.

① How long do you swim?

② When do you go swimming?

③ How far is the swimming pool from here?

④ How often do you go swimming?

⑤ How do you go to swimming pool?

[02~03] 다음 대화를 읽고 물음에 답하시오.

> B: What are you doing?
>
> G: I'm listening to old pop songs.
>
> B: Oh, do you like old pop songs?
>
> G: No, _____(A)_____ I just want to sing my grandma's favorite songs at her birthday party next week.
>
> B: Wow, (B)넌 정말 착한 손녀구나!

02 빈칸 (A)에 들어갈 말로 알맞은 것은?

① I'm into old pop songs.　　② I'm not interested in them.

③ I'm interested in them.　　④ I'm not interested in musicals.

⑤ I'm not interested in it.

03 밑줄 친 (B)의 우리말에 맞게 주어진 단어를 이용하여 영어로 쓰시오. (4 words)

> (nice / what)

➡ _____

04 다음 대화의 밑줄 친 부분의 의도로 알맞은 것은?

> B: How often do you play?
>
> G: Every weekend. I love playing table tennis. How about you?

① 능력 여부 묻기　　② 유감 표현하기　　③ 기대 표현하기

④ 빈도 묻기　　⑤ 보고하기

 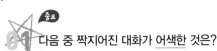
01 다음 중 짝지어진 대화가 <u>어색한</u> 것은?

① A: How often do you clean your room?

B: I clean my room once a week.

② A: What are you interested in?

B: I'm interested in Korean dramas.

③ A: What's your favorite sport, James?

B: I don't like sports much,

④ A: How often do you listen to the radio?

B: For two hours.

⑤ A: What winter sport are you interested in?

B: I'm interested in ice skating.

[02~03] 다음 대화를 읽고 물음에 답하시오.

B: _____(A)_____, Hana?

G: Well, I'm going to play table tennis with my dad and brother.

B: How often do you play?

G: Every weekend. I love playing table tennis. How about you?

B: I like playing soccer. _____(B)

서답형

02 위 대화의 빈칸 (A)에 주어진 〈조건〉대로 문장을 완성하시오.

┌─── 조건 ───
• 이번 주말 계획을 묻는 말을 쓸 것.
• 'any special plans'를 사용할 것.
└──────────

➡ _____

03 위 대화의 빈칸 (B)에 들어갈 말로 알맞은 것은?

① I'm not interested in outdoor sports.

② I enjoy outdoor sports.

③ I don't like playing baseball.

④ I'm interested in indoor sports.

⑤ I prefer indoor sports to outdoor ones.

04 다음 대화의 빈칸에 들어갈 말로 알맞은 것은?

G: _____, James?

B: I don't like sports much, but I sometimes go swimming.

G: How often do you go swimming?

B: Not very often. I only go swimming once a month.

① What are you interested in

② What makes you think so

③ What's your favorite sport

④ Are you interested in music

⑤ Do you like to go swimming

[05~06] 다음 대화를 읽고 물음에 답하시오.

B: What are you ①doing?

G: ②I'm listening to old pop songs.

B: Oh, do you like old pop songs?

G: No, I'm not ③interested in them. I just want ④to sing my grandma's favorite songs at her birthday party next week.

B: Wow, ⑤how a nice granddaughter!

05 밑줄 친 ①~⑤ 중 어법상 <u>어색한</u> 것은?

① ② ③ ④ ⑤

서답형

06 다음 영영풀이에 해당하는 단어를 대화에서 찾아 쓰시오.

> best liked or most enjoyed

➡ _____

[07~08] 다음 대화를 읽고 물음에 답하시오.

Anna: Do you have any special plans for the winter break?

Suho: I'm going to go to my grandparents' place in Pyeongchang. I'll go skating and sledding there. I love winter sports.

Anna: Good for you! I love winter sports, too. My favorite is ice hockey.

Suho: Oh, I've never played ice hockey, but _____ (A) _____

Anna: Really? I can teach you how to play.

Suho: That's awesome. Is ice hockey the most popular sport in Canada?

Anna: Yes, it is. Everyone I know loves watching it and playing it.

Suho: How often did you play ice hockey when you were in Canada?

Anna: I played at least two or three times a week in the winter.

Suho: Wow, I'm sure you're really good at ice hockey. I can't wait to learn from you.

07 위 대화의 빈칸 (A)에 들어갈 말로 알맞은 것은?

① my favorite winter sport is skiing.

② I'm interested in watching the Winter Olympics.

③ I'm interested in drawing cartoons.

④ I'm interested in learning how to play it.

⑤ I only go swimming once a month.

중요

08 위 대화를 읽고 답할 수 없는 질문은?

① Where is Suho going to go during winter break?

② What is Suho going to do in Pyeongchang?

③ How often did Anna play ice hockey when she was in Canada?

④ What winter sport is Suho interested in learning?

⑤ What winter sport is popular in Korea?

[09~10] 다음 대화를 읽고 물음에 답하시오.

M: _____ (A) _____ Then, be sure to watch MBS Sports to enjoy our __(a)__ broadcasts from 6 p.m. to 11 p.m. At 11 p.m. every night, you can also enjoy our __(b)__ of the most interesting games of the day.

서답형

09 위 대화의 빈칸 (A)에 주어진 〈조건〉에 맞게 영어로 쓰시오.

> ┌─── 조건 ───
> • 동계 올림픽을 보는 데 관심 있는지 묻는 표현을 쓸 것
> • 'interested'를 사용하고, 'watch the Winter Olympics'를 활용할 것

➡ _____

중요

10 빈칸 (a)와 (b)에 들어갈 말로 알맞은 것은?

① living – highlights

② living – spotlights

③ live – highlights

④ live – spotlights

⑤ alive – highlights

[01~02] 다음 대화를 읽고 물음에 답하시오.

James: Do you have any special plans for this weekend, Hana?

Hana: Well, I'm going to play table tennis with my dad and brother.

James: (A)얼마나 자주 하는데? (play)

Hana: Every weekend. I love playing table tennis. How about you?

James: I like playing soccer. I enjoy outdoor sports.

01 What sport does Hana play and how often does she play it? (6단어의 한 문장으로 쓰시오.)

➡ _____

02 밑줄 친 (A)의 우리말에 맞게 주어진 단어를 이용하여 영작하시오. (5단어로 쓸 것)

➡ _____

[03~04] 다음 대화를 읽고 물음에 답하시오.

Anna: Do you have any special plans for the winter break?

Suho: I'm going to go to my grandparents' place in Pyeongchang. I'll go skating and sledding there. I love winter sports.

Anna: Good for you! I love winter sports, too. My favorite is ice hockey.

Suho: Oh, I've never played ice hockey, but _____ (A) _____.

Anna: Really? I can teach you how to play.

Suho: That's awesome. Is ice hockey the most popular sport in Canada?

Anna: Yes, it is. (B) 내가 아는 모든 사람들은 아이스하키를 보는 것과 직접 하는 것을 정말 좋아해.

Suho: How often did you play ice hockey when you were in Canada?

Anna: I played at least two or three times a week in the winter.

Suho: Wow, I'm sure you're really good at ice hockey. I can't wait to learn from you.

03 빈칸 (A)에 주어진 조건에 맞게 영작하시오.

┌─ 조건 ─
• 관심을 표현하기
• how + to부정사를 사용할 것
• 'learn', 'play it'을 이용할 것
└─

➡ _____

04 밑줄 친 (B)의 우리말 해석에 맞게 주어진 단어를 알맞은 순서로 배열하시오.

(everyone / watching / I / playing / know / loves / it / and / it)

➡ _____

05 다음 글을 읽고 마지막 문장의 질문에 답을 하시오. (주어진 단어를 이용할 것)

M: It's important to show your love for the people around you. How often do you tell everyone in your family that you love them?

➡ I tell them that _____. (every day)

Grammar

교과서

① 지각동사

> • Gunnar **saw** the river ice **cracking**. Gunnar는 강의 얼음이 갈라지는 것을 보았다.

■ 지각동사는 지각을 묘사할 때 사용하는 동사로 '보다, 듣다, 느끼다'의 의미를 갖는 see, look at, watch, hear, listen to, feel 등의 동사를 말하며, 일반적으로 '지각동사+목적어'의 형태나, '지각동사+목적어+목적격보어'의 형태로 많이 쓰인다. 지각동사의 목적격보어로는 보통 동사원형이나 현재분사(동사+-ing)가 온다. 두 목적격보어의 차이는 현재분사에 진행의 의미가 들어간다는 점이다.

   • I **saw** Tom **get** into his car. 나는 Tom이 차 안으로 들어가는 것을 보았다. 〈동사원형: 동작 전체〉

   • I **saw** Tom **getting** into his car. 나는 Tom이 차 안으로 들어가고 있는 것을 보았다. 〈현재분사: 진행의 의미를 강조〉

■ '지각동사+목적어+원형부정사[현재분사]'로 쓰이는 경우에는 목적어와 목적격보어는 능동 관계가 되며, '지각동사+목적어+과거분사'로 쓰이는 경우에는 목적어와 목적격보어의 관계는 수동이다.

   • I **heard** him **call[calling]** my name. 나는 그가 내 이름을 부르는 것을 들었다. 〈원형부정사[현재분사]: 목적어와 목적격보어가 능동 관계〉

   • I **heard** my name **called**. 나는 내 이름이 불리는 것을 들었다. 〈과거분사: 목적어와 목적격보어가 수동 관계〉

■ 사역동사 make, have, let과 혼동하지 않도록 한다. 사역동사도 목적어와 목적격보어를 취하지만, 사역동사의 목적격보어로는 현재분사가 나오지 않는다.

   • He **made** me **do** the dishes. 그는 나에게 설거지를 하라고 시켰다.

   • He **had** his bike **repaired**. 그는 그의 자전거가 수리되도록 했다.

핵심 Check

1. 다음 괄호 안에서 알맞은 말을 고르시오.

   (1) I saw my sister (draw / to draw) a butterfly.

   (2) I heard my sister (opening / to open) the window.

   (3) I noticed him (injuring / injured).

② tell/want/ask+목적어+to부정사

• Gunnar **told** Balto **to continue** on. Gunnar는 Balto에게 계속 가라고 말했다.

■ 동사 다음에 목적어와 to부정사가 쓰여 '(목적어)에게 …하기를 말하다/원하다/요청하다'라는 의미를 나타낸다. 목적어 다음의 to부정사가 목적격보어이다.

■ **to부정사를 목적격보어로 취하는 동사**

tell, ask, expect, hope, want, advise, allow, enable, get, permit 등

• He **told** me **to throw** away the trash. 그는 내게 쓰레기를 버리라고 말했다.

• Mary **asked** me **to play** the piano. Mary는 내게 피아노를 쳐달라고 부탁했다.

■ 목적격보어로 쓰인 to부정사의 부정형은 'not to 동사원형'으로 쓴다.

• I **wanted** him **not to do** it again. 나는 그가 그것을 다시 하지 않기를 바랐다.

■ **동사에 따른 목적격보어**

지각동사 (see, hear 등)	동사원형, 현재분사, 과거분사
사역동사 (make, have, let)	동사원형, 과거분사
tell, want, ask 등	to부정사
make, keep, find 등	형용사

핵심 Check

2. 다음 괄호 안에서 알맞은 것을 고르시오.

　(1) I asked my sister (draw / to draw) a tree.

　(2) I told my sister (opening / to open) the window.

　(3) I wanted him (listening / to listen) to me.

01 다음 문장에서 어법상 어색한 부분을 바르게 고쳐 쓰시오.

(1) I saw a man took a picture.

_____ ➡ _____

(2) He heard some birds to sing.

_____ ➡ _____

(3) She asked me mailing the letter.

_____ ➡ _____

(4) Hana told me to not lose heart.

_____ ➡ _____

02 주어진 단어를 어법에 맞게 빈칸에 쓰시오.

(1) They heard the dog _____. (bark)
(2) He looked at the house _____ blue. (paint)
(3) We went there to watch it _____. (burn)
(4) Ben felt the snow _____ with his hands. (melt)

03 다음 우리말을 영어로 바르게 옮긴 것은?

> 경찰관은 그들에게 멈추라고 말했다.

① The police officer told them stop.
② The police officer told them stopped.
③ The police officer told them stopping.
④ The police officer told them to stop.
⑤ The police officer told them to stopping.

04 주어진 단어에 한 단어를 추가하고 바르게 배열하여 다음 우리말을 영어로 쓰시오.

> • 그는 빵이 타는 냄새를 맡고 그녀에게 토스터를 끄라고 말했다.
> (he, her, the bread, the toaster, burning, turn, smelled, told, and, off)

➡ _____

01 다음 빈칸에 알맞은 말이 순서대로 바르게 짝지어진 것은?

> • I saw two girls _____ coffee.
> • My friend wants me _____ a walk with him.

① drink – take
② drank – taking
③ drank – to take
④ drinking – taking
⑤ drinking – to take

02 다음 빈칸에 들어갈 말로 적절한 것을 <u>모두</u> 고르시오.

> He thought he heard someone _____ for help.

① cries   ② cry   ③ cried
④ crying   ⑤ to cry

03 ^{중요} 다음 빈칸에 들어갈 말로 적절한 것을 고르시오.

> I asked him _____ the door.

① to close   ② closing   ③ closed
④ closes   ⑤ close

^{서답형}
04 주어진 단어를 이용하여 다음 우리말을 영어로 쓰시오. (10단어)

> 우리는 Kate가 사랑스러운 노래를 부르는 것을 들었다.
> (hear / lovely)

➡ _____

 ^{중요}
05 다음 중 어법상 바르지 <u>않은</u> 것은?

① Our teacher tells us to read lots of books.
② She asked me to join the club with her.
③ The doctor advised him not smoke and drink.
④ My friend wants me to write a letter to her.
⑤ My mom allowed me to watch TV after dinner.

^{서답형}
06 괄호 안에서 알맞은 것을 고르시오.

(1) I heard someone (sing / sang) a song.
(2) I was surprised to see him (to meet / meeting) a client in person there.
(3) Elisa listened to the wood (popping / popped) as it burned.
(4) Melanie smelled something (burn / burning) in the kitchen.
(5) Did you make him (fix / fixed) your computer?
(6) He told Balto (to continue / continue) on.
(7) Mike asked Yuri (closing / to close) the window.
(8) Her mother warned her (to not / not to) talk to strangers.

07 다음 중 어법상 바르지 <u>않은</u> 것은?

> I ①heard ②someone ③to play the piano ④late ⑤at night.

①   ②   ③   ④   ⑤

서답형

08 다음 문장에서 어법상 **틀린** 부분을 찾아 바르게 고쳐 쓰시오.

> Sue's mom wants Sue reads more history books.

_____ ➡ _____

[09~10] 다음 우리말을 영어로 바르게 옮긴 것을 고르시오.

09 (2 개)

> 나는 내 남동생이 내 이메일을 읽고 있는 것을 보았다.

① I saw my brother reads my e-mail.
② I saw my brother to read my e-mail.
③ I saw my brother read my e-mail.
④ I saw my brother reading my e-mail.
⑤ I saw my brother to reading my e-mail.

10

> 내가 너를 박물관까지 데려다 주길 원하니?

① Do you want me take you to the museum?
② Do you want me to take you to the museum?
③ Do you want me taking you to the museum?
④ Do you want me to taking you to the museum?
⑤ Do you want me you took to the museum?

11 다음 중 어법상 바르지 <u>않은</u> 것은?

① Alex gets angry when he sees his brother using his phone.
② She could feel somebody touching her shoulder.
③ The students listened to Ruth introduce herself.
④ I watched him to sleep soundly on the sofa.
⑤ I heard a girl singing on my way to school.

12 다음 (A)~(C)에서 어법상 옳은 것끼리 바르게 짝지은 것은?

> • I saw a woman (A)(riding / to ride) a scooter.
> • Did you listen to him (B)(tell / to tell) interesting stories?
> • He found the bird under the tree (C) (injure / injured).

	(A)	(B)	(C)
①	to ride	tell	injure
②	to ride	to tell	injured
③	riding	tell	injured
④	riding	tell	injure
⑤	riding	to tell	injure

서답형

13 다음 대화의 빈칸에 알맞은 말을 3단어로 쓰시오.

> A: I can't find Edan anywhere. Do you know if he went out?
> B: I think so. I heard _____.

➡ _____

14 다음 빈칸에 들어갈 괄호 안에 주어진 동사의 형태가 <u>다른</u> 하나는?

① We told the children _____ basketball in the park. (play)
② Sheryll got her boy friend _____ for her outside. (wait)
③ I didn't allow them _____ everything on television. (watch)
④ Tell me what made you _____ today. (smile)
⑤ Tim asked me _____ him with his homework. (help)

서답형

15 다음 문장에서 어법상 <u>어색한</u> 부분을 바르게 고치시오.

(1) A gorilla saw him to fall inside and caught him.

_____ ➡ _____

(2) They watched me uploaded the report on the Internet.

_____ ➡ _____

(3) I will have him to check your computer.

_____ ➡ _____

(4) My mom wants me clean my desk every day.

_____ ➡ _____

(5) We asked Minho helped us with our art project.

_____ ➡ _____

(6) I told him bringing his passport next time.

_____ ➡ _____

서답형

16 다음 그림을 보고 괄호 안의 동사를 이용하여 주어진 문장의 빈칸을 알맞게 채우시오.

I asked him _____ for some information on the Internet. (search)

중요

17 다음 주어진 문장의 밑줄 친 부분과 쓰임이 같은 것은?

I told him <u>to come</u> early.

① She was happy <u>to meet</u> him.
② My plan is <u>to visit</u> London this year.
③ We asked her <u>to help</u> us.
④ It is important <u>to exercise</u> regularly.
⑤ I need a pen <u>to write</u> with.

서답형

18 다음 괄호 안에 주어진 단어를 이용하여 우리말을 영어로 옮기시오.

(1) Alex는 종종 학교로 가는 길에 새들이 노래하는 것을 듣는다. (often, on his way)

➡ _____

_____

(2) 무언가 타고 있는 냄새가 난다. (smell, something, I, burn)

➡ _____

_____

(3) 그는 내게 그와 결혼해 달라고 요청했다. (ask, marry)

➡ _____

_____

01 다음 문장에서 어법상 어색한 부분을 바르게 고쳐 다시 쓰시오.

(1) Alex usually gives a hand when he sees someone carrys something heavy.

　➡ _____

(2) A neighbor finally heard the dog to bark and called 911.

　➡ _____

(3) Tim just felt the ground shook.

　➡ _____

(4) He heard his name calling.

　➡ _____

(5) The Greek general ordered a soldier telling the people of Athens about their victory.

　➡ _____

(6) Years of training enabled him won the match.

　➡ _____

(7) I expect you keep good company when you go abroad.

　➡ _____

02 다음 두 문장이 비슷한 의미를 갖도록 빈칸을 알맞은 말로 채우시오.

> They said to him, "Please be careful."
> → They asked him _____.

　➡ _____

03 다음 두 문장을 〈보기〉와 같이 지각동사를 이용하여 한 문장으로 완성하시오.

> ┤ 보기 ├
> • He saw his son.
> • His son was sleeping on the sofa.
> → He saw his son sleeping on the sofa.

> • We watched a man.
> • He was running outside.

　➡ _____

04 다음 두 문장이 비슷한 의미가 되도록 빈칸에 알맞은 말을 쓰시오.

(1) I think that you had better come to my birthday party.

　➡ I want you _____ to my birthday party.

(2) Sam told her that she must not forget to turn off the light.

　➡ Sam warned her _____ to turn off the light.

(3) The teacher said to her students that they should clean the classroom every day.

　➡ The teacher ordered her students _____ the classroom every day.

(4) She said to Jaden that he should eat more vegetables.

　➡ She advised Jaden _____ more vegetables.

(5) I said to her, "We believe you are a good painter. You can do it."

　➡ I encouraged her _____ a good painter.

05 다음 그림을 참고하여 단어 listen을 알맞은 형태로 빈칸에 쓰시오.

➡ I saw a girl _____ to the music.

06 〈보기〉에서 의미상 적절한 단어를 골라 빈칸에 알맞은 형태로 쓰시오.

┌─── 보기 ───┐
paint   carry   touch   be
└────────────┘

(1) He told the children _____ quiet.

(2) He saw the house _____ on his way to the shopping mall.

(3) She felt someone _____ her.

(4) Mom had him _____ the chairs.

07 다음 우리말을 괄호 안에 주어진 어휘를 이용하여 주어진 단어 수대로 영작하시오.

(1) 나는 누군가 나의 이름을 부르고 있는 것을 들었다. (someone, call, 6단어)

➡ _____

(2) Kate는 무언가가 타고 있는 냄새를 맡았다. (something, burn, 4단어)

➡ _____

(3) Jake는 그의 동생이 자기의 전화기를 사용하고 있는 것을 발견했다. (find, brother, use, his phone, 7단어)

➡ _____

(4) 그가 돌아와서 그것이 도난당했다는 것을 알았을 때 그는 매우 화가 났다. (come back, steal, see, get, angry, very, 12단어)

➡ _____
_____

(5) 우리 담임 선생님은 우리에게 늘 학교에 제시간에 오라고 말씀하신다. (our teacher, always, on time, 11단어)

➡ _____
_____

(6) 그는 내가 그 일에 참여하는 것을 용납하지 않을 것이다. (will, permit, take part, 10단어)

➡ _____

(7) 나는 그에게 문을 닫지 말아달라고 부탁했다. (ask, close, the door, 8단어)

➡ _____

(8) 그녀는 내가 컴퓨터 게임을 하도록 했다. (let, computer games, 6단어)

➡ _____

08 그림을 보고 괄호 안에 주어진 단어들을 바르게 배열하여 문장을 완성하시오.

┌────────────────────────┐
Jaden's mom _____
after finishing homework. (him, allow, watch TV)
└────────────────────────┘

Grammar **79**

Reading

The Most Heart-Warming Winter Sport

In early March every year, the world's biggest sled dog race takes
place in Alaska. It is called the Iditarod Trail Sled Dog Race. Around
80 teams of 12 to 16 dogs take part in this race. Each team has to cover
about 1,800 km from Anchorage to Nome. The race can take more than
two weeks, and the teams often race through snowstorms. The Iditarod
Race began in 1973 in memory of the dogs that saved Nome.

One cold winter day in 1925, a terrible thing happened in Nome.
Some children got very sick, and the disease kept spreading. The
people of Nome needed medicine right away, but the town did not have
any. Someone had to get it from a hospital in Anchorage. Because of
the heavy snow, a dog sled relay was the only way to get the medicine
from Anchorage to Nome. Soon, the race to Nome began.

Twenty-one dog teams were in the relay. On January 27, the first
team left, and the others waited at different points. Gunnar was the
driver of the 20th team. The strongest dog on his team was Balto, so he
made Balto his lead dog.

race: 경주
trail: 자국, 흔적, 오솔길, (특정 목적을 위해 따라 가는) 루트[코스]
snowstorm: 눈보라
terrible: 끔찍한
medicine: 약
relay: 릴레이 경주, 계주

확인문제

● 다음 문장이 본문의 내용과 일치하면 T, 일치하지 않으면 F를 쓰시오.

1 The world's biggest sled dog race takes place in Alaska in early March every year. ☐

2 Around 12 to 16 teams of 80 dogs take part in the Iditarod Trail Sled Dog Race. ☐

3 A dog sled relay was the only way to get the medicine from Anchorage to Nome. ☐

4 The other teams waited at the same points. ☐

When Gunnar and Balto finally got the medicine, the snow was
~할 때, 시간의 부사절을 이끄는 접속사

so heavy that Gunnar could not see his own hands. However, Balto
so+형용사+that절: 너무 ~해서 …하다   (접속부사) 그러나

was able to stay on the trail. When they were crossing a frozen river,
            (특정 목적을 위한) 루트[코스]를 따라가는   과거진행형

Balto suddenly stopped. Then, Gunnar saw the river ice cracking.
                                    지각동사 see는 목적격보어로 동사원형이나 현재분사가 올 수 있다.

The whole team was saved because Balto stopped just in time. When
                                                            제때에

Balto and Gunnar reached the final team, they were sleeping. Gunnar

told Balto to continue on.
tell+목적어+to부정사: ~에게 …하라고 말하다

"Here's the medicine, Doctor!" shouted Gunnar. On February 2,

Gunnar and his team finally arrived in Nome. The town was saved.

This heart-warming story is now celebrated every year by the Iditarod
본문 전체에 걸쳐 나온, 개썰매를 통해 놈을 구한 이야기를 말한다.

Race, the biggest sled dog race in the world.
the Iditarod Race와 the biggest sled dog race in the world는 동격

crack: 갈라지다, 금이 가다

reach: ~에 이르다[닿다/도달하다]

continue: 계속되다, 계속하다

📎 **확인문제**

● 다음 문장이 본문의 내용과 일치하면 T, 일치하지 <u>않으면</u> F를 쓰시오.

1   When Gunnar and Balto finally got the medicine, Gunnar could not see his own

   hands because of the heavy snow. ☐

2   Balto wasn't able to stay on the trail. ☐

3   The whole team was saved because Balto saw the river ice cracking and stopped

   just in time. ☐

4   When Balto and Gunnar reached the final team, they were ready to start. ☐

5   This heart-warming story is now celebrated every month by the Iditarod Race, the

   biggest sled dog race in the world. ☐

● 우리말을 참고하여 빈칸에 알맞은 말을 쓰시오.

1 The _____ Heart-Warming Winter Sport

2 In early March every year, the world's biggest sled dog race _____ _____ in Alaska.

3 _____ _____ _____ the Iditarod Trail Sled Dog Race.

4 Around 80 teams of 12 to 16 dogs _____ _____ _____ this race.

5 Each team _____ _____ _____ about 1,800 km from Anchorage to Nome.

6 The race can _____ more than two weeks, and the teams often _____ _____ _____.

7 The Iditarod Race began in 1973 _____ _____ _____ the dogs that saved Nome.

8 One cold winter day in 1925, _____ _____ _____ _____ in Nome.

9 Some children got very sick, and the disease _____ _____.

10 The people of Nome needed medicine _____ _____, but the town _____ _____ _____ _____.

11 Someone _____ _____ _____ _____ from a hospital in Anchorage.

12 Because of the heavy snow, a dog sled relay was the only way _____ _____ _____ _____ from Anchorage to Nome.

13 Soon, _____ _____ _____ _____ began.

14 Twenty-one dog teams were _____ _____.

1	가장 가슴 따뜻한 겨울 스포츠
2	매년 3월 초에 알래스카(Alaska)에서는 세계 최대의 개썰매 경주가 열린다.
3	그것은 아이디타로드 개썰매 경주(Iditarod Trail Sled Dog Race)라고 불린다.
4	12~16마리 개로 구성된 80여 팀이 이 경주에 참여한다.
5	각 팀은 앵커리지(Anchorage)에서 놈(Nome)까지 약 1,800 km를 달려야 한다.
6	이 경주는 2주 이상 걸릴 수 있으며, 팀들은 종종 눈보라를 뚫고 경주한다.
7	아이디타로드 경주는 놈을 구한 개들을 기념하여 1973년에 시작되었다.
8	1925년의 어느 추운 겨울날, 놈 마을에서는 끔찍한 일이 일어났다.
9	몇몇 아이들이 매우 아팠고 병이 계속 퍼졌다.
10	놈의 사람들은 당장 약이 필요했지만 마을에는 약이 하나도 없었다.
11	누군가는 앵커리지에 있는 병원에서 약을 가져와야 했다.
12	폭설 때문에 개썰매 릴레이가 앵커리지에서 놈으로 약을 가져오는 유일한 방법이었다.
13	곧, 놈으로 향하는 질주가 시작되었다.
14	21개의 개 팀이 릴레이에 참여했다.

15 On January 27, the first team left, and _____ _____ waited _____ _____ _____.

16 Gunnar was the driver _____ _____ _____ _____.

17 The strongest dog on his team was Balto, so he _____ Balto _____ _____ _____.

18 When Gunnar and Balto finally got the medicine, the snow was _____ heavy _____ Gunnar _____ _____ see his own hands.

19 _____, Balto was able to _____ _____ _____ _____.

20 When they were crossing a _____ river, Balto suddenly stopped.

21 Then, Gunnar saw the river ice _____.

22 The whole team _____ _____ because Balto stopped _____ _____ _____.

23 When Balto and Gunnar _____ the final team, they were sleeping.

24 Gunnar told Balto _____ _____ _____.

25 "_____ the medicine, Doctor!" _____ Gunnar.

26 _____ February 2, Gunnar and his team finally _____ _____ Nome.

27 The town _____ _____.

28 This heart-warming story _____ _____ _____ every year by the Iditarod Race, _____ _____ _____ _____ _____ in the world.

---

15 1월 27일에 첫 번째 팀이 출발했고, 나머지 팀들은 서로 다른 지점에서 기다렸다.

16 Gunnar는 20번째 팀의 몰이꾼이었다.

17 그의 팀에서 가장 강한 개는 Balto였기 때문에, 그는 Balto를 그의 선두 개로 삼았다.

18 Gunnar와 Balto가 마침내 약을 받았을 때, 눈발이 너무 거세서 Gunnar는 자신의 손조차도 볼 수 없었다.

19 그러나, Balto는 코스를 제대로 따라갈 수 있었다.

20 그들이 얼어붙은 강을 건너고 있을 때 Balto는 갑자기 멈췄다.

21 그때, Gunnar는 강의 얼음이 갈라지는 것을 보았다.

22 Balto가 바로 제때 멈췄기 때문에 팀 전체가 목숨을 구할 수 있었다.

23 Balto와 Gunnar가 마지막 팀에 다다랐을 때, 그들은 자고 있었다.

24 Gunnar는 Balto에게 계속 가라고 말했다.

25 "여기 약이 있습니다, 의사 선생님!"이라고 Gunnar가 소리쳤다.

26 2월 2일에 Gunnar와 그의 팀은 마침내 놈에 도착했다.

27 놈 마을 사람들은 목숨을 구할 수 있었다.

28 이 가슴 따뜻한 이야기는 세계에서 가장 큰 개썰매 경주인 아이디타로드 경주를 통해 오늘날 매년 기념되고 있다.

● 우리말을 참고하여 본문을 영작하시오.

1 가장 가슴 따뜻한 겨울 스포츠

➡ _____

2 매년 3월 초에 알래스카(Alaska)에서는 세계 최대의 개썰매 경주가 열린다.

➡ _____

3 그것은 아이디타로드 개썰매 경주(Iditarod Trail Sled Dog Race)라고 불린다.

➡ _____

4 12~16마리 개로 구성된 80여 팀이 이 경주에 참여한다.

➡ _____

5 각 팀은 앵커리지(Anchorage)에서 놈(Nome)까지 약 1,800 km를 달려야 한다.

➡ _____

6 이 경주는 2주 이상 걸릴 수 있으며, 팀들은 종종 눈보라를 뚫고 경주한다.

➡ _____

7 아이디타로드 경주는 놈을 구한 개들을 기념하여 1973년에 시작되었다.

➡ _____

8 1925년의 어느 추운 겨울날, 놈 마을에서는 끔찍한 일이 일어났다.

➡ _____

9 몇몇 아이들이 매우 아팠고 병이 계속 퍼졌다.

➡ _____

10 놈의 사람들은 당장 약이 필요했지만 마을에는 약이 하나도 없었다.

➡ _____

11 누군가는 앵커리지에 있는 병원에서 약을 가져와야 했다.

➡ _____

12 폭설 때문에 개썰매 릴레이가 앵커리지에서 놈으로 약을 가져오는 유일한 방법이었다.

➡ _____

13 곧, 놈으로 향하는 질주가 시작되었다.

➡ _____

14 21개의 개 팀이 릴레이에 참여했다.

➡ _____

15 1월 27일에 첫 번째 팀이 출발했고, 나머지 팀들은 서로 다른 지점에서 기다렸다.

➡ _____

16 Gunnar는 20번째 팀의 몰이꾼이었다.

➡ _____

17 그의 팀에서 가장 강한 개는 Balto였기 때문에, 그는 Balto를 그의 선두 개로 삼았다.

➡ _____

18 Gunnar와 Balto가 마침내 약을 받았을 때, 눈발이 너무 거세서 Gunnar는 자신의 손조차도 볼 수 없었다.

➡ _____

_____

19 그러나, Balto는 코스를 제대로 따라갈 수 있었다.

➡ _____

20 그들이 얼어붙은 강을 건너고 있을 때 Balto는 갑자기 멈췄다.

➡ _____

21 그때, Gunnar는 강의 얼음이 갈라지는 것을 보았다.

➡ _____

22 Balto가 바로 제때 멈췄기 때문에 팀 전체가 목숨을 구할 수 있었다.

➡ _____

23 Balto와 Gunnar가 마지막 팀에 다다랐을 때, 그들은 자고 있었다.

➡ _____

24 Gunnar는 Balto에게 계속 가라고 말했다.

➡ _____

25 "여기 약이 있습니다, 의사 선생님!"이라고 Gunnar가 소리쳤다.

➡ _____

26 2월 2일에 Gunnar와 그의 팀은 마침내 놈에 도착했다.

➡ _____

27 놈 마을 사람들은 목숨을 구할 수 있었다.

➡ _____

28 이 가슴 따뜻한 이야기는 세계에서 가장 큰 개썰매 경주인 아이디타로드 경주를 통해 오늘날 매년 기념되고 있다.

➡ _____

_____

[01~04] 다음 글을 읽고 물음에 답하시오.

ⓐIn early March every year, the world's biggest sled dog race is taken place in Alaska. It is called the Iditarod Trail Sled Dog Race. ⓑAround 80 teams of 12 to 16 dogs take part in ⓒthis race. Each team has to cover about 1,800 km from Anchorage to Nome. The race can take more than two weeks, and the teams often race through snowstorms. The Iditarod Race began in 1973 in memory of the dogs that saved Nome.

서답형

01 위 글의 밑줄 친 ⓐ에서 어법상 틀린 부분을 찾아 고치시오.

_____ ➡ _____

02 위 글의 밑줄 친 ⓑAround와 같은 의미로 쓰인 것을 고르시오.

① I could hear laughter all around.

② They walked around the lake.

③ There were papers lying around all over the floor.

④ He arrived around five o'clock.

⑤ The house is built around a central courtyard.

서답형

03 위 글의 밑줄 친 ⓒthis race가 가리키는 것을 본문에서 찾아 쓰시오.

➡ _____

중요

04 위 글의 내용과 일치하지 않는 것은?

① 매년 3월 초에 알래스카에서는 세계 최대의 개썰매 경주가 열린다.

② 12~16마리 개로 구성된 80여 팀이 경주에 참여한다.

③ 개썰매 경주에 참여한 각 팀은 앵커리지에서 놈까지 약 1,800 km를 달려야 한다.

④ 이 개썰매 경주는 2주 이상 걸릴 수 있으며, 팀들은 종종 눈보라를 뚫고 경주한다.

⑤ 아이디타로드 경주는 앵커리지를 구한 개들을 기념하여 1973년에 시작되었다.

[05~08] 다음 글을 읽고 물음에 답하시오.

When Gunnar and Balto finally got the medicine, the snow was so heavy that Gunnar could not see his own hands. ___(A)___, Balto was able to stay on the trail. When they were crossing a frozen river, Balto suddenly stopped. Then, ⓐGunnar는 강의 얼음이 갈라지는 것을 보았다. The whole team was saved because Balto stopped just in time. When Balto and Gunnar reached the final team, they were sleeping. Gunnar told Balto ___(B)___ on.

"Here's the medicine, Doctor!" shouted Gunnar. On February 2, Gunnar and his team finally arrived in Nome. ⓑThe town saved. This heart-warming story is now celebrated every year by the Iditarod Race, the biggest sled dog race in the world.

05 위 글의 빈칸 (A)에 들어갈 알맞은 말을 고르시오.

① In addition ② However

③ As a result ④ For example

⑤ Thus

서답형

06 위 글의 빈칸 (B)에 continue를 알맞은 형태로 쓰시오.

➡ _____

서답형

07 위 글의 밑줄 친 ⓐ의 우리말에 맞게 주어진 어휘를 이용하여 6단어로 영작하시오.

crack

➡ _____

서답형

08 위 글의 밑줄 친 ⓑ에서 어법상 <u>틀린</u> 부분을 찾아 고치시오.

_____ ➡ _____

[09~11] 다음 글을 읽고 물음에 답하시오.

One cold winter day in 1925, a terrible thing happened in Nome. (①) Some children got very sick, and the disease kept ___ⓐ___. (②) Someone had to get it from a hospital in Anchorage. (③) Because of the heavy snow, a dog sled relay was the only way to get the medicine from Anchorage to Nome. (④) Soon, the race to Nome began. (⑤)

Twenty-one dog teams were in the relay. On January 27, the first team left, and the others waited at different points. Gunnar was the driver of the 20th team. The strongest dog on his team was Balto, so he made Balto his lead dog.

서답형

09 위 글의 빈칸 ⓐ에 spread를 알맞은 형태로 쓰시오.

➡ _____

10 위 글의 흐름으로 보아, 주어진 문장이 들어가기에 가장 적절한 곳은?

The people of Nome needed medicine right away, but the town did not have any.

①　　②　　③　　④　　⑤

11 위 글의 주제로 알맞은 것을 고르시오.

① a terrible thing which happened in Nome
② people who needed medicine right away
③ a dog sled relay, the only way to get the medicine from Anchorage to Nome
④ twenty-one dog teams which were in the relay
⑤ the other teams waiting at different points

[12~14] 다음 글을 읽고 물음에 답하시오.

One cold winter day, a man left home ⓐto get wood for a fire.

He slipped and broke his neck. He could not move, but no one was near him.

His dog came ⓑto his rescue. She barked and barked for 19 hours.

A neighbor finally heard the dog barking and called 911.

12 위 글의 밑줄 친 ⓐto get과 to부정사의 용법이 <u>다른</u> 것을 고르시오. (2개)

① I have no book to read.
② He awoke to find himself famous.
③ He went abroad to study economics.
④ It is difficult to know oneself.
⑤ I am glad to meet you.

서답형

13 Why couldn't the man move? Answer in English. (7 words)

➡ _____

서답형

14 위 글의 밑줄 친 ⓑ와 같은 뜻이 되도록 to부정사를 써서 바꿔 쓰시오.

➡ _____

[15~17] 다음 글을 읽고 물음에 답하시오.

One cold winter day in 1925, a terrible thing happened in Nome. Some children got very sick, and the disease kept spreading. The people of Nome needed medicine ⓐ right away, but the town did not have any. Someone had to get it from a hospital in Anchorage. ⓑBecause of the heavy snow, a dog sled relay was the only way to get the medicine from Anchorage to Nome. Soon, the race to Nome began.

Twenty-one dog teams were in the relay. On January 27, the first team left, and the others waited at different points. Gunnar was the driver of the 20th team. ⓒ그의 팀에서 가장 강한 개는 Balto였기 때문에, 그는 Balto를 그의 선두 개로 삼았다.

15 위 글의 밑줄 친 ⓐright away와 바꿔 쓸 수 없는 말을 고르시오.

① immediately   ② at once
③ closely   ④ right now
⑤ without delay

서답형

16 위 글의 밑줄 친 ⓑ를 Because를 사용하여 바꿔 쓰시오.

➡ _____

서답형

17 위 글의 밑줄 친 ⓒ의 우리말에 맞게, 주어진 어휘를 알맞게 배열하시오.

made / on his team / Balto / the strongest dog / Balto / his lead dog / so / was / he

➡ _____

_____

[18~20] 다음 글을 읽고 물음에 답하시오.

(A)[In / On] early March every year, the world's biggest sled dog race takes place in Alaska. ⓐIt is called the Iditarod Trail Sled Dog Race. Around 80 teams of 12 to 16 dogs take part in this race. Each team has to ⓑ cover about 1,800 (B)[km / kilometer] from Anchorage to Nome. The race can (C)[spend / take] more than two weeks, and the teams often race through snowstorms. The Iditarod Race began in 1973 in memory of the dogs that saved Nome.

서답형

18 위 글의 괄호 (A)~(C)에서 어법상 알맞은 낱말을 골라 쓰시오.

➡ (A) _____ (B) _____ (C) _____

서답형

19 위 글의 밑줄 친 ⓐ를 능동태로 고치시오.

➡ _____

20 위 글의 밑줄 친 ⓑcover와 같은 의미로 쓰인 것을 고르시오.

① Did she cover her face with her hands?
② The surveys cover all sides of the business.
③ The cars cover 200 miles a day.
④ The BBC will cover all the major games of the tournament.
⑤ He will cover the loss with insurance.

[21~24] 다음 글을 읽고 물음에 답하시오.

When Gunnar and Balto finally got the medicine, the snow was so heavy that Gunnar could not see his own hands. However, Balto was able to stay ____@____ the trail. When they were crossing a frozen river, Balto suddenly stopped. Then, Gunnar saw the river ice cracking. The whole team was saved because Balto stopped just in time. When Balto and Gunnar reached the final team, they were sleeping. Gunnar told Balto to continue ____ⓑ____.

"Here's the medicine, Doctor!" shouted Gunnar. ____ⓒ____ February 2, Gunnar and his team finally arrived in Nome. The town was saved. This heart-warming story is now celebrated every year by the Iditarod Race, the biggest sled dog race in the world.

21 위 글의 빈칸 @~ⓒ에 공통으로 들어갈 전치사를 고르시오. (대·소문자 무시)

① from   ② by
③ in   ④ for
⑤ on

22 What's the Iditarod Race? Answer in English in a full sentence. (9~10 words)

➡ _____

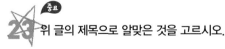

위 글의 제목으로 알맞은 것을 고르시오.

① Gunnar Couldn't See His Own Hands
② Balto Was Able to Stay on the Trail
③ The Team Was Saved Thanks to Balto
④ Gunnar Finally Arrived in Nome
⑤ The Origin of the Iditarod Race

위 글을 읽고 대답할 수 <u>없는</u> 질문은?

① When did Gunnar and Balto get the medicine?
② Why couldn't Gunnar see his own hands?
③ When Balto and Gunnar reached the final team, why did Gunnar tell Balto to continue going?
④ When did Gunnar and his team finally arrive in Nome?
⑤ Was the town saved?

[25~27] 다음 글을 읽고 물음에 답하시오.

One summer day, there were lots of people around a gorilla cage at a zoo.

A boy was ____@____ excited ____ⓑ____ he climbed over the wall.

One of the gorillas saw him falling inside and caught him.

ⓒShe ⓓtook care of the boy until help arrived.

25 위 글의 빈칸 @와 ⓑ에 들어갈 알맞은 말을 쓰시오.

➡ @ _____ ⓑ _____

26 위 글의 밑줄 친 ⓒShe가 가리키는 것을 본문에서 찾아 쓰시오.

➡ _____

27 위 글의 밑줄 친 ⓓtook care of와 바꿔 쓸 수 있는 말을 쓰시오.

➡ _____

[01~02] 다음 글을 읽고 물음에 답하시오.

In early March every year, the world's biggest sled dog race ⓐtakes place in Alaska. It is called the Iditarod Trail Sled Dog Race. Around 80 teams of 12 to 16 dogs take part in this race. Each team has to cover about ⓑ 1,800 km from Anchorage to Nome. The race can take more than two weeks, and the teams often race through snowstorms. The Iditarod Race began in 1973 ⓒ~을 기념하여 the dogs that saved Nome.

01 위 글의 밑줄 친 ⓐtakes place와 바꿔 쓸 수 있도록 hold를 변형하여 쓰시오.

➡ _____

02 위 글의 밑줄 친 ⓑ를 읽는 법을 영어로 쓰시오.

➡ _____

[03~05] 다음 글을 읽고 물음에 답하시오.

When Gunnar and Balto finally got the medicine, ⓐthe snow was so heavy that Gunnar could not see his own hands. However, Balto was able to stay on the trail. When they were crossing a frozen river, Balto suddenly stopped. Then, Gunnar saw the river ice cracking. The whole team was saved because Balto stopped just in time. When Balto and Gunnar reached the final team, they were sleeping. Gunnar told Balto to continue on.

"Here's the medicine, Doctor!" shouted Gunnar. On February 2, Gunnar and his team finally ⓑarrived in Nome. ⓒThe town was saved.

03 위 글의 밑줄 친 ⓐ를 다음과 같이 바꿔 쓸 때 빈칸에 들어갈 알맞은 말을 쓰시오.

➡ the snow was _____ heavy for Gunnar _____ see his own hands

04 위 글의 밑줄 친 ⓑarrived in과 바꿔 쓸 수 있는 단어를 본문에서 찾아 쓰시오.

➡ _____

05 위 글의 밑줄 친 ⓒThe town이 가리키는 것을 본문에서 찾아 쓰시오.

➡ _____

[06~08] 다음 글을 읽고 물음에 답하시오.

One cold winter day in ⓐ1925, a terrible thing happened in Nome. Some children got very sick, and the disease kept spreading. The people of Nome needed medicine right away, but the town did not have any. ⓑSomeone must get it from a hospital in Anchorage. Because of the heavy snow, a dog sled relay was the only way to get the medicine from Anchorage to Nome. Soon, the race to Nome began.

Twenty-one dog teams were in the relay. _____(A)_____ January 27, the first team left, and the others waited at different points. Gunnar was the driver of the 20th team. The strongest dog on his team was Balto, so he made Balto his lead dog.

06 위 글의 빈칸 (A)에 들어갈 알맞은 전치사를 쓰시오.

➡ _____

07 위 글의 밑줄 친 ⓐ1925를 읽는 법을 영어로 쓰시오.

➡ _____

08 위 글의 밑줄 친 ⓑ에서 어법상 틀린 부분을 찾아 고치시오.

_____ ➡ _____

[09~11] 다음 글을 읽고 물음에 답하시오.

One cold winter day in 1925, a terrible thing happened in Nome. Some children got very sick, and the disease kept spreading. The people of Nome needed medicine right away, but the town did not have ⓐany. Someone had to get it from a hospital in Anchorage. (A)[Because / Because of] the heavy snow, a dog sled relay was the only way to get the medicine from Anchorage to Nome. Soon, the race to Nome began.

Twenty-one dog teams were in the relay. On January 27, the first team left, and (B)[others / the others] waited at different points. Gunnar was the driver of the 20th team. The strongest dog on his team was Balto, (C)[as / so] he made Balto his lead dog.

09 위 글의 괄호 (A)~(C)에서 문맥이나 어법상 알맞은 낱말을 골라 쓰시오.

➡ (A) _____ (B) _____ (C) _____

10 위 글의 밑줄 친 ⓐany 뒤에 생략된 말을 쓰시오.

➡ _____

11 본문의 내용과 일치하도록 다음 빈칸 (A)와 (B)에 알맞은 단어를 쓰시오.

When the people of Nome needed medicine right away, a (A)_____ _____ _____ was the only way to get the medicine from Anchorage to Nome. Soon, the race to Nome began and (B)_____ _____ _____ took part in the relay.

[12~13] 다음 글을 읽고 물음에 답하시오.

When Gunnar and Balto finally got the medicine, the snow was so heavy that Gunnar could not see his own hands. However, Balto was able to stay on the trail. When they were crossing a frozen river, Balto suddenly stopped. ⓐThen, Gunnar saw the river ice to crack. The whole team was saved because Balto stopped just in time. When Balto and Gunnar reached the final team, they were sleeping. Gunnar told Balto to continue on.

"Here's the medicine, Doctor!" shouted Gunnar. On February 2, Gunnar and his team finally arrived in Nome. The town was saved. ⓑThis heart-warming story is now celebrated every year by the Iditarod Race, the biggest sled dog race in the world.

12 위 글의 밑줄 친 ⓐ에서 어법상 틀린 부분을 찾아 고치시오.

_____ ➡ _____

13 위 글의 밑줄 친 ⓑ를 능동태로 고치시오.

➡ _____
_____

해석

Link - Share

Are you interested in <u>learning</u> the history of the marathon? The first marathon
전치사의 목적어(동명사)

<u>was run by</u> Pheidippides in 490 B.C. The Greek army in Marathon ordered
수동태   to부정사를 목적격보어로 받는 동사

<u>him to tell</u> the people of Athens about their victory. He ran 40 km <u>from</u>
목적격보어   ~에서

Marathon <u>to</u> Athens.
···까지

구문해설 • army: 군대, 육로   • victory: 승리

마라톤의 역사를 배우는 것에 관심이 있나요? 최초의 마라톤은 Pheidippides에 의해 기원전 490년에 달려졌습니다. 마라톤에 있던 그리스 군대는 그들의 승리에 관해 아테네의 사람들에게 말하라고 그에게 명령했습니다. 그는 마라톤에서 아테네까지 40km를 달렸습니다.

Write

One cold winter day, a man left home to <u>get</u> wood for a fire. He <u>slipped</u> and
to부정사의 부사적 용법(목적)   slip의 과거

broke his neck. He could not move, but <u>no one</u> was near him. His dog came
아무도 없었다

to his rescue. <u>She</u> barked and barked for 19 hours. A neighbor <u>finally</u> heard the
= to rescue him   = His dog   = at last

dog <u>barking</u> and called 911.
지각동사 hear의 목적격보어로 쓰인 현재분사

구문해설 • slip: 미끄러지다   • neck: 목   • rescue: 구하다, 구조하다   • bark: (개가) 짖다

어느 추운 겨울날, 한 남자가 불을 피울 나무를 구하기 위해 집을 떠났다. 그는 미끄러져서 목을 부러뜨렸다. 그는 움직일 수 없었지만, 그 주변에 아무도 없었다. 그의 개가 그를 구하기 위해 왔다. 그녀는 19시간 동안 짖고 또 짖었다. 한 이웃이 마침내 개가 짖는 소리를 듣고 911에 전화했다.

Culture Project - Share

<u>Every</u> winter, you can <u>see</u> many people <u>jumping</u> into the sea at Haeundae
every+단수 명사   지각동사+목적어+현재분사: '···가 ~하는 것을 보다'

Beach. <u>It's</u> a way of wishing for good health in the New Year.
= Jumping into the sea

구문해설 • jump into: ~로 뛰어들다   • beach: 해변   • way: 방법   • wish: 바라다
        • New Year: 새해

매년 겨울, 많은 사람들이 해운대 해변에서 바다로 뛰어드는 모습을 볼 수 있다. 이것은 새해에 건강하기를 비는 방법이다.

01 다음 두 단어의 관계가 같도록 빈칸에 주어진 철자로 단어를 쓰시오.

> shout : yell = arrive in[at] : _____

02 우리말에 맞게 빈칸을 완성하시오.

> 그 경주는 2주 이상 걸릴 수 있으며, 팀들은 종종 눈보라를 뚫고 경주한다.
>
> ➡ The race can _____ more than two weeks, and the teams often race through _____s.

03 〈보기〉의 단어를 사용하여 자연스러운 문장을 만들 수 없는 것은? (대 · 소문자 무시)

> ┌─ 보기 ┐
> medicine / polar / heart-warming / terrible / victory

① The car racer started to drive faster to catch up with the _____ car.

② _____ bears are large and white.

③ She cried when she heard the _____ story.

④ I had a _____ dream last night.

⑤ Our _____ will be remembered forever.

04 다음 우리말에 해당하는 단어를 세 단어로 쓰시오.

> 아이디타로드 경주는 Nome을 구한 개들을 기념하여 1973년에 시작되었다.
> The Iditarod Race began in 1973 _____ the dogs that saved Nome.

05 다음 빈칸에 어울리는 말을 고르시오.

> _____ the heavy snow, a dog sled relay was the only way to get the medicine from Anchorage to Nome.

① Because   ② Despite

③ Though   ④ Because of

⑤ In spite of

06 다음 글의 ⓐ~ⓔ 중 어법상 어색한 것은?

> M: ⓐIt's important ⓑshow your love for the people around you. ⓒHow often do you tell everyone in your family ⓓthat you love ⓔthem?

① ⓐ   ② ⓑ   ③ ⓒ   ④ ⓓ   ⑤ ⓔ

[07~08] 다음 대화를 읽고 물음에 답하시오.

> A: What winter sport are you interested in?
> B: _____ (A) _____
> A: How often do you go ice skating?
> B: (B)한 달에 한두 번 가.

07 위 대화의 빈칸 (A)에 들어갈 표현을 〈조건〉에 맞게 쓰시오.

> ┌─ 보기 ┐
> • 'ice skating'에 관심을 나타내는 표현을 쓸 것
> • 명사 'an interest'를 사용할 것

➡ _____

08 위 대화의 밑줄 친 (B)의 우리말에 맞게 주어진 단어를 이용하여 쓰시오.

> go / twice

➡ _____

09 두 사람의 대화가 <u>어색한</u> 것은?

① A: Are you interested in reading novels?
  B: Yes, reading novels is my favorite.
② A: What are you doing?
  B: I'm listening to old pop songs.
③ A: What TV programs are you interested in?
  B: I'm fascinated by Korean history and culture.
④ A: How often do you watch comedy programs?
  B: I watch them every day.
⑤ A: Sumi, are you interested in watching movies?
  B: Yes, I am.

[10~11] 다음 대화를 읽고 물음에 답하시오.

G: _____(A)_____, James?
B: I don't like sports much, but I sometimes go swimming.
G: How often do you go swimming?
B: Not very often. _____(B)_____

10 빈칸 (A)에 들어갈 말로 알맞은 것은?

① What are you going to do
② Are you interested in watching movies
③ What are you doing
④ What's your favorite sport
⑤ Do you have any special plans for this weekend

11 빈칸 (B)에 들어갈 말로 알맞은 것은?

① I only go swimming once a month.
② I always go swimming.
③ I'm not interested in going swimming.
④ I'll go skating and sledding.
⑤ I go swimming almost every day.

[12~13] 다음 대화를 읽고 물음에 답하시오.

Anna: Do you have any special plans for the winter break?
Suho: I'm going to go to my grandparents' place in Pyeongchang. I'll go skating and sledding there. I love winter sports.
Anna: Good for you! I love winter sports, too. My favorite is ice hockey.
Suho: Oh, I've never played ice hockey, but I'm interested in learning how to play it.
Anna: Really? I can teach you how to play.
Suho: That's awesome. Is ice hockey the most popular sport in Canada?
Anna: Yes, it is. Everyone I know loves watching it and playing it.
Suho: _____(A)_____ when you were in Canada?
Anna: I played at least two or three times a week in the winter.
Suho: Wow, I'm sure you're really good at ice hockey. I can't wait to learn from you.

12 위 대화의 빈칸 (A)에 들어갈 말로 알맞은 것은?

① What did you usually do
② What city did you live in
③ What were you interested in
④ Were you into ice hockey
⑤ How often did you play ice hockey

13 위 대화의 내용과 일치하지 <u>않는</u> 것은?

① Suho is going to his grandparents' place during the winter vacation.
② Both Suho and Anna love winter sports.
③ Suho goes skating two or three times a week in the winter.
④ Ice hockey is the most popular sport in Canada.
⑤ Suho thinks Anna is really good at ice hockey.

Grammar

14 다음 빈칸에 알맞은 말이 순서대로 짝지어진 것은?

> • Gunnar saw the river ice _____.
> • Mr. Kim told me _____ on time.

① crack – come
② cracks – comes
③ cracked – came
④ to crack – coming
⑤ cracking – to come

15 다음 그림을 보고 괄호 안에 주어진 어휘를 이용하여 빈칸에 알맞은 말을 쓰시오.

I saw David _____ fishing with his father. (go)

16 다음 중 어법상 바르지 <u>않은</u> 것은?

① She made me bake the bread yesterday.
② I watched her talked on the phone.
③ Did you see the man walking his dog?
④ They asked Molly to help them.
⑤ Anne told me to stay longer.

17 다음 주어진 문장의 밑줄 친 부분과 쓰임이 같은 것은?

> I caught him <u>reading</u> my diary.

① We spent a few days at the shelter, <u>waiting</u> for the heavy snow to stop.
② When they were <u>crossing</u> a frozen river, Balto suddenly stopped.
③ I saw him <u>walking</u> across the street.
④ My dream was <u>becoming</u> a B-boy dancer.
⑤ Some children got very sick, and the disease kept <u>spreading</u>.

18 다음 두 문장을 〈보기〉와 같이 한 문장으로 고쳐 쓰시오.

> ┤ 보기 ├
> • I saw her.
> • She was crossing the road.
> = I saw her crossing the road.

(1) • He looked at the baby.
   • The baby was sleeping on the bed.
   ➡ _____

(2) • I heard Amy.
   • She was locking her room.
   ➡ _____

19 다음 문장에서 어법상 <u>어색한</u> 부분을 찾아 바르게 고쳐 다시 쓰시오.

(1) Do you want me believing that false story?

➡ _____

(2) Can you ask him return the book to the library tomorrow?

➡ _____

_____

(3) I heard somebody cried while I took a walk to the park.

➡ _____

_____

(4) I saw Ann to wait for a bus at the bus stop.

➡ _____

_____

Reading

[20~22] 다음 글을 읽고 물음에 답하시오.

In early March every year, the world's biggest sled dog race takes place in Alaska. It is called the Iditarod Trail Sled Dog Race. Around 80 teams of 12 to 16 dogs take part in this race. Each team has to cover ⓐabout 1,800 km ___(A)___ Anchorage to Nome. The race can take more than two weeks, and the teams often race ___(B)___ snowstorms. The Iditarod Race began in 1973 in memory of the dogs that saved Nome.

20 위 글의 빈칸 (A)와 (B)에 들어갈 전치사가 바르게 짝지어진 것은?

① for – through　② from – by
③ at – in　④ at – in
⑤ from – through

21 위 글의 밑줄 친 ⓐabout과 바꿔 쓸 수 있는 단어를 본문에서 찾아 쓰시오.

➡ _____

22 위 글을 읽고 대답할 수 <u>없는</u> 질문은?

① When does the world's biggest dog race take place?
② What is the world's biggest sled dog race called?
③ How many teams take part in this race?
④ How long does it take for the winning team of the race to finish it?
⑤ When did the Iditarod Race begin?

[23~25] 다음 글을 읽고 물음에 답하시오.

One cold winter day in 1925, a terrible thing happened in Nome. Some children got very sick, and the disease kept spreading. The people of Nome needed medicine right away, but the town did not have any. Someone had to get it from a hospital in Anchorage. Because of the heavy snow, a dog sled relay was the only way ⓐto get the medicine from Anchorage to Nome. Soon, the race to Nome began.

Twenty-one dog teams were in the relay. On January 27, the first team left, and ___(A)___ waited at different points. Gunnar was the driver of the 20th team. The strongest dog on his team was Balto, so he made Balto his lead dog.

23 위 글의 빈칸 (A)에 들어갈 알맞은 말을 고르시오.

① one　② the other
③ another　④ the others
⑤ others

24 아래 〈보기〉에서 위 글의 밑줄 친 ⓐto get과 문법적 쓰임이 같은 것의 개수를 고르시오.

┌─ 보기 ├─
① I was surprised to see my cousin there.
② I want something cold to drink.
③ It is difficult to answer the question.
④ He use the computer to do his homework.
⑤ Is there a knife to cut this bread with?

① 1개　② 2개　③ 3개　④ 4개　⑤ 5개

25 위 글의 내용과 일치하지 <u>않는</u> 것은?

① 1925년의 어느 추운 겨울날, 놈 마을의 몇몇 아이들이 매우 아팠고 병이 계속 퍼졌다.
② 놈의 사람들은 당장 약이 필요했지만 마을에는 약이 하나도 없었다.
③ 폭설 때문에 개썰매 릴레이가 앵커리지에서 놈으로 약을 가져오는 유일한 방법이었다.
④ 21개의 개 팀이 릴레이에 참여했다.
⑤ 1월 27일에 첫 번째 팀이 출발했고, 나머지 팀들은 모두 같은 지점에서 기다렸다.

[26~27] 다음 글을 읽고 물음에 답하시오.

When Gunnar and Balto finally got the medicine, the snow was so heavy that Gunnar could not see his own hands. However, ⓐ Balto는 코스를 제대로 따라갈 수 있었다. When they were crossing a frozen river, Balto suddenly stopped. Then, Gunnar saw the river ice cracking. The whole team was saved because Balto stopped just in time. When Balto and Gunnar reached the final team, they were sleeping. Gunnar told Balto to continue on.

"Here's the medicine, Doctor!" shouted Gunnar. On February 2, Gunnar and his team ⓑfinally arrived in Nome. The town was saved. This heart-warming story is now celebrated every year by the Iditarod Race, the biggest sled dog race in the world.

26 위 글의 밑줄 친 ⓐ의 우리말에 맞게 주어진 어휘를 이용하여 8단어로 영작하시오.

┌─────────────────────────┐
│　　able, stay, trail　　│
└─────────────────────────┘

➡ _____

27 위 글의 밑줄 친 ⓑfinally와 바꿔 쓸 수 <u>없는</u> 말을 <u>모두</u> 고르시오.

① at last　　　　② in the end
③ at least　　　④ in the long run
⑤ actually

[28~29] 다음 글을 읽고 물음에 답하시오.

One summer day, there were lots of people around a gorilla cage at a zoo.
A boy was so (A)[exciting / excited] that he climbed over the wall.
One of the (B)[gorilla / gorillas] saw him (C) [to fall / falling] inside and ___ⓐ___ him.
She took care of the boy until help arrived.

28 위 글의 괄호 (A)~(C)에서 문맥이나 어법상 알맞은 낱말을 골라 쓰시오.

➡ (A) _____ (B) _____ (C) _____

29 위 글의 빈칸 ⓐ에 catch를 알맞은 형태로 쓰시오.

➡ _____

01 다음 두 단어의 관계가 같도록 빈칸에 알맞은 말을 쓰시오. (a로 시작하여 쓸 것.)

| popular : unpopular = terrible : _____ |

02 우리말에 맞게 빈칸에 알맞은 단어를 쓰시오.

- 그의 팀에서 가장 강한 개는 Balto였기 때문에, 그는 Balto를 그의 선두 개로 삼았다.
  ➡ The strongest dog on his team was Balto, so he made Balto his (A)_____ dog.
- 그들이 얼어붙은 강을 건너고 있을 때 Balto는 갑자기 멈췄다.
  ➡ When they were crossing a (B)_____ river, Balto suddenly stopped.

[03~04] 다음 영영풀이에 해당하는 단어를 찾으시오.

03

| to break or to make something break, either so that it gets lines on its surface, or so that it breaks into pieces |

① cost   ② slip
③ crack   ④ reach
⑤ cut

04

| to cover, reach, or have an effect on a wider or increasing area |

① cross   ② spread
③ shout   ④ spend
⑤ save

05 자연스러운 대화가 되도록 알맞은 순서로 배열한 것은?

| (A) I'm interested in ice skating.
(B) How often do you go ice skating?
(C) What sport are you interested in?
(D) I go once or twice a month. |

① (A) – (B) – (D) – (C)
② (B) – (A) – (C) – (D)
③ (C) – (A) – (B) – (D)
④ (C) – (D) – (A) – (D)
⑤ (D) – (A) – (B) – (D)

06 다음 글의 밑줄 친 우리말에 맞게 주어진 〈조건〉을 보고 영작하시오.

| M: 크리스마스에 이런 가난한 사람들을 돕는 것은 중요합니다. |

─ 조건 ─
- 가주어, 진주어 to부정사를 이용할 것.
- 'these', 'help', 'at'을 사용할 것.

➡ _____

07 빈칸에 들어갈 말로 알맞은 것은?

| G: What's your favorite TV show, Jason?
B: I don't watch TV, but I listen to the radio.
G: _____
B: Almost every day. |

① How often do you watch it?
② How often do you clean your room?
③ How many times a week do you play soccer?
④ How often do you listen to the radio?
⑤ How long have you been interested in listening to the radio?

08 다음 대화를 읽고 아래의 요약문을 완성하시오.

> B: What are you doing?
> G: I'm listening to old pop songs.
> B: Oh, do you like old pop songs?
> G: No, I'm not interested in them. I just want to sing my grandma's favorite songs at her birthday party next week.
> B: Wow, what a nice granddaughter!

⬇

> The girl is listening to _____ to sing her _____ songs at her _____ next week.

[09~10] 다음 대화를 읽고 물음에 답하시오.

Anna: Do you have any special plans for the winter break?

Suho: I'm going to go to my grandparents' place in Pyeongchang. (A)거기서 스케이트와 썰매를 타러 갈 거야. I love winter sports.

Anna: Good for you! I love winter sports, too. My favorite is ice hockey.

Suho: Oh, I've never played ice hockey, but I'm interested ⓐin learning how to play it.

Anna: Really? I can teach you ⓑhow to play.

Suho: That's awesome. Is ice hockey ⓒthe most popular sport in Canada?

Anna: Yes, it is. Everyone I know ⓓlove watching it and playing it.

Suho: How often did you play ice hockey when you were in Canada?

Anna: I played at least ⓔtwo or three times a week in the winter.

Suho: Wow, I'm sure you're really good at ice hockey. I can't wait to learn from you.

09 위 대화의 밑줄 친 ⓐ~ⓔ 중, 어법상 어색한 것은?

① ⓐ   ② ⓑ   ③ ⓒ   ④ ⓓ   ⑤ ⓔ

10 위 대화의 밑줄 친 (A)의 우리말에 맞게 주어진 단어를 활용하여 영작하시오.

> go / skate / sled

➡ _____

11 다음 빈칸에 들어갈 말이 바르게 짝지어진 것은?

> • I saw the moon _____ from my bedroom window.
> • This problem is easy _____ for everybody to solve.

① rising – too   ② rising – enough
③ rose – too   ④ rose – enough
⑤ rise – to

[12~13] 다음 중 어법상 어색한 문장을 고르시오.

12 ① I felt somebody look at me.
② In Canada, you can see many people to sail on the ice in small boats.
③ I smell something burning.
④ He was listening to her play the piano.
⑤ I heard them yelling each other.

13 ① My parents want me to do better next time.
② Ms. Lee told her dog to bring her the stick.
③ Simon encouraged his son studying science harder.
④ She asked me to speak slowly.
⑤ My mom made me clean my room.

14 빈칸에 들어갈 말이 바르게 짝지어진 것은? (출제율 90%)

> • Mr. Kim tells his students _____ lunch tomorrow.
> • Every winter, you can see many people _____ into the sea at Haeundae Beach.

① bring – jumping
② bring – to jump
③ to bring – jumping
④ to bring – to jump
⑤ to bringing – jumped

15 다음 중 어법상 틀린 문장의 개수는? (출제율 100%)

> ⓐ The doctor told him not to eat salty food.
> ⓑ We never allow our children playing with toy guns.
> ⓒ I didn't expect her to dance with me last night.
> ⓓ I want you coming to my birthday party.
> ⓔ We heard a baby crying loudly.
> ⓕ We watched an old man to run outside.
> ⓖ We were so surprised to see the snow to fall from the sky.

① 1개   ② 2개   ③ 3개   ④ 4개   ⑤ 5개

16 주어진 단어를 이용하여 다음 우리말을 영어로 쓰시오. (출제율 90%)

> 나는 Jake가 농구하는 것을 보았다.
> (see, play)

➡ _____

17 다음 우리말을 영어로 바르게 옮긴 것은? (출제율 95%)

> 그에게 그것을 고쳐 달라고 부탁해 보는 게 어때?

① Why don't you ask him fixes it?
② Why don't you ask him fix it?
③ Why don't you ask him fixing it?
④ Why don't you ask him to fix it?
⑤ Why don't you ask him to fixing it?

[18~20] 다음 글을 읽고 물음에 답하시오.

> In early March every year, the world's biggest sled dog race takes place in Alaska. It is called the Iditarod Trail Sled Dog Race. ⓐ 12~16마리 개로 구성된 80여 팀이 이 경주에 참여한다. Each team has to cover about 1,800 km from Anchorage to Nome. The race can take ⓑmore than two weeks, and the teams often race through snowstorms. The Iditarod Race began in 1973 in memory of the dogs ⓒthat saved Nome.

18 위 글의 밑줄 친 ⓐ의 우리말에 맞게 한 단어를 보충하여, 주어진 어휘를 알맞게 배열하시오. (출제율 95%)

> this race / of / dogs / 80 teams / 12 / 16 / take part in / around

➡ _____
_____

19 위 글의 밑줄 친 ⓑmore than과 바꿔 쓸 수 있는 한 단어를 쓰시오. (출제율 90%)

➡ _____

20 위 글의 밑줄 친 ⓒthat과 문법적 쓰임이 같은 것을 모두 고르시오.

① He is the greatest novelist that has ever lived.

② The fact is that he said so.

③ I'm glad that I found you.

④ He was the first man that came here.

⑤ It is natural that they should respect each other.

[21~23] 다음 글을 읽고 물음에 답하시오.

ⓐOne cold winter day in 1925, a terrible thing was happened in Nome. Some children got very sick, and the disease kept spreading. The people of Nome needed medicine right away, but the town did not have any. Someone had to get it from a hospital in Anchorage. Because of the heavy snow, a dog sled relay was the only way to get the medicine from Anchorage to Nome. Soon, the race to Nome began.

Twenty-one dog teams were in the relay. On January 27, the first team left, and the others waited at different points. Gunnar was the driver of the 20th team. The strongest dog on his team was Balto, so ⓑhe made Balto his lead dog.

21 위 글의 밑줄 친 ⓐ에서 어법상 틀린 부분을 찾아 고치시오.

_____ ➡ _____

22 위 글의 밑줄 친 ⓑhe가 가리키는 것을 본문에서 찾아 쓰시오.

➡ _____

23 위 글을 읽고 대답할 수 없는 질문은?

① When did a terrible thing happen in Nome?

② Did the town have any medicine?

③ How many dog teams were in the dog sled relay?

④ Why was Gunnar the driver of the 20th team?

⑤ What was the name of the strongest dog on Gunnar's team?

[24~25] 다음 글을 읽고 물음에 답하시오.

One cold winter day, a man left home to get wood for a fire.

He slipped and broke his neck. He could not move, but no one was near him.

His dog came to his rescue. ⓐShe barked and barked for 19 hours.

A neighbor finally heard the dog barking and called 911.

24 위 글의 밑줄 친 ⓐShe가 가리키는 것을 본문에서 찾아 쓰시오.

➡ _____

25 위 글의 내용과 일치하지 않는 것은?

① 어느 추운 겨울날, 한 남자가 불을 피울 나무를 구하기 위해 집을 떠났다.

② 그는 미끄러져서 목이 부러졌다.

③ 그는 움직일 수 없었지만, 그 주변에 아무도 없었다.

④ 그는 19시간 동안 계속 고함을 질렀다.

⑤ 한 이웃이 911에 전화했다.

[01~02] 다음 대화를 읽고 물음에 답하시오.

> Anna: Do you have any special plans for the winter break?
>
> Suho: I'm going to go to my grandparents' place in Pyeongchang. I'll go skating and sledding there. I love winter sports.
>
> Anna: Good for you! I love winter sports, too. My favorite is ice hockey.
>
> Suho: Oh, I've never played ice hockey, but I'm interested in learning how to play it.
>
> Anna: Really? I can teach you how to play.
>
> Suho: That's awesome. Is ice hockey the most popular sport in Canada?
>
> Anna: Yes, it is. Everyone I know loves watching it and playing it.
>
> Suho: _____(A)_____
>
> Anna: I played ice hockey at least two or three times a week in the winter.
>
> Suho: Wow, I'm sure you're really good at ice hockey. I can't wait to learn from you.

01 위 대화의 빈칸 (A)에 들어갈 표현을 주어진 〈조건〉과 밑줄 친 Anna의 대답을 참고하여 영어로 쓰시오.

> ┤ 조건 ├
> • '얼마나 자주 ~을 했니?'라고 빈도를 묻는 표현을 쓸 것.
> • 'when'을 이용하여 '캐나다에 있었을 때'를 사용할 것.

➡ _____

_____

02 위 대화의 요약문의 빈칸을 완성하시오.

> The girl and the boy both like _____.
> The boy is going to go to Pyeongchang

and _____ and _____ there _____ the winter break. The girl likes _____. The boy is interested in _____ ice hockey, so the girl is going to teach him _____ it.

03 다음 대화의 빈칸 (A)와 (B)에 들어갈 말을 주어진 조건에 맞게 영어로 쓰시오.

> A: _____(A)_____
> B: I'm interested in comedy programs.
> A: _____(B)_____
> B: I watch them every day.

> ┤ 조건 ├
> • (A)는 'interested'를 사용하여 '어떤 TV 프로그램에 관심이 있는지' 묻는 표현을 쓸 것.
> • (B)는 대명사 'them'을 사용하여 '얼마나 자주 코미디 프로그램을 보는지' 묻는 표현을 쓸 것.

➡ (A) _____

(B) _____

04 다음 대화를 요약하여 한 문장으로 쓸 때 빈칸을 알맞게 채우시오.

(1) Dad: Minji, are you hungry?

Minji: Yes, Dad. I want to have pizza. Will you order one for me?

➡ Minji asked _____.

(2) Stuart: We will go to the beach tomorrow. Don't forget to wear suncream.

Susie: Okay, I will.

➡ Stuart told Susie _____.

05 다음 두 문장을 하나의 문장으로 쓰시오.

(1) • Julia closed the door.
　　• Did you hear it?

➡ _____

(2) • Ms. Park saw her son.
　　• He was reading a book.

➡ _____

[06~07] 다음 글을 읽고 물음에 답하시오.

　One cold winter day in 1925, a terrible thing happened in Nome. ⓐ몇몇 아이들이 매우 아팠고 병이 계속 퍼졌다. The people of Nome needed medicine right away, but the town did not have any. Someone had to get it from a hospital in Anchorage. Because of the heavy snow, a dog sled relay was the only way to get the medicine from Anchorage to Nome. Soon, the race to Nome began.

　Twenty-one dog teams were in the relay. On January 27, the first team left, and the others waited at different points. Gunnar was the driver of the 20th team. ⓑThe strongest dog on his team was Balto, so he made Balto his lead dog.

06 위 글의 밑줄 친 ⓐ의 우리말에 맞게 주어진 어휘를 이용하여 10단어로 영작하시오.

got, sick, disease, kept

➡ _____

_____

중요

07 위 글의 밑줄 친 ⓑ를 다음과 같이 바꿔 쓸 때 빈칸에 들어갈 알맞은 말을 쓰시오.

➡ _____ the strongest dog on his team was Balto, he made Balto his lead dog.

[08~10] 다음 글을 읽고 물음에 답하시오.

　When Gunnar and Balto finally got the medicine, the snow was so heavy that Gunnar could not see his own hands. However, Balto was able to stay on the trail. When they were (A)[crossing / crossed] a frozen river, Balto suddenly stopped. Then, Gunnar saw the river ice cracking. The whole team was saved because Balto stopped ⓐ바로 제때. When Balto and Gunnar (B)[reached / reached to] the final team, they were sleeping. Gunnar told Balto to continue on.

　"Here's the medicine, Doctor!" shouted Gunnar. On February 2, Gunnar and his team finally arrived in Nome. The town was saved. This (C)[heart-warming / heart-warmed] story is now celebrated every year by the Iditarod Race, the biggest sled dog race in the world.

08 위 글의 괄호 (A)~(C)에서 문맥이나 어법상 알맞은 낱말을 골라 쓰시오.

➡ (A) _____ (B) _____ (C) _____

중요

09 위 글의 밑줄 친 ⓐ의 우리말을 세 단어로 쓰시오.

➡ _____

10 본문의 내용과 일치하도록 다음 빈칸 (A)와 (B)에 알맞은 단어를 쓰시오.

In spite of all the difficulties, Gunnar and his team finally arrived in Nome and (A)_____ the town. This heart-warming story is now (B)_____ every year by the Iditarod Race, the biggest sled dog race in the world.

01 다음에 주어진 일을 얼마나 자주 하는지 묻고 대답하는 말을 〈보기〉와 같이 세 문장을 완성하시오.

[What]
• clean your room   • wash your hands   • play the piano   • go on a trip
[How often]
• once a week   • very often   • three times a day   • twice a month

―― 보기 ――
• What: go to the movies   • How often: twice a month
A: How often do you go to the movies?
B: I go to the movies twice a month.

02 〈보기〉에 주어진 어휘와 지각동사를 이용하여 공원에서 볼 수 있는 다양한 사람들을 묘사하는 문장을 세 문장 이상 쓰시오.

―― 보기 ――
ride a bike   eat a piece of pizza
take a picture   wait for someone

(1) _____
(2) _____
(3) _____
(4) _____

03 다음 내용을 바탕으로 감동적인 이야기를 담은 네 컷 만화의 대본을 쓰시오.

Characters: a boy, his parents, a gorilla
Setting: on a summer day at a zoo
Beginning: A boy climbed over the wall to see the gorillas.
Middle: A gorillas saw him falling inside and caught him.
End: The gorilla took care of him until help arrived.

One summer day, there were lots of people around a gorilla cage (A)_____.
A boy was so excited that he climbed (B)_____.
One of the gorillas saw him (C)_____ inside and caught him.
She (D)_____ the boy until help arrived.

단원별 모의고사

01 다음 단어에 대한 영어 설명이 <u>어색한</u> 것은?

① reach: to arrive at a place, especially after spending a long time or a lot of effort travelling

② terrible: extremely severe in a way that causes harm or damage

③ medicine: a substance, especially in the form of a liquid or a pill, that is a treatment for illness or injury

④ race: a running or swimming race between two or more teams in which each person in the team runs or swims part of the race

⑤ snowstorm: a heavy fall of snow that is blown by strong winds

02 다음 우리말에 맞게 빈칸에 알맞은 단어를 쓰시오.

(1) 너는 겨울 방학 때 특별한 계획이 있니?
➡ Do you have any _____ plans for the winter break?

(2) 그는 미끄러져 목이 부러졌다.
➡ He _____ and broke his neck

03 다음 영영풀이에 해당하는 단어를 고르시오.

> a long line or a series of marks that have been left by someone or something

① rescue   ② trail
③ crack   ④ memory
⑤ relay

04 주어진 우리말에 맞게 빈칸에 알맞은 단어를 쓰시오. (단, 분사 형태로 쓸 것)

> 그들이 얼어붙은 강을 건너고 있을 때 Balto는 갑자기 멈췄다. 그때, Gunnar는 강의 얼음이 갈라지는 것을 보았다.
> ➡ When they were crossing a ⓐ_____ river, Balto suddenly stopped. Then, Gunnar saw the river ice ⓑ_____.

05 다음 대화의 빈칸에 들어갈 알맞은 말은?

> B: Do you have any special plans for this weekend, Hana?
> G: Well, I'm going to play table tennis with my dad and brother.
> B: How often do you play?
> G: _____ I love playing table tennis. How about you?
> B: I like playing soccer. I enjoy outdoor sports.

① I don't like sports much.
② I'm interested in playing table tennis.
③ Every weekend.
④ I play table tennis.
⑤ I had a great time.

06 다음 대화의 빈칸에 들어갈 말로 <u>어색한</u> 것은?

> B: What are you doing?
> G: I'm listening to old pop songs.
> B: Oh, do you like old pop songs?
> G: Yes, _____

① I'm into old pop songs.
② I enjoy old pop songs.
③ I like old pop songs.
④ I don't listen to pop songs very often.
⑤ I have an interest in old pop songs.

07 다음 대화의 빈칸에 들어갈 말로 적절한 것은?

> B: What are you doing?
> G: I'm practicing badminton.
> B: Do you like playing badminton?
> G: _____ I just want to pass the badminton test next week.
> B: O.K. Good luck!

① Yes, I love playing badminton.
② No, I don't. I'm into playing badminton.
③ I play badminton twice a week.
④ What makes you think so?
⑤ No, I'm not interested in it.

08 다음 중 짝지어진 대화가 <u>어색한</u> 것은?

① A: Are you interested in dolphins?
　B: Yes, I'm interested in smart animals.
② A: How often do you eat fast food?
　B: Eating fast food is not good for your health.
③ A: Jimin, are you interested in sports?
　B: No, I'm not.
④ A: What are you interested in?
　B: I'm interested in art.
⑤ A: How often do you exercise?
　B: I never exercise.

[09~10] 다음 대화를 읽고 아래 요약문의 빈칸을 완성하시오.

09

> G: What's your favorite sport, James?
> B: I don't like sports much, but I sometimes go swimming.
> G: How often do you go swimming?
> B: Not very often. I only go swimming once a month.

⬇

> James _____ sports much, but he goes _____ _____ a _____.

10

> B: Do you have any special plans for this weekend, Hana?
> G: Well, I'm going to play table tennis with my dad and brother.
> B: How often do you play?
> G: Every weekend. I love playing table tennis. How about you?
> B: I like playing soccer. I enjoy outdoor sports.

⬇

> Hana is going to play _____ with her dad and brother _____. She plays table tennis _____.

[11~12] 다음 대화를 읽고 물음에 답하시오.

> Anna: Do you have any special plans for the winter break?
> Suho: I'm going to go to my grandparents' place in Pyeongchang. I'll go skating and sledding there. I love winter sports.
> Anna: Good for you! I love winter sports, too. My favorite is ice hockey.
> Suho: Oh, I've never played ice hockey, but I'm interested in learning how to play it.
> Anna: Really? I can teach you how to play.
> Suho: That's awesome. Is ice hockey the most popular sport in Canada?
> Anna: Yes, it is. Everyone I know loves watching it and playing it.
> Suho: How often did you play ice hockey when you were in Canada?
> Anna: I played at least two or three times a week in the winter.
> Suho: Wow, I'm sure you're really good at ice hockey. (A)너한테 빨리 배우고 싶다.

11 위 대화를 읽고 다음 질문에 영어로 답하시오.

> Q: What winter sport is Suho interested in learning?

➡ _____

12 위 대화의 밑줄 친 (A)의 우리말에 맞게 주어진 조건에 따라 영어로 쓰시오.

> ┌ 조건 ┐
> • 'can't wait'을 사용할 것.

➡ _____

13 다음 중 밑줄 친 부분의 쓰임이 바르지 <u>못한</u> 것은?

① Jaden asks Minji <u>to review</u> his Korean essay after school.
② She advised me <u>staying</u> in bed for a few days.
③ They won't let you <u>use</u> a plastic bag.
④ I saw her <u>crying</u> in the room.
⑤ He told me <u>to send</u> the card.

14 다음 중 어법상 바르지 <u>않은</u> 것은?

① I heard her opened the window.
② She saw James talk on the phone.
③ They watched Pheidippides running from Marathon to Athens.
④ I felt the ground shake.
⑤ He listened to her sing a song.

15 주어진 단어를 이용하여 다음 우리말을 영어로 쓰시오.

(1) 그는 누군가가 자기를 보고 있는 것을 느꼈다.
(feel, someone, look)

➡ _____

(2) 나는 그에게 여권을 가져오라고 말했다.
(tell, bring, his passport)

➡ _____

16 다음 문장에서 어법상 <u>어색한</u> 부분을 바르게 고치시오.

(1) I saw an old woman to walk her dog.
_____ ➡ _____

(2) I heard my sister cried.
_____ ➡ _____

(3) Have you ever heard Russian speaking?
_____ ➡ _____

(4) I want my parents listening to me more.
_____ ➡ _____

(5) Ms. Kim told us being not late for class.
_____ ➡ _____

17 다음 빈칸에 fix를 어법에 맞게 쓰시오.

> • I watched him _____ my computer.
> • I saw my computer _____.

[18~20] 다음 글을 읽고 물음에 답하시오.

> In early March every year, the world's biggest sled dog race takes place in Alaska. ⓐ It is called the Iditarod Trail Sled Dog Race. Around 80 teams of 12 to 16 dogs ⓑtake part in this race. Each team has to cover about 1,800 km from Anchorage to Nome. The race can take more than two weeks, and the teams often race through snowstorms. The Iditarod Race began in 1973 in memory of the dogs that saved Nome.

18 위 글의 밑줄 친 ⓐIt이 가리키는 것을 본문에서 찾아 쓰시오.

➡ _____

19 위 글의 밑줄 친 ⓑtake part in과 바꿔 쓸 수 있는 말을 모두 고르시오.

① take place　　② participate in
③ perform　　　④ carry out
⑤ join

20 위 글을 읽고 the Iditarod Trail Sled Dog Race에 대해 알 수 <u>없는</u> 것을 고르시오.

① 개최 시기　　② 개최 장소
③ 참가팀의 규모　④ 개의 품종
⑤ 시작 연도

[21~22] 다음 글을 읽고 물음에 답하시오.

One cold winter day ①in 1925, a (A) [terrible / terrific] thing happened in Nome. Some children got very sick, and the disease kept spreading. The people of Nome needed medicine right away, but the town did not have (B)[any / none]. Someone had to get it ②from a hospital in Anchorage. Because of the heavy snow, a dog sled relay was the only way to get the medicine from Anchorage to Nome. Soon, the race ③to Nome began.

Twenty-one dog teams were in the relay. On January 27, the first team left, and the others waited ④at different points. Gunnar was the driver of the (C)[20 / 20th] team. The strongest dog ⑤from his team was Balto, so he made Balto his lead dog.

21 위 글의 밑줄 친 ①~⑤에서 전치사의 쓰임이 적절하지 <u>않</u>은 것을 찾아 알맞게 고치시오.

_____ 번 ➡ _____

22 위 글의 괄호 (A)~(C)에서 문맥이나 어법상 알맞은 낱말을 골라 쓰시오.

➡ (A) _____　(B) _____　(C) _____

[23~25] 다음 글을 읽고 물음에 답하시오.

When Gunnar and Balto finally got the medicine, ⓐ눈발이 너무 거세서 Gunnar는 자신의 손조차도 볼 수 없었다. However, Balto was able to stay on the trail. When they were crossing a frozen river, Balto suddenly stopped. Then, Gunnar saw the river ice cracking. The whole team was saved because Balto stopped just in time. When Balto and Gunnar reached the final team, they were sleeping. Gunnar told Balto to continue on.

"Here's the medicine, Doctor!" shouted Gunnar. On February 2, Gunnar and his team finally arrived in Nome. The town ___(A)___. This heart-warming story is now celebrated every year by the Iditarod Race, the biggest sled dog race in the world.

23 위 글의 빈칸 (A)에 save를 알맞은 형태로 쓰시오.

➡ _____

24 위 글의 밑줄 친 ⓐ의 우리말에 맞게 한 단어를 보충하여, 주어진 어휘를 알맞게 배열하시오.

Gunnar / heavy / the snow / that / his own hands / could not see / was

➡ _____

25 위 글의 내용과 일치하지 <u>않는</u> 것은?

① Gunnar와 Balto가 마침내 약을 받았을 때, 눈발이 너무 거셌다.
② Balto는 코스를 제대로 따라갈 수 없었다.
③ Balto와 Gunnar가 마지막 팀에 다다랐을 때, 그들은 자고 있었다.
④ Gunnar는 Balto에게 계속 가라고 말했다.
⑤ 2월 2일에 Gunnar와 그의 팀은 마침내 놈에 도착했다.

INSIGHT
on the textbook

교과서 파헤치기

※ 다음 영어를 우리말로 쓰시오.

01	single	_____	22	bleach	_____
02	chief	_____	23	enough	_____
03	darkness	_____	24	packed	_____
04	spread	_____	25	popular	_____
05	electricity	_____	26	surprisingly	_____
06	foundation	_____	27	remain	_____
07	amusement park	_____	28	roof	_____
08	blackout	_____	29	safe	_____
09	shelter	_____	30	village	_____
10	impossible	_____	31	work	_____
11	ceiling	_____	32	save	_____
12	widely	_____	33	less	_____
13	bend	_____	34	amazing	_____
14	charity	_____	35	pay for	_____
15	install	_____	36	at least	_____
16	shout	_____	37	light up	_____
17	invent	_____	38	not ~ anymore	_____
18	shake	_____	39	forget to부정사	_____
19	magic	_____	40	turn up	_____
20	leftover	_____	41	thanks to	_____
21	whole	_____	42	come up with	_____
			43	just like	_____

※ 다음 우리말을 영어로 쓰시오.

01 구부리다, 휘다

02 천장

03 흔들다, 털다

04 자선단체

05 어둠, 암흑

06 어려운

07 전체의

08 대규모 정전 사태

09 널리, 폭넓게

10 남은 음식

11 주요한; 우두머리, 부장

12 더 적은

13 불가능한

14 외치다

15 전기

16 단 하나의

17 작동하다

18 구하다

19 놀이공원

20 재단

21 지붕

22 마법의, 신기한

23 주거지, 쉼터

24 마을

25 인기 있는

26 설치하다

27 남아 있다

28 안전한

29 지속되다

30 놀랍게도

31 표백제

32 꽉 들어찬

33 충분한

34 발명하다

35 ~을 환하게 밝히다

36 ~ 덕분에

37 더 이상 ~ 않다

38 ~을 말리다

39 지불하다

40 ~할 것을 잊다

41 ~을 생각해 내다, ~을 만들어 내다

42 (소리 등을) 높이다

43 A를 B로 채우다

※ 다음 영영풀이에 알맞은 단어를 <보기>에서 골라 쓴 후, 우리말 뜻을 쓰시오.

1 _____ : to continue to exist: _____

2 _____ : a very small town located in a country area: _____

3 _____ : the covering that forms the top of a building, vehicle, etc.: _____

4 _____ : food that has not been finished at a meal: _____

5 _____ : a time when there is no light or power because of an electricity failure: _____

6 _____ : to keep someone or something safe from death, harm, loss, etc.: _____

7 _____ : the inside surface of a room that you can see when you look above you: _____

8 _____ : liked or enjoyed by a large number of people: _____

9 _____ : a device for giving light, especially one that has a covering: _____

10 _____ : to cover, reach, or have an effect on a wider or increasing area: _____

11 _____ : to design and/or create something that has never been made before: _____

12 _____ : a strong chemical used for cleaning things or removing colour from things: _____

13 _____ : to put furniture, a machine, or a piece of equipment into position and make it ready to use: _____

14 _____ : the period between the time when the sun rises and the time it goes down, or the part of the day that is neither evening nor night: _____

15 _____ : a form of energy that can be produced in several ways and that provides power to devices that create light, heat, etc.: _____

16 _____ : a system of giving money, food, or help free to those who are in need because they are ill, poor, or have no home, or any organization that has the purpose of providing money or helping in this way _____

보기			
charity	blackout	roof	village
bleach	install	spread	leftover
ceiling	electricity	daytime	save
last	lamp	invent	popular

※ 다음 우리말과 일치하도록 빈칸에 알맞은 말을 쓰시오.

Listen & Speak 1-A

1. **G:** Can you _____ _____ the volume on your phone? I like this song.

   B: I can't _____ _____ _____ _____. It's the _____ volume.

   G: _____ me just _____ your phone in a glass. _____ _____ a glass _____ _____ a speaker.

   B: _____ _____ _____ _____ _____! _____ try it now.

2. **B:** _____ _____ that a movie star _____ _____ to our school.

   G: That's _____. She's my _____ _____.

   B: Oh, who is she?

   G: Miranda Kim. She _____ the _____ _____ in the movie *Jupiter*.

   B: Wow, I _____ _____ _____ _____ _____ her!

1. **G:** 네 휴대폰 소리를 키워줄 수 있겠니? 이 노래가 좋아.
   B: 소리를 더는 키울 수 없어. 음량이 이미 가장 높은데.
   G: 그냥 네 휴대폰을 유리잔 안에 넣게 해 줘. 유리잔이 스피커처럼 쓰인다고 들었어.
   B: 재미있는 생각이야! 지금 해 보자.

2. **B:** 우리 학교에 영화 배우가 온다고 들었어.
   G: 맞아. 내가 가장 좋아하는 여배우야.
   B: 오, 누군데?
   G: Miranda Kim이야. 영화 《주피터》에서 책임 과학자를 연기했어.
   B: 우와, 빨리 만나보고 싶은데!

Listen & Speak 2-A

1. **W:** Excuse me, are you _____ with your _____?

   M: Yes, it was really _____.

   W: Do you _____ _____ _____ the _____ home?

   M: Yes, _____.

   W: _____ _____ _____ _____ _____ the leftovers by tomorrow.

2. **B:** What's _____ _____ _____ this _____?

   G: _____ _____ _____ visit Hong Kong _____ _____ _____.

   B: That _____. What are you _____ _____ _____ there?

   G: I'm _____ _____ _____ to an _____ park. I'm also going _____ _____ _____ of food.

   B: Good. _____ _____ _____ _____ some dim sum.

1. **W:** 실례합니다, 식사를 마치셨나요?
   M: 네, 정말 좋았어요.
   W: 남은 음식을 집에 가져가시겠어요?
   M: 네, 부탁합니다.
   W: 내일까지는 남은 음식을 다 드시는 걸 잊지 마세요.

2. **B:** 이번 겨울 방학에는 뭘 할 거야?
   G: 부모님과 홍콩에 갈 거야.
   B: 신나겠는걸. 거기서 뭘 할 거니?
   G: 놀이공원에 갈 거야. 그리고 온갖 음식들을 먹어 볼 거야.
   B: 좋은데. 딤섬을 먹어 보는 걸 잊지 마.

Communicate A

Yuri: _____ _____, Jaden?

Jaden: My science homework is too _____.

Yuri: What do you _____ _____ do?

Jaden: I need to find _____ _____ _____ _____ _____ trees.

Yuri: That's easy. _____ _____ _____ we _____ _____ trees _____ _____ _____ paper.

Jaden: Oh, I think _____ _____ _____, _____. Then, I can just _____ _____ _____ _____.

Yuri: Yes! You _____ _____ _____ just one paper towel _____ _____ _____ your hands.

Jaden: That's _____. I need _____ _____ two or three paper towels.

Yuri: Just _____ your hands _____ you use a paper towel. Then, one will be _____ _____ _____.

Jaden: Oh, that's a good idea, Yuri! I'll _____ that _____ _____.

Yuri: Good! Just _____ _____ _____ _____ your hands _____ _____ 10 _____.

Communicate B

A: _____ _____ _____ that _____ _____ _____ is the _____ _____ _____ _____ the Earth.

B: I've _____ _____, _____. What can we do to _____ _____?

A: _____ _____ we _____ _____ the light _____ we're not using it?

B: That's a good idea. _____ _____ to _____ _____ the light _____ you _____ your room.

Progress Check

1. B: _____ _____ _____ a famous baseball player _____ _____ to our school.

   G: That's right. He's _____ _____ _____ _____.

   B: Oh, who is he?

   G: I'm _____ _____ _____ tell you. It's a _____!

2. B: What's your _____ _____ this _____ _____?

   G: I'm going _____ _____ Vietnam _____ my parents.

   B: That _____ _____. What are you _____ to do there?

   G: I'm going to _____ some time on the _____ and eat lots of _____.

   B: Good. _____ _____ _____ _____ the fruit there, too.

   G: O.K., I _____ _____.

유리: 무슨 일 있니, Jaden?

Jaden: 과학 숙제가 너무 어려워.

유리: 뭘 해야 하는데?

Jaden: 나무들을 살리는 방법을 찾아야 해.

유리: 그건 쉬워. 나는 종이를 덜 사용함으로써 나무들을 살릴 수 있다고 들었어.

Jaden: 아, 나도 들어 본 것 같아. 그럼, 종이컵 쓰는 걸 멈추면 되겠네.

유리: 맞아! 그리고 손을 말리는 데 종이 수건을 한 장만 쓸 수도 있지.

Jaden: 그건 불가능해. 나는 종이 수건이 적어도 두세 장은 필요해.

유리: 종이 수건을 쓰기 전에 손을 털어 봐. 그럼, 한 장으로 충분하고도 남을 거야.

Jaden: 오, 좋은 생각이야, 유리야! 다음에 해 봐야겠어.

유리: 좋아! 손을 적어도 열 번은 털어야 한다는 걸 잊지 마.

A: 전기를 절약하는 게 지구를 살리는 데 가장 좋은 방법이라고 들었어.

B: 나도 들었어. 전기를 절약하기 위해 무엇을 할 수 있을까?

A: 사용하지 않을 때는 전기를 끄는 게 어때?

B: 좋은 생각이야. 방을 나갈 때 불 끄는 것을 잊지 마.

1. B: 유명한 야구 선수가 우리 학교로 온다고 들었어.

   G: 맞아. 그는 내가 가장 좋아하는 선수야.

   B: 오, 누군데?

   G: 말해주지 않을 거야. 놀라게 할 거야!

2. B: 이번 겨울 방학에 무슨 계획이 있니?

   G: 부모님과 함께 베트남에 갈 거야.

   B: 재미있겠다. 거기서 뭘 할 거야?

   G: 바닷가에서 시간을 좀 보내고 해산물을 많이 먹을 거야.

   B: 좋아. 거기 과일을 먹어 보는 것도 잊지 마.

   G: 알겠어, 잊지 않을게.

※ 다음 우리말에 맞도록 대화를 영어로 쓰시오.

Listen & Speak 1-A

1. G: _____

   B: _____

   G: _____

   B: _____

2. B: _____

   G: _____

   B: _____

   G: _____

   B: _____

해석

1. G: 네 휴대폰 소리를 키워줄 수 있겠니? 이 노래가 좋아.
   B: 소리를 더는 키울 수 없어. 음량이 이미 가장 높은데.
   G: 그냥 네 휴대폰을 유리잔 안에 넣게 해 줘. 유리잔이 스피커처럼 쓰인다고 들었어.
   B: 재미있는 생각이야! 지금 해 보자.

2. B: 우리 학교에 영화 배우가 온다고 들었어.
   G: 맞아. 내가 가장 좋아하는 여배우야.
   B: 오, 누군데?
   G: Miranda Kim이야. 영화 《주피터》에서 책임 과학자를 연기했어.
   B: 우와, 빨리 만나보고 싶은데!

Listen & Speak 2-A

1. W: _____

   M: _____

   W: _____

   M: _____

   W: _____

2. B: _____

   G: _____

   B: _____

   G: _____

   B: _____

1. W: 실례합니다, 식사를 마치셨나요?
   M: 네, 정말 좋았어요.
   W: 남은 음식을 집에 가져가시겠어요?
   M: 네, 부탁합니다.
   W: 내일까지는 남은 음식을 다 드시는 걸 잊지 마세요.

2. B: 이번 겨울 방학에는 뭘 할 거야?
   G: 부모님과 홍콩에 갈 거야.
   B: 신나겠는걸. 거기서 뭘 할 거니?
   G: 놀이공원에 갈 거야. 그리고 온갖 음식들을 먹어 볼 거야.
   B: 좋은데. 딤섬을 먹어 보는 걸 잊지 마.

Communicate A

Yuri: _____

Jaden: _____

Yuri: _____

Jaden: _____

Yuri: _____

Jaden: _____

Yuri: _____

Jaden: _____

Yuri: _____

Jaden: _____

Yuri: _____

유리: 무슨 일 있니, Jaden?

Jaden: 과학 숙제가 너무 어려워.

유리: 뭘 해야 하는데?

Jaden: 나무들을 살리는 방법을 찾아야 해.

유리: 그건 쉬워. 나는 종이를 덜 사용함으로써 나무들을 살릴 수 있다고 들었어.

Jaden: 아, 나도 들어 본 것 같아. 그럼, 종이컵 쓰는 걸 멈추면 되겠네.

유리: 맞아! 그리고 손을 말리는 데 종이 수건을 한 장만 쓸 수도 있지.

Jaden: 그건 불가능해. 나는 종이 수건이 적어도 두세 장은 필요해.

유리: 종이 수건을 쓰기 전에 손을 털어봐. 그럼, 한 장으로 충분하고도 남을 거야.

Jaden: 오, 좋은 생각이야, 유리야! 다음에 해 봐야겠어.

유리: 좋아! 손을 적어도 열 번은 털어야 한다는 걸 잊지 마.

Communicate B

A: _____

B: _____

A: _____

B: _____

A: 전기를 절약하는 게 지구를 살리는 데 가장 좋은 방법이라고 들었어.

B: 나도 들었어. 전기를 절약하기 위해 무엇을 할 수 있을까?

A: 사용하지 않을 때는 전기를 끄는 게 어때?

B: 좋은 생각이야. 방을 나갈 때 불 끄는 것을 잊지 마.

Progress Check

1. B: _____

   G: _____

   B: _____

   G: _____

2. B: _____

   G: _____

   B: _____

   G: _____

   B: _____

   G: _____

1. B: 유명한 야구 선수가 우리 학교로 온다고 들었어.
   G: 맞아. 그는 내가 가장 좋아하는 선수야.
   B: 오, 누군데?
   G: 말해주지 않을 거야. 놀라게 할 거야!

2. B: 이번 겨울 방학에 무슨 계획이 있니?
   G: 부모님과 함께 베트남에 갈 거야.
   B: 재미있겠다. 거기서 뭘 할 거야?
   G: 바닷가에서 시간을 좀 보내고 해산물을 많이 먹을 거야.
   B: 좋아. 거기 과일을 먹어 보는 것도 잊지 마.
   G: 알겠어, 잊지 않을게.

※ 다음 우리말과 일치하도록 빈칸에 알맞은 것을 골라 쓰시오.

1 _____ Magic _____
   A. Lamps   B. One-Dollar

2 "Wow, I can _____ a book in my room now!" _____ Marco, a boy in a _____ in the Philippines.
   A. shouted   B. village   C. read

3 His house has no _____ just _____ all the _____ houses in the _____.
   A. other   B. village   C. like   D. electricity

4 People in the village are _____ poor _____ _____ for electricity.
   A. pay   B. to   C. too

5 Even _____ the _____, they live in darkness _____ the houses are _____ close together.
   A. because   B. daytime   C. packed   D. during

6 Now _____ are changing _____ _____ a _____ plastic bottle.
   A. of   B. because   C. single   D. things

7 One plastic bottle in the ceiling can _____ _____ a whole room _____ _____ any electricity.
   A. without   B. light   C. using   D. up

8 This amazing plastic bottle is _____ a Moser lamp _____ it was _____ _____ Alfredo Moser.
   A. invented   B. called   C. by   D. because

9 In 2002, _____ _____ many _____ in his town in Brazil.
   A. blackouts   B. were   C. there

10 These blackouts made him _____ up _____ a new _____ to _____ his house.
   A. come   B. light   C. with   D. way

11 A Moser lamp can be _____ _____ about one dollar and _____ for _____ 10 years.
   A. for   B. made   C. about   D. lasts

12 It is _____ very _____.
   A. safe   B. also

---

1 1달러짜리 마법의 전구

2 "우와, 이젠 제 방에서 책을 읽을 수 있어요!" 필리핀의 한 마을에 사는 소년인 Marco가 외쳤다.

3 그의 집은 마을의 다른 모든 집들과 마찬가지로 전기가 없다.

4 마을 사람들은 너무나 가난해서 전기세를 낼 수가 없다.

5 심지어 낮 동안에도, 집들이 빽빽하게 들어차 있어서 그들은 어둠 속에 살아간다.

6 이제 플라스틱병 하나 때문에 상황이 바뀌고 있다.

7 천장에 있는 플라스틱병 하나는 전기를 쓰지 않고 방 전체를 밝힐 수 있다.

8 이 놀라운 플라스틱병은 Moser 램프라고 불리는데, 그것이 Alfredo Moser에 의해 발명되었기 때문이다.

9 2002년, 브라질에 있는 그의 마을에는 정전이 잦았다.

10 이 정전들은 그가 집을 밝히는 새로운 방법을 생각해 내도록 만들었다.

11 Moser 램프는 1달러 정도로 만들 수 있고 10년 정도 지속된다.

12 그것은 또한 매우 안전하다.

13 It can _____ _____ a house _____.

    A. fire   B. start   C. never

14 _____, it is very _____ to _____ this magic lamp.

    A. easy   B. surprisingly   C. make

15 _____ to _____ a Moser lamp _____ a bottle

    A. from   B. how   C. make

16 1. _____ a _____ plastic bottle _____ water.

    A. with   B. fill   C. clear

17 2. _____ some bleach _____ _____ the water _____.

    A. clear   B. keep   C. add   D. to

18 3. Make a hole in the _____, and _____ the bottle _____ the _____.

    A. hole   B. into   C. push   D. roof

19 4. _____ a _____ of the bottle _____ _____ the roof.

    A. remain   B. third   C. let   D. above

20 5. Sunlight _____ _____ by the water in the bottle and _____ _____ the room.

    A. spreads   B. bent   C. around   D. is

21 _____ the Philippines, Moser lamps are _____ _____ _____ the My Shelter Foundation.

    A. used   B. by   C. in   D. widely

22 The _____ also teaches _____ people _____ to make and _____ the lamps.

    A. install   B. charity   C. how   D. local

23 _____ _____ the charity, _____ _____ homes in the Philippines now have Moser lamps.

    A. of   B. thanks   C. thousands   D. to

24 It _____ also _____ Moser lamps popular in _____ countries, _____ as Argentina, India, and Fiji.

    A. has   B. other   C. made   D. such

25 Moser lamps will _____ _____ the lives of many people _____ many _____ to come.

    A. for   B. light   C. years   D. up

13 그것은 절대 집에 불을 낼 수 없다.

14 놀랍게도, 이 신기한 램프를 만드는 것은 매우 쉽다.

15 병으로 Moser 램프를 만드는 법

16 1. 투명한 플라스틱병에 물을 채운다.

17 2. 물을 깨끗이 유지하기 위해 표백제를 조금 넣는다.

18 3. 지붕에 구멍을 내고, 병을 구멍 안으로 넣는다.

19 4. 병의 3분의 1은 지붕 위에 남아 있도록 한다.

20 5. 햇빛이 병 속의 물에 의해 굴절되어 방에 퍼진다.

21 필리핀에서 Moser 램프는 My Shelter 재단에 의해 널리 사용된다.

22 또한 그 자선단체는 지역 사람들에게 램프를 만들고 설치하는 법을 가르친다.

23 이 자선단체 덕분에, 필리핀의 수천 가구가 이제 Moser 램프를 갖고 있다.

24 그 단체는 아르헨티나, 인도, 피지와 같은 다른 나라들에서도 Moser 램프가 유명해 지도록 만들었다.

25 Moser 램프는 앞으로 오랫동안 많은 사람들의 삶을 밝혀 줄 것이다.

※ 다음 우리말과 일치하도록 빈칸에 알맞은 말을 쓰시오.

1 _____ _____ Lamps

2 "Wow, I can read a book in my room now!" _____ Marco, a boy in a village _____ _____ _____.

3 His house _____ _____ _____ just like _____ _____ _____ _____ in the village.

4 People in the village are _____ poor _____ _____ _____ _____.

5 Even _____ the daytime, they live in darkness _____ the houses _____ _____ _____ _____.

6 Now things _____ _____ _____ _____ _____ a single plastic bottle.

7 One plastic bottle _____ _____ _____ can _____ _____ a whole room _____ _____ any electricity.

8 This amazing plastic bottle _____ _____ a Moser lamp _____ it _____ _____ Alfredo Moser.

9 In 2002, there _____ _____ _____ _____ in his town in Brazil.

10 These blackouts made him _____ _____ _____ a new _____ _____ _____ his house.

11 A Moser lamp can _____ _____ _____ about one dollar and _____ _____ _____ 10 years.

12 It is also _____ _____.

1 1달러짜리 마법의 전구

2 "우와, 이젠 제 방에서 책을 읽을 수 있어요!" 필리핀의 한 마을에 사는 소년인 Marco가 외쳤다.

3 그의 집은 마을의 다른 모든 집들과 마찬가지로 전기가 없다.

4 마을 사람들은 너무나 가난해서 전기세를 낼 수가 없다.

5 심지어 낮 동안에도, 집들이 빽빽하게 들어차 있어서 그들은 어둠 속에 살아간다.

6 이제 플라스틱병 하나 때문에 상황이 바뀌고 있다.

7 천장에 있는 플라스틱병 하나는 전기를 쓰지 않고 방 전체를 밝힐 수 있다.

8 이 놀라운 플라스틱병은 Moser 램프라고 불리는데, 그것이 Alfredo Moser에 의해 발명되었기 때문이다.

9 2002년, 브라질에 있는 그의 마을에는 정전이 잦았다.

10 이 정전들은 그가 집을 밝히는 새로운 방법을 생각해 내도록 만들었다.

11 Moser 램프는 1달러 정도로 만들 수 있고 10년 정도 지속된다.

12 그것은 또한 매우 안전하다.

13 It can _____ _____ a house fire.

14 Surprisingly, it is very easy _____ _____ this magic lamp.

15 _____ _____ _____ a Moser lamp from a bottle

16 1. _____ a clear plastic bottle _____ water.

17 2. _____ some _____ _____ _____ the water _____ .

18 3. Make a hole in the roof, and _____ the bottle _____ the hole.

19 4. Let _____ _____ of the bottle _____ _____ the roof.

20 5. Sunlight _____ _____ _____ the water in the bottle and _____ _____ the room.

21 In the Philippines, Moser lamps _____ _____ _____ by the My Shelter Foundation.

22 _____ _____ also teaches local people _____ _____ _____ and _____ the lamps.

23 _____ _____ the charity, _____ _____ homes in the Philippines now have Moser lamps.

24 It _____ also _____ Moser lamps popular in _____ _____, _____ _____ _____ Argentina, India, and Fiji.

25 Moser lamps will _____ _____ the lives of many people _____ _____ _____ _____ _____ .

13 그것은 절대 집에 불을 낼 수 없다.

14 놀랍게도, 이 신기한 램프를 만드는 것은 매우 쉽다.

15 병으로 Moser 램프를 만드는 법

16 1. 투명한 플라스틱병에 물을 채운다.

17 2. 물을 깨끗이 유지하기 위해 표백제를 조금 넣는다.

18 3. 지붕에 구멍을 내고, 병을 구멍 안으로 넣는다.

19 4. 병의 3분의 1은 지붕 위에 남아 있도록 한다.

20 5. 햇빛이 병 속의 물에 의해 굴절되어 방에 퍼진다.

21 필리핀에서 Moser 램프는 My Shelter 재단에 의해 널리 사용된다.

22 또한 그 자선단체는 지역 사람들에게 램프를 만들고 설치하는 법을 가르친다.

23 이 자선단체 덕분에, 필리핀의 수천 가구가 이제 Moser 램프를 갖고 있다.

24 그 단체는 아르헨티나, 인도, 피지와 같은 다른 나라들에서도 Moser 램프가 유명해 지도록 만들었다.

25 Moser 램프는 앞으로 오랫동안 많은 사람들의 삶을 밝혀 줄 것이다.

※ 다음 문장을 우리말로 쓰시오.

1 ▶ One-Dollar Magic Lamps

➡ _____

2 ▶ "Wow, I can read a book in my room now!" shouted Marco, a boy in a village in the Philippines.

➡ _____

3 ▶ His house has no electricity just like all the other houses in the village.

➡ _____

4 ▶ People in the village are too poor to pay for electricity.

➡ _____

5 ▶ Even during the daytime, they live in darkness because the houses are packed close together.

➡ _____

6 ▶ Now things are changing because of a single plastic bottle.

➡ _____

7 ▶ One plastic bottle in the ceiling can light up a whole room without using any electricity.

➡ _____

8 ▶ This amazing plastic bottle is called a Moser lamp because it was invented by Alfredo Moser.

➡ _____

9 ▶ In 2002, there were many blackouts in his town in Brazil.

➡ _____

10 ▶ These blackouts made him come up with a new way to light his house.

➡ _____

11 ▶ A Moser lamp can be made for about one dollar and lasts for about 10 years.

➡ _____

12 ▶ It is also very safe.

➡ _____

13▸ It can never start a house fire.

➡ _____

14▸ Surprisingly, it is very easy to make this magic lamp.

➡ _____

15▸ How to make a Moser lamp from a bottle

➡ _____

16▸ 1. Fill a clear plastic bottle with water.

➡ _____

17▸ 2. Add some bleach to keep the water clear.

➡ _____

18▸ 3. Make a hole in the roof, and push the bottle into the hole.

➡ _____

19▸ 4. Let a third of the bottle remain above the roof.

➡ _____

20▸ 5. Sunlight is bent by the water in the bottle and spreads around the room.

➡ _____

21▸ In the Philippines, Moser lamps are widely used by the My Shelter Foundation.

➡ _____

22▸ The charity also teaches local people how to make and install the lamps.

➡ _____

23▸ Thanks to the charity, thousands of homes in the Philippines now have Moser lamps.

➡ _____

24▸ It has also made Moser lamps popular in other countries, such as Argentina, India, and Fiji.

➡ _____

25▸ Moser lamps will light up the lives of many people for many years to come.

➡ _____

※ 다음 괄호 안의 단어들을 우리말에 맞도록 바르게 배열하시오.

1 (Magic / One-Dollar / Lamps)
➡ _____

2 ("wow, / can / I / a / read / book / my / in / room / now!" / Marco, / shouted / boy / a / in / village / a / in / Philippines. / the)
➡ _____

3 (house / his / no / has / just / electricity / like / the / all / other / in / houses / village. / the)
➡ _____

4 (in / people / the / village / too / are / poor / pay / to / electricity. / for)
➡ _____

5 (during / even / daytime, / the / live / they / darkness / in / because / houses / the / packed / are / together. / close)
➡ _____

6 (things / now / changing / are / of / because / a / plastic / single / bottle.)
➡ _____

7 (plastic / one / in / bottle / the / ceiling / light / can / up / a / room / whole / using / without / electricity. / any)
➡ _____

8 (amazing / this / bottle / plastic / called / is / Moser / a / lamp / it / because / invented / was / by / Moser. / Alfredo)
➡ _____

9 (2002, / in / were / there / blcakouts / many / his / in / town / Brazil. / in)
➡ _____

10 (blackouts / these / him / made / come / with / up / a / way / new / light / to / house. / his)
➡ _____

11 (Moser / a / lamp / be / can / for / made / about / dollar / one / and / for / lasts / about / years. / 10)
➡ _____

12 (is / it / also / safe. / very)
➡ _____

1 1달러짜리 마법의 전구

2 "우와, 이젠 제 방에서 책을 읽을 수 있어요!" 필리핀의 한 마을에 사는 소년인 Marco가 외쳤다.

3 그의 집은 마을의 다른 모든 집들과 마찬가지로 전기가 없다.

4 마을 사람들은 너무나 가난해서 전기세를 낼 수가 없다.

5 심지어 낮 동안에도, 집들이 빽빽하게 들어차 있어서 그들은 어둠 속에 살아간다.

6 이제 플라스틱병 하나 때문에 상황이 바뀌고 있다.

7 천장에 있는 플라스틱병 하나는 전기를 쓰지 않고 방 전체를 밝힐 수 있다.

8 이 놀라운 플라스틱병은 Moser 램프라고 불리는데, 그것이 Alfredo Moser에 의해 발명되었기 때문이다.

9 2002년, 브라질에 있는 그의 마을에는 정전이 잦았다.

10 이 정전들은 그가 집을 밝히는 새로운 방법을 생각해 내도록 만들었다.

11 Moser 램프는 1달러 정도로 만들 수 있고 10년 정도 지속된다.

12 그것은 또한 매우 안전하다.

13 (it / never / can / a / start / fire. / house)

➡ _____

14 (surprisingly, / is / it / easy / very / make / to / magic / this / lamp.)

➡ _____

15 (to / how / a / make / lamp / Moser / a / from / bottle)

➡ _____

16 (1. / a / fill / plastic / clear / with / bottle / water.)

➡ _____

17 (2. / some / add / to / bleach / the / keep / clear. / water)

➡ _____

18 (3. / a / make / hole / the / in / roof, / and / the / push / into / bottle / hole. / the)

➡ _____

19 (4. / a / let / of / third / the / remain / bottle / above / roof. / the)

➡ _____

20 (5. / is / sunlight / bent / by / water / the / in / bottle / and / spreads / the / around / room.)

➡ _____

21 (the / in / Philippines, / lamps / Moser / widely / are / by / used / the / Shelter / My / Foundation.)

➡ _____

➡ _____

22 (charity / the / teaches / also / people / local / to / how / make / and / the / install / lamps.)

➡ _____

23 (to / thanks / charity, / the / of / thousands / homes / the / in / now / Philippines / have / lamps. / Moser)

➡ _____

➡ _____

24 (has / it / made / also / lamps / Moser / in / popular / countries, / other / as / such / India, / Argentina, / Fiji. / and)

➡ _____

➡ _____

25 (lamps / Moser / light / will / up / lives / the / many / of / for / people / years / many / come. / to)

➡ _____

➡ _____

13 그것은 절대 집에 불을 낼 수 없다.

14 놀랍게도, 이 신기한 램프를 만드는 것은 매우 쉽다.

15 병으로 Moser 램프를 만드는 법

16 1. 투명한 플라스틱병에 물을 채운다.

17 2. 물을 깨끗이 유지하기 위해 표백제를 조금 넣는다.

18 3. 지붕에 구멍을 내고, 병을 구멍 안으로 넣는다.

19 4. 병의 3분의 1은 지붕 위에 남아 있도록 한다.

20 5. 햇빛이 병 속의 물에 의해 굴절되어 방에 퍼진다.

21 필리핀에서 Moser 램프는 My Shelter 재단에 의해 널리 사용된다.

22 또한 그 자선단체는 지역 사람들에게 램프를 만들고 설치하는 법을 가르친다.

23 이 자선단체 덕분에, 필리핀의 수천 가구가 이제 Moser 램프를 갖고 있다.

24 그 단체는 아르헨티나, 인도, 피지와 같은 다른 나라들에서도 Moser 램프가 유명해 지도록 만들었다.

25 Moser 램프는 앞으로 오랫동안 많은 사람들의 삶을 밝혀 줄 것이다.

※ 다음 우리말을 영어로 쓰시오.

1 1달러짜리 마법의 전구

➡ _____

2 "우와, 이젠 제 방에서 책을 읽을 수 있어요!" 필리핀의 한 마을에 사는 소년인 Marco가 외쳤다.

➡ _____

3 그의 집은 마을의 다른 모든 집들과 마찬가지로 전기가 없다.

➡ _____

4 마을 사람들은 너무나 가난해서 전기세를 낼 수가 없다.

➡ _____

5 심지어 낮 동안에도, 집들이 빽빽하게 들어차 있어서 그들은 어둠 속에 살아간다.

➡ _____

6 이제 플라스틱병 하나 때문에 상황이 바뀌고 있다.

➡ _____

7 천장에 있는 플라스틱병 하나는 전기를 쓰지 않고 방 전체를 밝힐 수 있다.

➡ _____

8 이 놀라운 플라스틱병은 Moser 램프라고 불리는데, 그것이 Alfredo Moser에 의해 발명되었기 때문이다.

➡ _____

9 2002년, 브라질에 있는 그의 마을에는 정전이 잦았다.

➡ _____

10 이 정전들은 그가 집을 밝히는 새로운 방법을 생각해 내도록 만들었다.

➡ _____

11 Moser 램프는 1달러 정도로 만들 수 있고 10년 정도 지속된다.

➡ _____

12 그것은 또한 매우 안전하다.

➡ _____

13 그것은 절대 집에 불을 낼 수 없다.

➡ _____

14 놀랍게도, 이 신기한 램프를 만드는 것은 매우 쉽다.

➡ _____

15 병으로 Moser 램프를 만드는 법

➡ _____

16 1. 투명한 플라스틱병에 물을 채운다.

➡ _____

17 2. 물을 깨끗이 유지하기 위해 표백제를 조금 넣는다.

➡ _____

18 3. 지붕에 구멍을 내고, 병을 구멍 안으로 넣는다.

➡ _____

19 4. 병의 3분의 1은 지붕 위에 남아 있도록 한다.

➡ _____

20 5. 햇빛이 병 속의 물에 의해 굴절되어 방에 퍼진다.

➡ _____

21 필리핀에서 Moser 램프는 My Shelter 재단에 의해 널리 사용된다.

➡ _____

22 또한 그 자선단체는 지역 사람들에게 램프를 만들고 설치하는 법을 가르친다.

➡ _____

23 이 자선단체 덕분에, 필리핀의 수천 가구가 이제 Moser 램프를 갖고 있다.

➡ _____

24 그 단체는 아르헨티나, 인도, 피지와 같은 다른 나라들에서도 Moser 램프가 유명해 지도록 만들었다.

➡ _____

25 Moser 램프는 앞으로 오랫동안 많은 사람들의 삶을 밝혀 줄 것이다.

➡ _____

※ 다음 우리말과 일치하도록 빈칸에 알맞은 말을 쓰시오.

Link-Share

1. We thought we could _____ _____ _____ _____ with a glass bottle.

2. We made one lamp _____ _____ a plastic bottle and _____ _____ out of a glass bottle.

3. _____ _____ _____ _____ were the same.

4. We _____ _____ the glass bottle lamp was _____ _____ the plastic bottle lamp.

1. 우리는 우리가 램프를 유리병으로 더 밝게 만들 수 있다고 생각했다.
2. 우리는 플라스틱병으로 램프를 하나 만들고 유리병으로 또 다른 하나를 만들었다.
3. 다른 모든 단계는 똑같았다.
4. 우리는 유리병 램프가 플라스틱병 램프보다 더 밝다는 것을 알았다.

Write

1. You can make _____ _____ _____ things _____ a CD case.

2. You _____ _____ _____ a grass container.

3. First, _____ _____ _____ the CD case with soil and water, and _____ grass seeds _____ the soil.

4. Second, _____ the case and tape _____ _____ _____ _____.

5. _____, leave _____ in the sun _____ _____ ten days.

6. Now, your grass container _____ _____.

7. It will _____ _____ _____ when the grass grows.

1. 당신은 CD 케이스로 많은 것들을 만들 수 있다.
2. 당신은 심지어 잔디를 기르는 용기를 만들 수도 있다.
3. 먼저 CD 케이스의 절반을 흙과 물로 채우고, 잔디 씨앗을 흙 안에 넣어라.
4. 두 번째, 케이스를 닫고 모든 옆면에 테이프를 붙여라.
5. 마지막으로, 햇빛이 비치는 곳에 약 10일 동안 놓아 두어라.
6. 이제, 당신의 잔디를 기르는 용기가 준비되었다.
7. 잔디가 자랄 때 그것은 당신을 행복하게 만들어 줄 것이다.

Culture Project-Share

1. We'd _____ _____ _____ about a pot-in-pot cooler.

2. It _____ _____ _____ without electricity.

3. _____'s very easy _____ _____ one.

4. First, _____ a pot _____ a larger pot.

5. Then, _____ sand and water _____ these pots.

6. Just _____ the water _____ _____, and it'll _____ the food.

1. 우리는 pot-in-pot cooler(항아리 냉장고)에 대해 이야기하고 싶다.
2. 그것은 전기 없이 식품을 신선하게 유지할 수 있다.
3. 그것을 만드는 것은 매우 쉽다.
4. 우선, 항아리 하나를 더 큰 항아리에 넣는다.
5. 그리고 항아리들 사이에 모래와 물을 넣는다.
6. 물이 그저 마르게 두면, 그것이 음식을 시원하게 할 것이다.

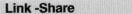
※ 다음 우리말을 영어로 쓰시오.

Link -Share

1. 우리는 우리가 램프를 유리병으로 더 밝게 만들 수 있다고 생각했다.
   ➡ _____

2. 우리는 플라스틱병으로 램프를 하나 만들고 유리병으로 또 다른 하나를 만들었다.
   ➡ _____

3. 다른 모든 단계는 똑같았다.
   ➡ _____

4. 우리는 유리병 램프가 플라스틱병 램프보다 더 밝다는 것을 알았다.
   ➡ _____

Write

1. 당신은 CD 케이스로 많은 것들을 만들 수 있다.
   ➡ _____

2. 당신은 심지어 잔디를 기르는 용기를 만들 수도 있다.
   ➡ _____

3. 먼저 CD 케이스의 절반을 흙과 물로 채우고, 잔디 씨앗을 흙 안에 넣어라.
   ➡ _____

4. 두 번째, 케이스를 닫고 모든 옆면에 테이프를 붙여라.
   ➡ _____

5. 마지막으로, 햇빛이 비치는 곳에 약 10일 동안 놓아 두어라.
   ➡ _____

6. 이제, 당신의 잔디를 기르는 용기가 준비되었다.
   ➡ _____

7. 잔디가 자랄 때 그것은 당신을 행복하게 만들어 줄 것이다.
   ➡ _____

Culture Project-Share

1. 우리는 pot-in-pot cooler(항아리 냉장고)에 대해 이야기하고 싶다.
   ➡ _____

2. 그것은 전기 없이 식품을 신선하게 유지할 수 있다.
   ➡ _____

3. 그것을 만드는 것은 매우 쉽다.
   ➡ _____

4. 우선, 항아리 하나를 더 큰 항아리에 넣는다.
   ➡ _____

5. 그리고 항아리들 사이에 모래와 물을 넣는다.
   ➡ _____

6. 물이 그저 마르게 두면, 그것이 음식을 시원하게 할 것이다.
   ➡ _____

※ 다음 영어를 우리말로 쓰시오.

01 bark		22 cover	
02 crack		23 granddaughter	
03 shout		24 slip	
04 awesome		25 trail	
05 reach		26 broadcast	
06 sled		27 highlight	
07 relay		28 language	
08 special		29 cage	
09 celebrate		30 happen	
10 grandparents' place		31 medicine	
11 save		32 disease	
12 heart-warming		33 heavy snow	
13 snowstorm		34 terrible	
14 outdoor		35 once a month	
15 rescue		36 take place	
16 spread		37 right away	
17 around		38 continue on	
18 frozen		39 take part in	
19 popular		40 in memory of	
20 race		41 keep -ing	
21 lead dog		42 be sure to부정사	
		43 get[become]+형용사	

※ 다음 우리말을 영어로 쓰시오.

01 굉장한, 엄청난 _____

02 (개가) 짖다 _____

03 폭설 _____

04 갈라지다, 금이 가다 _____

05 질병, 병, 질환 _____

06 언어 _____

07 미끄러지다 _____

08 눈보라 _____

09 끔찍한 _____

10 목 _____

11 얼어붙은 _____

12 발생하다, 일어나다 _____

13 대략 _____

14 가슴 따뜻한 _____

15 코스, 흔적 _____

16 경주하다, 달리다 _____

17 기념하다, 축하하다 _____

18 도달하다, 닿다 _____

19 (사람들 사이로) 퍼지다 _____

20 구하다, 구조하다 _____

21 방송 _____

22 우리 _____

23 썰매 _____

24 약 _____

25 실외의 _____

26 인기 있는 _____

27 구하다 _____

28 외치다 _____

29 특별한 _____

30 오르다, 올라가다 _____

31 생방송의, 생중계의 _____

32 썰매 타러 가다 _____

33 선두 개 _____

34 손녀, 외손녀 _____

35 ~에 참여[참가]하다 _____

36 ~을 기념[추모]하여 _____

37 곧바로, 즉시 _____

38 계속 ~하다 _____

39 개최되다, 일어나다 _____

40 적어도 _____

41 ~에 관심이 있다 _____

42 한 달에 한 번 _____

43 여행을 가다 _____

※ 다음 영영풀이에 알맞은 단어를 <보기>에서 골라 쓴 후, 우리말 뜻을 쓰시오.

1 _____ : a heavy fall of snow that is blown by strong winds: _____

2 _____ : extremely severe in a way that causes harm or damage: _____

3 _____ : to cover, reach, or have an effect on a wider or increasing area: _____

4 _____ : to happen, especially after being planned or arranged: _____

5 _____ : a competition in which all the competitors try to be the fastest and to finish first: _____

6 _____ : a long line or a series of marks that have been left by someone or something: _____

7 _____ : to keep happening, existing, or doing something, or to cause something or someone to do this: _____

8 _____ : a structure made of metal bars or wire in which animals or birds are kept: _____

9 _____ : to help someone or something out of a dangerous, harmful, or unpleasant situation: _____

10 _____ : a substance, especially in the form of a liquid or a pill, that is a treatment for illness or injury: _____

11 _____ : to slide a short distance by accident so that you fall or nearly fall: _____

12 _____ : to arrive at a place, especially after spending a long time or a lot of effort travelling: _____

13 _____ : an object used for travelling over snow and ice with long, narrow strips of wood or metal: _____

14 _____ : illness of people, animals, plants, etc., caused by infection or a failure of health rather than by an accident: _____

15 _____ : to break or to make something break, either so that it gets lines on its surface, or so that it breaks into pieces: _____

16 _____ : a running or swimming race between two or more teams in which each person in the team runs or swims part of the race: _____

보기			
race	reach	crack	rescue
disease	relay	continue	medicine
terrible	snowstorm	take place	cage
sled	spread	trail	slip

※ 다음 우리말과 일치하도록 빈칸에 알맞은 말을 쓰시오.

Listen & Speak 1-A

1. **B:** _____ are you _____?

   G: I'm _____ _____ old pop songs.

   B: Oh, _____ _____ _____ old pop songs?

   G: No, _____ _____ _____ _____ them. I just want _____ _____ my _____ _____ _____ at her birthday party next week.

   B: Wow, _____ _____ _____ granddaughter!

2. **M:** _____ _____ _____ _____ _____ the Winter Olympics? Then, _____ _____ _____ _____ MBS Sports to enjoy our _____ _____ from 6 p.m. to 11 p.m. At 11 p.m. _____ _____, you can also _____ our _____ of _____ _____ _____ games of the day.

Listen & Speak 2-A

1. **W:** What's your _____ sport, James?

   B: I don't like sports much, but I _____ _____ _____.

   G: _____ _____ do you _____ _____?

   B: _____ _____ _____. I only _____ _____ _____ _____ _____.

2. **B:** Do you have _____ _____ _____ for this weekend, Hana?

   G: Well, I'm _____ _____ _____ _____ _____ with my dad and brother.

   B: _____ _____ do you _____?

   G: _____ _____. I love _____ table tennis. _____ _____ you?

   B: I _____ _____ soccer. I _____ _____ sports.

1. **B:** 뭐 하고 있어?
   G: 오래된 팝송들을 듣고 있어.
   B: 오, 오래된 팝송들을 좋아하니?
   G: 아니, 거기에 관심이 있지는 않아. 그냥 다음 주 할머니 생신에 할머니께서 가장 좋아하시는 노래들을 불러 드리고 싶어.
   B: 우와, 정말 착한 손녀구나!

2. **M:** 동계 올림픽을 보는 것에 관심이 있나요? 그럼, 오후 6시에서 11시까지 하는 MBS Sports의 경기 생중계를 꼭 보세요. 또한 매일 밤 11시에, 여러분은 그날 가장 흥미진진했던 경기의 하이라이트를 즐길 수 있습니다.

1. **G:** James, 가장 좋아하는 스포츠가 뭐야?
   B: 스포츠를 많이 좋아하지는 않지만, 가끔 수영하러 가.
   G: 수영을 얼마나 자주 하러 가는데?
   B: 그렇게 자주는 아니야. 한 달에 한 번만 가.

2. **B:** 하나야, 이번 주말에 특별한 계획 있어?
   G: 음, 우리 아빠와 남동생하고 탁구를 할 거야.
   B: 얼마나 자주 하는데?
   G: 매주 주말. 탁구 하는 걸 정말 좋아하거든. 너는 어때?
   B: 나는 축구 하는 걸 좋아해. 야외 스포츠가 좋아.

Communicate A

Anna: Do you have any _____ _____ for the _____ _____?

Suho: I'm going _____ _____ to my _____ _____ in Pyeongchang. I'll _____ _____ and _____ there. I love _____ _____.

Anna: _____ _____ you! I love winter sports, too. My _____ is ice hockey.

Suho: Oh, I've _____ _____ ice hockey, but _____ _____ _____ _____ how _____ _____ it.

Anna: Really? I can teach you _____ _____ _____.

Suho: That's _____. Is ice hockey _____ _____ _____ sport in Canada?

Anna: Yes, it is. _____ I know _____ watching it and _____ it.

Suho: _____ did you play ice hockey _____ you were in Canada?

Anna: I played _____ _____ two or _____ _____ a week in the winter.

Suho: Wow, _____ _____ you're really _____ _____ ice hockey. I _____ _____ _____ _____ from you.

Communicate B

A: _____ _____ _____ are you _____ _____?

B: I'm _____ _____ _____ _____.

A: _____ _____ _____ you go ice skating?

B: I go _____ or _____ _____ _____.

Progress Check

1. B: What _____ you _____?
   G: I'm _____ _____.
   B: Do you like _____ badminton?
   G: No, I'm _____ _____ _____ it. I just want _____ _____ the badminton test _____ _____.
   B: O.K. _____ _____!

2. G: What's your _____ TV show, Jason?
   B: I don't watch TV, but I _____ _____ the radio.
   G: _____ _____ do you _____ _____ the radio?
   B: _____ _____ _____.

3. M: _____ important _____ _____ your love for the people around you. _____ _____ do you _____ everyone in your family _____ you love them?

Anna: 너는 겨울 방학 때 특별한 계획이 있니?

수호: 나는 평창에 계신 할머니 할아버지 댁에 갈 거야. 거기서 스케이트와 썰매를 타러 갈 거야. 난 겨울 스포츠를 정말 좋아하거든.

Anna: 잘됐다! 나도 겨울 스포츠를 정말 좋아해. 내가 제일 좋아하는 것은 아이스하키야.

수호: 오, 나는 아이스하키를 해 본 적은 없지만, 하는 법을 배우는 데에는 관심이 있어.

Anna: 정말? 내가 어떻게 하는지 가르쳐 줄 수 있어.

수호: 정말 잘 됐다. 캐나다에서는 아이스하키가 가장 인기 있는 스포츠니?

Anna: 응, 맞아. 내가 아는 모든 사람들은 아이스하키를 보는 것과 직접 하는 것을 정말 좋아해.

수호: 너는 캐나다에 있을 때 아이스하키를 얼마나 자주 했니?

Anna: 겨울에는 일주일에 적어도 두세 번은 했어.

수호: 우와, 네가 아이스하키를 정말 잘 할 거라고 확신해. 너한테 빨리 배우고 싶다.

A: 어떤 겨울 스포츠에 관심이 있니?
B: 스케이트 타기에 관심이 있어.
A: 얼마나 자주 스케이트 타러 가?
B: 한 달에 한두 번 가.

1. B: 뭐 하고 있어?
   G: 배드민턴을 연습하고 있어.
   B: 배드민턴 하는 걸 좋아해?
   G: 아니, 관심이 있지는 않아. 그냥 다음주에 있는 배드민턴 시험에 통과하고 싶어.
   B: 그렇구나. 행운을 빌어!

2. G: Jason, 네가 가장 좋아하는 TV 쇼는 뭐니?
   B: TV를 보지는 않지만, 라디오는 들어.
   G: 얼마나 자주 라디오를 들어?
   B: 거의 매일.

3. M: 당신의 사랑을 주변 사람들에게 보여주는 것은 중요합니다. 당신은 얼마나 자주 가족 모두에게 사랑한다고 말해 주나요?

※ 다음 우리말에 맞도록 대화를 영어로 쓰시오.

Listen & Speak 1-A

1. B: _____

   G: _____

   B: _____

   G: _____

   B: _____

2. M: _____

   _____

   _____

   _____

Listen & Speak 2-A

1. G: _____

   B: _____

   G: _____

   B: _____

2. B: _____

   G: _____

   B: _____

   G: _____

   B: _____

해석

1. B: 뭐 하고 있어?
   G: 오래된 팝송들을 듣고 있어.
   B: 오, 오래된 팝송들을 좋아하니?
   G: 아니, 거기에 관심이 있지는 않아. 그냥 다음 주 할머니 생신에 할머니께서 가장 좋아하시는 노래들을 불러 드리고 싶어.
   B: 우와, 정말 착한 손녀구나!

2. M: 동계 올림픽을 보는 것에 관심이 있나요? 그럼, 오후 6시에서 11시까지 하는 MBS Sports의 경기 생중계를 꼭 보세요. 또한 매일 밤 11시에, 여러분은 그날 가장 흥미진진했던 경기의 하이라이트를 즐길 수 있습니다.

1. G: James, 가장 좋아하는 스포츠가 뭐야?
   B: 스포츠를 많이 좋아하지는 않지만, 가끔 수영하러 가.
   G: 수영을 얼마나 자주 하러 가는데?
   B: 그렇게 자주는 아니야. 한 달에 한 번만 가.

2. B: 하나야, 이번 주말에 특별한 계획 있어?
   G: 음, 우리 아빠와 남동생하고 탁구를 할 거야.
   B: 얼마나 자주 하는데?
   G: 매주 주말. 탁구 하는 걸 정말 좋아하거든. 너는 어때?
   B: 나는 축구 하는 걸 좋아해. 야외 스포츠가 좋아.

Communicate A

Anna: _____

Suho: _____
_____

Anna: _____

Suho: _____
_____

Anna: _____

Suho: _____

Anna: _____

Suho: _____

Anna: _____

Suho: _____

Communicate B

A: _____

B: _____

A: _____

B: _____

Progress Check

1. B: _____

G: _____

B: _____

G: _____

B: _____

2. G: _____

B: _____

G: _____

B: _____

3. M: _____
_____

Anna: 너는 겨울 방학 때 특별한 계획이 있니?

수호: 나는 평창에 계신 할머니 할아버지 댁에 갈 거야. 거기서 스케이트와 썰매를 타러 갈 거야. 난 겨울 스포츠를 정말 좋아하거든.

Anna: 잘됐다! 나도 겨울 스포츠를 정말 좋아해. 내가 제일 좋아하는 것은 아이스하키야.

수호: 오, 나는 아이스하키를 해 본 적은 없지만, 하는 법을 배우는 데에는 관심이 있어.

Anna: 정말? 내가 어떻게 하는지 가르쳐 줄 수 있어.

수호: 정말 잘 됐다. 캐나다에서는 아이스하키가 가장 인기 있는 스포츠니?

Anna: 응, 맞아. 내가 아는 모든 사람들은 아이스하키를 보는 것과 직접 하는 것을 정말 좋아해.

수호: 너는 캐나다에 있을 때 아이스하키를 얼마나 자주 했니?

Anna: 겨울에는 일주일에 적어도 두세 번은 했어.

수호: 우와, 네가 아이스하키를 정말 잘 할 거라고 확신해. 너한테 빨리 배우고 싶다.

A: 어떤 겨울 스포츠에 관심이 있니?
B: 스케이트 타기에 관심이 있어.
A: 얼마나 자주 스케이트 타러 가?
B: 한 달에 한두 번 가.

1. B: 뭐 하고 있어?
G: 배드민턴을 연습하고 있어.
B: 배드민턴 하는 걸 좋아해?
G: 아니, 관심이 있지는 않아. 그냥 다음주에 있는 배드민턴 시험에 통과하고 싶어.
B: 그렇구나. 행운을 빌어!

2. G: Jason, 네가 가장 좋아하는 TV 쇼는 뭐니?
B: TV를 보지는 않지만, 라디오는 들어.
G: 얼마나 자주 라디오를 들어?
B: 거의 매일.

3. M: 당신의 사랑을 주변 사람들에게 보여주는 것은 중요합니다. 당신은 얼마나 자주 가족 모두에게 사랑한다고 말해 주나요?

※ 다음 우리말과 일치하도록 빈칸에 알맞은 것을 골라 쓰시오.

1 _____ _____ _____ Winter Sport

A. Heart-Warming　　B. Most　　　　C. The

2 In _____ March every year, the world's _____ sled dog race _____ _____ in Alaska.

A. take　　　　B. early　　　　C. place　　　　D. biggest

3 _____ _____ _____ the Iditarod Trail Sled Dog Race.

A. is　　　　B. it　　　　C. called

4 _____ 80 teams of 12 _____ 16 dogs take _____ in this race.

A. to　　　　B. part　　　　C. around

5 Each team _____ to _____ about 1,800 km _____ Anchorage to Nome.

A. cover　　　　B. from　　　　C. has

6 The race can _____ more _____ two weeks, and the teams often race _____ _____.

A. through　　　　B. take　　　　C. snowstorms　　　D. than

7 The Iditarod Race began in 1973 _____ _____ of the dogs that _____ Nome.

A. memory　　　　B. saved　　　　C. in

8 One _____ winter day in 1925, a _____ thing _____ in Nome.

A. happened　　　　B. cold　　　　C. terrible

9 Some children _____ very sick, and the disease _____ _____.

A. kept　　　　B. got　　　　C. spreading

10 The people of Nome _____ medicine _____ _____, but the town did not have _____.

A. away　　　　B. any　　　　C. right　　　　D. needed

11 Someone _____ _____ get it _____ a hospital in Anchorage.

A. to　　　　B. from　　　　C. had

12 _____ of the _____ snow, a dog sled relay was the only _____ to get the _____ from Anchorage to Nome.

A. heavy　　　　B. medicine　　　　C. because　　　　D. way

13 Soon, the _____ to Nome _____.

A. race　　　　B. began

14 _____ dog teams were _____ the _____.

A. relay　　　　B. twenty-dog　　　　C. in

1　가장 가슴 따뜻한 겨울 스포츠

2　매년 3월 초에 알래스카 (Alaska)에서는 세계 최대의 개 썰매 경주가 열린다.

3　그것은 아이디타로드 개썰매 경주(Iditarod Trail Sled Dog Race)라고 불린다.

4　12~16마리 개로 구성된 80여 팀이 이 경주에 참여한다.

5　각 팀은 앵커리지(Anchorage) 에서 놈(Nome)까지 약 1,800 km를 달려야 한다.

6　이 경주는 2주 이상 걸릴 수 있 으며, 팀들은 종종 눈보라를 뚫 고 경주한다.

7　아이디타로드 경주는 놈을 구한 개들을 기념하여 1973년에 시작 되었다.

8　1925년의 어느 추운 겨울날, 놈 마을에서는 끔찍한 일이 일어났 다.

9　몇몇 아이들이 매우 아팠고 병 이 계속 퍼졌다.

10　놈의 사람들은 당장 약이 필요 했지만 마을에는 약이 하나도 없었다.

11　누군가는 앵커리지에 있는 병원 에서 약을 가져와야 했다.

12　폭설 때문에 개썰매 릴레이가 앵커리지에서 놈으로 약을 가져 오는 유일한 방법이었다.

13　곧, 놈으로 향하는 질주가 시작 되었다.

14　21개의 개 팀이 릴레이에 참여 했다.

15 _____ January 27, the first team left, and the _____ waited _____ different _____.

    A. others   B. on   C. points   D. at

16 Gunnar was the driver _____ the _____ _____.

    A. of   B. team   C. 20th

17 The _____ dog on his team was Balto, so he _____ Balto his _____ dog.

    A. made   B. strongest   C. lead

18 When Gunnar and Balto _____ got the medicine, the snow was _____ heavy _____ Gunnar could not see his _____ hands.

    A. that   B. own   C. finally   D. so

19 _____, Balto was able to _____ on the _____.

    A. stay   B. however   C. trail

20 When they were _____ a _____ river, Balto suddenly _____.

    A. frozen   B. stopped   C. crossing

21 Then, Gunnar _____ the river ice _____.

    A. cracking   B. saw

22 The _____ team was saved _____ Balto stopped _____ in time.

    A. because   B. whole   C. just

23 When Balto and Gunnar _____ the _____ team, they were _____.

    A. sleeping   B. final   C. reached

24 Gunnar _____ Balto to _____ _____.

    A. continue   B. told   C. on

25 "_____ the _____, Doctor!" _____ Gunnar.

    A. shouted   B. here's   C. medicine

26 _____ February 2, Gunnar and his team finally _____ _____ Nome.

    A. in   B. on   C. arrived

27 The town _____ _____.

    A. saved   B. was

28 This heart-warming story _____ now _____ every year by the Iditarod Race, the _____ _____ dog race in the world.

    A. biggest   B. celebrated   C. is   D. sled

15 1월 27일에 첫 번째 팀이 출발 했고, 나머지 팀들은 서로 다른 지점에서 기다렸다.

16 Gunnar는 20번째 팀의 몰이꾼 이었다.

17 그의 팀에서 가장 강한 개는 Balto였기 때문에, 그는 Balto를 그의 선두 개로 삼았다.

18 Gunnar와 Balto가 마침내 약을 받았을 때, 눈발이 너무 거세서 Gunnar는 자신의 손조차도 볼 수 없었다.

19 그러나, Balto는 코스를 제대로 따라갈 수 있었다.

20 그들이 얼어붙은 강을 건너고 있을 때 Balto는 갑자기 멈췄다.

21 그때, Gunnar는 강의 얼음이 갈 라지는 것을 보았다.

22 Balto가 바로 제때 멈췄기 때문 에 팀 전체가 목숨을 구할 수 있 었다.

23 Balto와 Gunnar가 마지막 팀에 다다랐을 때, 그들은 자고 있었 다.

24 Gunnar는 Balto에게 계속 가라 고 말했다.

25 "여기 약이 있습니다. 의사 선생 님!"이라고 Gunnar가 소리쳤다.

26 2월 2일에 Gunnar와 그의 팀은 마침내 놈에 도착했다.

27 놈 마을 사람들은 목숨을 구할 수 있었다.

28 이 가슴 따뜻한 이야기는 세계 에서 가장 큰 개썰매 경주인 아 이디타로드 경주를 통해 오늘날 매년 기념되고 있다.

※ 다음 우리말과 일치하도록 빈칸에 알맞은 말을 쓰시오.

1 The _____ _____ Winter Sport

2 In early March _____ _____, the world's _____ _____ _____ race _____ _____ in Alaska.

3 _____ _____ _____ the Iditarod Trail Sled Dog Race.

4 _____ 80 teams of 12 to 16 dogs _____ _____ _____ this race.

5 Each team _____ _____ _____ about 1,800 km _____ Anchorage _____ Nome.

6 The race can _____ _____ _____ two weeks, and the teams often _____ _____ _____.

7 The Iditarod Race began in 1973 _____ _____ _____ the dogs that saved Nome.

8 One cold winter day in 1925, _____ _____ _____ _____ in Nome.

9 Some children _____ very _____, and the disease _____ _____.

10 The people of Nome needed medicine _____ _____, but the town _____ _____ _____ _____ _____.

11 Someone _____ _____ _____ _____ _____ from a hospital in Anchorage.

12 _____ _____ the heavy snow, a dog sled relay was the only way _____ _____ _____ _____ from Anchorage to Nome.

13 Soon, _____ _____ _____ _____ began.

14 Twenty-one dog teams were _____ _____ _____.

---

1 가장 가슴 따뜻한 겨울 스포츠

2 매년 3월 초에 알래스카 (Alaska)에서는 세계 최대의 개 썰매 경주가 열린다.

3 그것은 아이디타로드 개썰매 경주(Iditarod Trail Sled Dog Race)라고 불린다.

4 12~16마리 개로 구성된 80여 팀이 이 경주에 참여한다.

5 각 팀은 앵커리지(Anchorage) 에서 놈(Nome)까지 약 1,800 km를 달려야 한다.

6 이 경주는 2주 이상 걸릴 수 있 으며, 팀들은 종종 눈보라를 뚫 고 경주한다.

7 아이디타로드 경주는 놈을 구한 개들을 기념하여 1973년에 시작 되었다.

8 1925년의 어느 추운 겨울날, 놈 마을에서는 끔찍한 일이 일어났 다.

9 몇몇 아이들이 매우 아팠고 병 이 계속 퍼졌다.

10 놈의 사람들은 당장 약이 필요 했지만 마을에는 약이 하나도 없었다.

11 누군가는 앵커리지에 있는 병원 에서 약을 가져와야 했다.

12 폭설 때문에 개썰매 릴레이가 앵커리지에서 놈으로 약을 가져 오는 유일한 방법이었다.

13 곧, 놈으로 향하는 질주가 시작 되었다.

14 21개의 개 팀이 릴레이에 참여 했다.

15 On January 27, the first team left, and _____ _____ waited _____ _____ _____.

16 Gunnar was the driver _____ _____ _____ _____.

17 The _____ _____ on his team was Balto, so he _____ Balto _____ _____ _____.

18 When Gunnar and Balto finally got the medicine, the snow was _____ heavy _____ Gunnar _____ _____ see his own hands.

19 _____, Balto was _____ _____.

20 When they were crossing a _____ river, Balto _____ _____.

21 Then, Gunnar saw the river ice _____.

22 The whole team _____ _____ because Balto stopped _____ _____ _____.

23 When Balto and Gunnar _____ the final team, they were sleeping.

24 Gunnar told Balto _____ _____ _____.

25 "_____ the _____, Doctor!" _____ Gunnar.

26 _____ February 2, Gunnar and his team finally _____ _____ Nome.

27 The town _____ _____.

28 This heart-warming story _____ _____ _____ every year by the Iditarod Race, _____ _____ _____ _____ _____ in the world.

15 1월 27일에 첫 번째 팀이 출발했고, 나머지 팀들은 서로 다른 지점에서 기다렸다.

16 Gunnar는 20번째 팀의 몰이꾼이었다.

17 그의 팀에서 가장 강한 개는 Balto였기 때문에, 그는 Balto를 그의 선두 개로 삼았다.

18 Gunnar와 Balto가 마침내 약을 받았을 때, 눈발이 너무 거세서 Gunnar는 자신의 손조차도 볼 수 없었다.

19 그러나, Balto는 코스를 제대로 따라갈 수 있었다.

20 그들이 얼어붙은 강을 건너고 있을 때 Balto는 갑자기 멈췄다.

21 그때, Gunnar는 강의 얼음이 갈라지는 것을 보았다.

22 Balto가 바로 제때 멈췄기 때문에 팀 전체가 목숨을 구할 수 있었다.

23 Balto와 Gunnar가 마지막 팀에 다다랐을 때, 그들은 자고 있었다.

24 Gunnar는 Balto에게 계속 가라고 말했다.

25 "여기 약이 있습니다, 의사 선생님!"이라고 Gunnar가 소리쳤다.

26 2월 2일에 Gunnar와 그의 팀은 마침내 놈에 도착했다.

27 놈 마을 사람들은 목숨을 구할 수 있었다.

28 이 가슴 따뜻한 이야기는 세계에서 가장 큰 개썰매 경주인 아이디타로드 경주를 통해 오늘날 매년 기념되고 있다.

본문 Test **31**

※ 다음 문장을 우리말로 쓰시오.

1 The Most Heart-Warming Winter Sport

➡ _____

2 In early March every year, the world's biggest sled dog race takes place in Alaska.

➡ _____

3 It is called the Iditarod Trail Sled Dog Race.

➡ _____

4 Around 80 teams of 12 to 16 dogs take part in this race.

➡ _____

5 Each team has to cover about 1,800 km from Anchorage to Nome.

➡ _____

6 The race can take more than two weeks, and the teams often race through snowstorms.

➡ _____

7 The Iditarod Race began in 1973 in memory of the dogs that saved Nome.

➡ _____

8 One cold winter day in 1925, a terrible thing happened in Nome.

➡ _____

9 Some children got very sick, and the disease kept spreading.

➡ _____

10 The people of Nome needed medicine right away, but the town did not have any.

➡ _____

11 Someone had to get it from a hospital in Anchorage.

➡ _____

12 Because of the heavy snow, a dog sled relay was the only way to get the medicine from Anchorage to Nome.

➡ _____

13 Soon, the race to Nome began.

➡ _____

14 Twenty-one dog teams were in the relay.

➡ _____

15 On January 27, the first team left, and the others waited at different points.

➡ _____

16 Gunnar was the driver of the 20th team.

➡ _____

17 The strongest dog on his team was Balto, so he made Balto his lead dog.

➡ _____

18 When Gunnar and Balto finally got the medicine, the snow was so heavy that Gunnar could not see his own hands.

➡ _____

19 However, Balto was able to stay on the trail.

➡ _____

20 When they were crossing a frozen river, Balto suddenly stopped.

➡ _____

21 Then, Gunnar saw the river ice cracking.

➡ _____

22 The whole team was saved because Balto stopped just in time.

➡ _____

23 When Balto and Gunnar reached the final team, they were sleeping.

➡ _____

24 Gunnar told Balto to continue on.

➡ _____

25 "Here's the medicine, Doctor!" shouted Gunnar.

➡ _____

26 On February 2, Gunnar and his team finally arrived in Nome.

➡ _____

27 The town was saved.

➡ _____

28 This heart-warming story is now celebrated every year by the Iditarod Race, the biggest sled dog race in the world.

➡ _____

※ 다음 괄호 안의 단어들을 우리말에 맞도록 바르게 배열하시오.

1 (Most / The / Winter / Heart-Warming / Sport)
➡ _____

2 (early / in / every / March / year, / world's / the / sled / biggest / dog / takes / race / place / Alaska. / in)
➡ _____
_____

3 (is / it / the / called / Trail / Iditarod / Dog / Sled / Race.)
➡ _____

4 (80 / around / of / teams / 12 / to / dogs / 16 / part / take / race. / in / this)
➡ _____

5 (team / each / to / has / cover / 1,800km / about / to / Anchorage / from / Nome.)
➡ _____

6 (race / the / take / can / than / more / weeks, / two / and / teams / the / race / often / snowstorms. / through)
➡ _____
_____

7 (Iditarod / the / Race / in / began / 1973 / memory / in / the / of / dogs / saved / that / Nome.)
➡ _____

8 (cold / one / day / winter / 1925, / in / terrible / a / thing / in / happened / Nome.)
➡ _____

9 (children / some / very / got / sick, / and / disease / the / spreading. / kept)
➡ _____

10 (people / the / of / needed / Nome / right / away, / medicine / the / but / town / not / did / any. / have)
➡ _____
_____

11 (had / someone / get / to / it / from / in / hospital / a / Anchorage.)
➡ _____

12 (of / because / the / snow, / heavy / dog / a / sled / was / relay / only / the / to / way / get / medicine / the / to / Anchorage / from / Nome.)
➡ _____
_____

13 (soon, / race / the / Nome / to / began.)
➡ _____

14 (dog / twenty-one / were / teams / in / relay. / the)
➡ _____

1 가장 가슴 따뜻한 겨울 스포츠

2 매년 3월 초에 알래스카 (Alaska)에서는 세계 최대의 개 썰매 경주가 열린다.

3 그것은 아이디타로드 개썰매 경주(Iditarod Trail Sled Dog Race)라고 불린다.

4 12~16마리 개로 구성된 80여 팀이 이 경주에 참여한다.

5 각 팀은 앵커리지(Anchorage) 에서 놈(Nome)까지 약 1,800 km를 달려야 한다.

6 이 경주는 2주 이상 걸릴 수 있 으며, 팀들은 종종 눈보라를 뚫 고 경주한다.

7 아이디타로드 경주는 놈을 구한 개들을 기념하여 1973년에 시작 되었다.

8 1925년의 어느 추운 겨울날, 놈 마을에서는 끔찍한 일이 일어났 다.

9 몇몇 아이들이 매우 아팠고 병 이 계속 퍼졌다.

10 놈의 사람들은 당장 약이 필요 했지만 마을에는 약이 하나도 없었다.

11 누군가는 앵커리지에 있는 병원 에서 약을 가져와야 했다.

12 폭설 때문에 개썰매 릴레이가 앵커리지에서 놈으로 약을 가져 오는 유일한 방법이었다.

13 곧, 놈으로 향하는 질주가 시작 되었다.

14 21개의 개 팀이 릴레이에 참여 했다.

15 (January / on / 27, / team / the / first / left, / and / others / the / waited / different / points. / at)

➡ _____

16 (was / Gunnar / the / of / driver / the / team. / 20th)

➡ _____

17 (the / dog / strongest / on / team / his / was / so / Balto, / made / he / his / Balto / dog. / lead)

➡ _____

18 (Gunnar / when / and / finally / Balto / the / got / medicine, / snow / the / was / heavy / so / that / could / Gunnar / see / not / own / hands. / his)

➡ _____

19 (Balto / however, / able / was / to / on / stay / trail. / the)

➡ _____

20 (they / when / crossing / were / a / river, / frozen / suddenly / Balto / stopped.)

➡ _____

21 (Gunnar / then, / the / saw / ice / river / cracking.)

➡ _____

22 (whole / the / team / saved / was / because / stopped / Balto / in / time. / just)

➡ _____

23 (Balto / when / and / reached / Gunnar / the / team, / final / were / they / sleeping.)

➡ _____

24 (told / Gunnar / Balto / continue / to / on.)

➡ _____

25 (the / "here's / Doctor!" / medicine, / Gunnar. / shouted)

➡ _____

26 (February / on / 2, / Gunnar / and / team / his / arrived / finally / Nome. / in)

➡ _____

27 (town / the / saved. / was)

➡ _____

28 (heart-warming / this / story / now / is / every / celebrated / year / by / Iditarod / the / Race, / biggest / the / dog / sled / race / the / world. / in)

➡ _____

---

15 1월 27일에 첫 번째 팀이 출발했고, 나머지 팀들은 서로 다른 지점에서 기다렸다.

16 Gunnar는 20번째 팀의 몰이꾼이었다.

17 그의 팀에서 가장 강한 개는 Balto였기 때문에, 그는 Balto를 그의 선두 개로 삼았다.

18 Gunnar와 Balto가 마침내 약을 받았을 때, 눈발이 너무 거세서 Gunnar는 자신의 손조차도 볼 수 없었다.

19 그러나, Balto는 코스를 제대로 따라갈 수 있었다.

20 그들이 얼어붙은 강을 건너고 있을 때 Balto는 갑자기 멈췄다.

21 그때, Gunnar는 강의 얼음이 갈라지는 것을 보았다.

22 Balto가 바로 제때 멈췄기 때문에 팀 전체가 목숨을 구할 수 있었다.

23 Balto와 Gunnar가 마지막 팀에 다다랐을 때, 그들은 자고 있었다.

24 Gunnar는 Balto에게 계속 가고 말했다.

25 "여기 약이 있습니다. 의사 선생님!"이라고 Gunnar가 소리쳤다.

26 2월 2일에 Gunnar와 그의 팀은 마침내 놈에 도착했다.

27 놈 마을 사람들은 목숨을 구할 수 있었다.

28 이 가슴 따뜻한 이야기는 세계에서 가장 큰 개썰매 경주인 아이디타로드 경주를 통해 오늘날 매년 기념되고 있다.

※ 다음 우리말을 영어로 쓰시오.

1 가장 가슴 따뜻한 겨울 스포츠

➡ _____

2 매년 3월 초에 알래스카(Alaska)에서는 세계 최대의 개썰매 경주가 열린다.

➡ _____

3 그것은 아이디타로드 개썰매 경주(Iditarod Trail Sled Dog Race)라고 불린다.

➡ _____

4 12~16마리 개로 구성된 80여 팀이 이 경주에 참여한다.

➡ _____

5 각 팀은 앵커리지(Anchorage)에서 놈(Nome)까지 약 1,800 km를 달려야 한다.

➡ _____

6 이 경주는 2주 이상 걸릴 수 있으며, 팀들은 종종 눈보라를 뚫고 경주한다.

➡ _____

7 아이디타로드 경주는 놈을 구한 개들을 기념하여 1973년에 시작되었다.

➡ _____

8 1925년의 어느 추운 겨울날, 놈 마을에서는 끔찍한 일이 일어났다.

➡ _____

9 몇몇 아이들이 매우 아팠고 병이 계속 퍼졌다.

➡ _____

10 놈의 사람들은 당장 약이 필요했지만 마을에는 약이 하나도 없었다.

➡ _____

11 누군가는 앵커리지에 있는 병원에서 약을 가져와야 했다.

➡ _____

12 폭설 때문에 개썰매 릴레이가 앵커리지에서 놈으로 약을 가져오는 유일한 방법이었다.

➡ _____

13 곧, 놈으로 향하는 질주가 시작되었다.

➡ _____

14 21개의 개 팀이 릴레이에 참여했다.

➡ _____

15 1월 27일에 첫 번째 팀이 출발했고, 나머지 팀들은 서로 다른 지점에서 기다렸다.

➡ _____

16 Gunnar는 20번째 팀의 몰이꾼이었다.

➡ _____

17 그의 팀에서 가장 강한 개는 Balto였기 때문에, 그는 Balto를 그의 선두 개로 삼았다.

➡ _____

18 Gunnar와 Balto가 마침내 약을 받았을 때, 눈발이 너무 거세서 Gunnar는 자신의 손조차도 볼 수 없었다.

➡ _____

_____

19 그러나, Balto는 코스를 제대로 따라갈 수 있었다.

➡ _____

20 그들이 얼어붙은 강을 건너고 있을 때 Balto는 갑자기 멈췄다.

➡ _____

21 그때, Gunnar는 강의 얼음이 갈라지는 것을 보았다.

➡ _____

22 Balto가 바로 제때 멈췄기 때문에 팀 전체가 목숨을 구할 수 있었다.

➡ _____

23 Balto와 Gunnar가 마지막 팀에 다다랐을 때, 그들은 자고 있었다.

➡ _____

24 Gunnar는 Balto에게 계속 가라고 말했다.

➡ _____

25 "여기 약이 있습니다, 의사 선생님!"이라고 Gunnar가 소리쳤다.

➡ _____

26 2월 2일에 Gunnar와 그의 팀은 마침내 놈에 도착했다.

➡ _____

27 놈 마을 사람들은 목숨을 구할 수 있었다.

➡ _____

28 이 가슴 따뜻한 이야기는 세계에서 가장 큰 개썰매 경주인 아이디타로드 경주를 통해 오늘날 매년 기념되고 있다.

➡ _____

_____

※ 다음 우리말과 일치하도록 빈칸에 알맞은 말을 쓰시오.

Link-Share

1. _____ you _____ _____ _____ the history of the marathon?

2. The first marathon _____ _____ _____ Pheidippides in 490 _____.

3. The Greek army in Marathon _____ _____ _____ _____ the people of Athens about their victory.

4. He _____ 40 km _____ Marathon _____ Athens.

1. 마라톤의 역사를 배우는 것에 관심이 있나요?
2. 최초의 마라톤은 Pheidippides에 의해 기원전 490년에 달려졌습니다.
3. 마라톤에 있던 그리스 군대는 그들의 승리에 관해 아테네의 사람들에게 말하라고 그에게 명령했습니다.
4. 그는 마라톤에서 아테네까지 40km를 달렸습니다.

Write

1. One cold winter day, a man _____ home _____ _____ _____ for a fire.

2. He _____ and _____ _____ _____.

3. He could _____ _____, but _____ _____ was _____ him.

4. His dog _____ _____ _____ _____.

5. She _____ _____ _____ _____ 19 hours.

6. A neighbor finally _____ _____ _____ _____ and _____ 911.

1. 어느 추운 겨울날, 한 남자가 불을 피울 나무를 구하기 위해 집을 떠났다.
2. 그는 미끄러져서 목을 부러뜨렸다.
3. 그는 움직일 수 없었지만, 그 주변에 아무도 없었다.
4. 그의 개가 그를 구하기 위해 왔다.
5. 그녀는 19시간 동안 짖고 또 짖었다.
6. 한 이웃이 마침내 개가 짖는 소리를 듣고 911에 전화했다.

Culture Project-Share

1. _____ _____, you can _____ _____ _____ _____ _____ into the sea at Haeundae Beach.

2. It's _____ _____ _____ _____ for good health in the New Year.

1. 매년 겨울, 많은 사람들이 해운대 해변에서 바다로 뛰어 드는 모습을 볼 수 있다.
2. 이것은 새해에 건강하기를 비는 방법이다.

※ 다음 우리말을 영어로 쓰시오.

Link-Share

1. 마라톤의 역사를 배우는 것에 관심이 있나요?

   ➡ _____

2. 최초의 마라톤은 Pheidippides에 의해 기원전 490년에 달려졌습니다.

   ➡ _____

3. 마라톤에 있던 그리스 군대는 그들의 승리에 관해 아테네의 사람들에게 말하라고 그에게 명령했습니다.

   ➡ _____

4. 그는 마라톤에서 아테네까지 40km를 달렸습니다.

   ➡ _____

Write

1. 어느 추운 겨울날, 한 남자가 불을 피울 나무를 구하기 위해 집을 떠났다.

   ➡ _____

2. 그는 미끄러져서 목을 부러뜨렸다.

   ➡ _____

3. 그는 움직일 수 없었지만, 그 주변에 아무도 없었다.

   ➡ _____

4. 그의 개가 그를 구하기 위해 왔다.

   ➡ _____

5. 그녀는 19시간 동안 짖고 또 짖었다.

   ➡ _____

6. 한 이웃이 마침내 개가 짖는 소리를 듣고 911에 전화했다.

   ➡ _____

Culture Project-Share

1. 매년 겨울, 많은 사람들이 해운대 해변에서 바다로 뛰어 드는 모습을 볼 수 있다.

   ➡ _____

2. 이것은 새해에 건강하기를 비는 방법이다.

   ➡ _____

MEMO

영어 기출 문제집

적중 100

2학기

정답 및 해설

미래 | 최연희

중 2

영어 기출 문제집

적중100

2학기

정답 및 해설

미래 | 최연희

중 2

Think Big, Start Small

시험대비 실력평가   p.08

01 whole   02 ④   03 ⑤   04 ①
05 ③   06 ④   07 come up with
08 a[one] third of

01 둘은 반의어 관계이다. 어려운 : 쉬운 = 일부분의 : 전체의
02 방에서 책을 읽을 수 없다고 소리치고 있으므로 그의 집에 전기가 없다는 것이 적절하다.
03 Alfredo Moser에 의해 발명되었다가 적절하다.
04 '특히 덮개가 있는 빛을 제공하는 장치'의 의미로 'lamp(등, 램프)'가 적절하다.
05 '여러 가지 방법으로 생산될 수 있고 빛, 열 등을 만드는 장치에 동력을 제공하는 에너지의 형태'라는 의미로 '전기'가 적절하다.
06 ④의 'chief'는 명사로 사용되었다. '장, 우두머리'의 의미이다.
07 'come up with'는 '~을 생각해 내다'라는 뜻이다.
08 '~의 1/3'은 'a[one] third of'를 사용한다.

서술형 시험대비   p.09

01 (1) daytime, 낮   (2) ceiling, 천장   (3) blackout, 정전
02 (1) light up   (2) bent, spreads
03 (1) leftover   (2) Foundation
04 (1) chief   (2) bleach   (3) widely
05 (1) hole, hole   (2) magic

01 (1) 해가 뜨는 시간과 지는 시간 사이의 기간이나 저녁도 밤도 아닌 하루의 부분 (2) 위쪽을 바라볼 때 볼 수 있는 방의 안쪽 표면 (3) 전기 시스템의 고장으로 빛이나 전력이 없는 때
02 (1) light up: ~을 밝히다 (2) bend가 수동태로 과거분사 bent가 적절하고, '퍼지다'는 'spread'를 사용하고 주어가 3인칭 단수 'sunlight'이므로 'spreads'로 쓴다.
03 (1) 남은 음식: leftover (2) 재단: foundation
04 (1) 그녀는 영화 '주피터'에서 책임 과학자를 연기했어. (2) 물을 깨끗이 유지하기 위해 표백제를 조금 넣어라. (3) 오늘날 가스는 요리할 때 널리 쓰인다. / 형용사 'wide'는 동사 'is used'를 수식할 때 부사 'widely'가 되어야 한다.
05 (1) 물체의 표면에 개구부가 있거나 물체를 완전히 관통하는 개구부가 있는 물체의 빈 공간 (2) 특별한 힘을 가진 또는 비정상적이거나 예상치 못한 방식으로 또는 쉽게 또는 빠르게 발생하는

핵심 Check   p.10~11

1 ②   2 ③

교과서 대화문 익히기

Check(√) True or False   p.12

1 T   2 F   3 T   4 F

교과서 확인학습   p.14~15

Listen & Speak 1-A

(1) turn up, turn it up anymore, highest / Let, put, I've heard, works like / What an interesting idea, Let's
(2) I've heard, is coming / favorite actress / played, chief / can't wait to

Listen & Speak 2-A

(1) finished, good, want to take, leftovers / Don't forget to eat
(2) your plan for, winter break / I'm going to / exciting, going to do / going to go, amusement, all kinds / Don't forget to try

Communicate A

wrong / difficult / have to / to save / I've heard that, by using less / I've heard that, too, stop using / to dry off / impossible, at least / shake, before, more than enough / try, next time / don't forget to shake, at least, times

Communicate B

I've heard, saving electricity, to save / heard that, too, save / turn off, when / Don't forget, turn off, when, leave

Progress Check

(1) I've heard that, is coming / favorite / surprise
(2) plan for / to visit / sounds exciting / spend, beach, seafood / Don't forget to try / won't forget

시험대비 기본평가   p.16

01 ③   02 are you finished with your meal?   03 ⑤

01 빈칸에는 어떤 사실을 들어서 알고 있음을 말하는 표현이 온다. B의 마지막 말에 'who is he?'라고 그가 누군지 모르고 있기 때문에 ⑤는 자연스럽지 않다.
02 be동사 의문문으로 'be finished with'는 '~을 마치다'는 의미다.
03 (B)에는 'Don't forget to부정사'를 이용하여 '~할 것을 잊지 마라'는 당부의 말이 적절하다. remember / forget + 동명사는 '~한 것을 기억하다[잊다]'의 뜻으로 과거의 일을 나타낸다.

01 ②   02 ④   03 ③   04 ⑤
05 dim sum   06 ④   07 ④   08 ①
09 ③

01 'A: 무슨 일 있어?'라는 물음에 'B: '내일 내 과학 숙제 가져올 것을 잊지 마.'라는 대답은 자연스럽지 못하다.

02 B의 첫 번째 말에서 더 이상 볼륨을 올릴 수 없다고 했으므로 빈 칸 (A)는 볼륨을 올려달라는 부탁의 말이 적절하다.

03 B의 마지막 말에 '정말 재미있는 생각이야!'라고 말하는 것으로 보아 빈칸에는 '유리잔이 스피커처럼 작동한다.'는 말이 적절하다.

04 (A) 미래의 계획을 말할 때 'I'm going to부정사'를 사용하고, (B) '~할 것을 잊지 마'라는 상기시켜 주는 표현으로 'Don't forget to부정사'나 'Remember to부정사'를 사용한다.

05 튀기거나 증기로 익힌 여러 음식을 포함하는 중국식 식사 또는 간단한 간식 요리

06 Yuri의 '손을 말리는 데 좋은 종이 수건을 한 장만 쓸 수도 있지.'라는 말에 대한 Jaden의 반응으로 (④)가 적절하다.

07 종이컵을 사용하는 것을 멈추는 것은 Jaden이 한 말이다.

08 대화의 내용상 '전기를 절약하는 것'이 적절하다.

09 '~하는 게 어때?', '~하자'는 표현으로 'Why don't we+동사원형 ~?'을 사용할 수 있다.

01 she try the fruit there   02 I won't forget.
03 I've heard that we can save trees by using less paper.
04 don't forget to shake your hands at least 10 times.
05 Don't forget to
06 I've heard that a movie star is coming to our school.

01 소년은 여행에서 과일을 먹어 보라고 제안하고 있다.

02 '~하지 않을 거야'는 will not의 축약형 won't를 사용하여 3단 어로 만든다.

03 'I've heard (that) ~.' 표현을 이용하고, '~함으로써'는 'by -ing'를 사용한다. '덜' 사용한다는 것은 little을 비교급 less로 바꾸어 준다.

05 소녀는 날씨가 나쁠까봐 걱정을 하고 있으므로 '우산을 가져갈 것을 잊지 마.'라는 충고가 적절하다. '~하는 것을 잊지 마'라는 뜻으로 상대방에게 해야 할 일을 상기시켜 줄 때 'Don't forget to부정사'를 사용한다.

06 어떤 사실을 들어서 알고 있음을 말할 때 'I've heard (that) ~.' 표현을 쓴다. 현재진행형 'is coming'이 미래의 일을 나타낼 때 사용될 수 있다.

Grammar

1 (1) famous   (2) happy
2 (1) wash   (2) painted   (3) to do   (4) to sign

01 (1) to laugh → laugh   (2) finishing → finish
   (3) sadly → sad   (4) tiring → tired
02 (1) throw   (2) thrown   (3) to meet
   (4) do(또는 to do)
03 ②   04 Let me know her name.

01 (1), (2) 사역동사의 목적어와 목적격보어의 관계가 능동일 경 우 목적격보어로 원형부정사를 쓰는 것이 적절하다. (3) 동사 make의 보어로 부사가 아닌 형용사가 적절하다. (4) 내가 지치 게 되는 것이므로 tired가 적절하다.

02 (1) 사역동사의 목적격보어는 목적어와의 관계가 능동일 경우 원형부정사가 쓰인다. (2) 사역동사의 목적격보어는 목적어와의 관계가 수동일 경우 과거분사가 쓰인다. (3) get이 '~하게 하다' 라는 사역동사의 뜻으로 쓰일 때에는 목적격보어로 to부정사를 쓴다. (4) help는 목적격보어로 동사원형이나 to부정사가 나오 며 뜻의 차이는 없다.

03 동사 make의 보어로 부사가 아닌 형용사가 적절하며 소설이 그 녀를 유명하게 만든 것이므로 The novel이 주어가 되어야 한 다.

04 사역동사 let의 목적격보어로 목적어와의 관계가 능동일 경우 원형부정사를 쓴다.

01 ⑤   02 ①, ⑤   03 ①
04 The pot can keep the fruit cold.   05 ③
06 (1) learn   (2) see   (3) cleaned   (4) help
   (5) to read   (6) interesting   (7) regularly, healthy
07 ③   08 ②   09 steal → stolen
10 ③, ④   11 ④   12 ⑤   13 ④
14 ②, ③   15 ⑤
16 (1) the test was   (2) he is silly
17 (1) to wear → wear   (2) write → to write
   (3) steal → stolen
18 (1) My father keeps his car clean.
   (2) Rainy days make me sad.
   (3) Her new book made her famous.

01 목적어와의 관계가 능동이므로 사역동사 let의 목적격보어로 원형부정사가 적절하고, 동사 found의 보어로 부사가 아닌 형용사가 적절하다.

02 help는 준사역동사로 목적어와 목적격보어의 관계가 능동일 경우 목적격보어로 원형부정사 또는 to부정사를 취한다.

03 5형식을 만들 수 있는 동사로 형용사를 목적격보어로 받을 수 있는 동사가 나와야 한다. call은 call A B(명사) 형태로 쓰이며, ask, order, beg 등은 목적격보어로 to부정사가 나온다.

04 '주어+동사+목적어+목적격보어'의 어순으로 쓰는데 동사 keep의 목적격보어로 형용사를 써야 하는 것에 주의한다.

05 이름이 불리는 것으로 목적어와의 관계가 수동이므로 사역동사 have의 목적격보어로 과거분사가 적절하다. Her wish was to have her son's name mentioned at graduation.

06 (1), (2) 사역동사 have와 let의 목적격보어로 동사원형이 적절하다. (3) 방이 청소되는 것이므로 목적격보어로 수동의 의미를 갖는 과거분사가 적절하다. (4) help는 준사역동사로 목적격보어로 원형부정사 또는 to부정사를 받는다. (5) get이 '~하게 하다'라는 사역동사의 뜻으로 쓰일 때에는 목적격보어로 to부정사를 쓴다. (6) 동사 find의 목적격보어로 형용사가 적절하다. (7) 첫 번째 괄호에는 동사를 수식하는 부사가 알맞으므로 regularly, 두 번째 괄호에는 keep의 목적격보어로 형용사를 쓴다.

07 목적격보어로 부사가 아닌 형용사가 사용된다는 것에 주의한다. ④ well은 부사이므로 형용사 good이 적절하다. Reading a lot of books will make me good at English.

08 소고기가 무엇을 요리하는 것이 아니라 요리되도록 하는 것이므로 사역동사 have의 목적격보어로 과거분사 cooked를 쓰는 것이 적절하다.

09 지갑이 무엇을 훔치는 것이 아니라 훔쳐진[도난당한] 것이므로 수동의 의미를 갖는 과거분사가 적절하다.

10 Marie가 의자에 앉는 것으로 목적어와의 관계가 능동이므로 사역동사 help의 목적격보어로 원형부정사 혹은 to부정사가 적절하다.

11 '주어(I)+동사(keep)+목적어(the baby)+목적격보어(safe)'의 어순으로 쓰는데 동사 keep의 목적격보어로 형용사를 써야 하는 것에 주의한다.

12 get은 사역동사의 뜻으로 쓰일 때 목적어와 목적격보어의 관계가 능동일 경우 목적격보어로 to부정사를 쓴다.

13 ④번은 4형식으로 쓰였고 나머지는 5형식이다.

14 ② Elizabeth had the meat roasted in the garden. ③ Morris got the girl to stand up in front of students.

15 (A) 사역동사 make의 목적어와 목적격보어의 관계가 능동이

므로 원형부정사가 적절하다. (B) 동사 get의 목적어와 목적격보어의 관계가 능동이므로 to부정사가 적절하다. (C) 사역동사의 목적어와 목적격보어의 관계가 수동이므로 과거분사가 적절하다.

16 목적어와 목적격보어를 that절의 주어와 동사로 써서 문장을 바꿔 쓴다.

17 (1) 목적어와 목적격보어의 관계가 능동이므로 목적격보어로 원형부정사가 적절하다. (2) 목적어와 목적격보어의 관계가 능동이므로 get의 목적격보어로 to부정사가 적절하다. (3) 목적어와 목적격보어의 관계가 수동이므로 목적격보어로 과거분사가 적절하다. handcuffs: 수갑

18 (1)~(3) '주어+동사+목적어+목적격보어'의 어순으로 쓰는데 동사의 목적격보어로 형용사를 써야 하는 것에 주의한다. (4), (5), (6) 목적어와 목적격보어의 관계가 능동이므로 사역동사의 목적격보어로 원형부정사를 이용한다.

19 형용사를 목적격보어로 받을 수 있는 동사가 나와야 한다.

20 get은 사역동사의 뜻으로 쓰일 때 목적어와 목적격보어의 관계가 능동일 경우 목적격 보어로 to부정사를 쓴다.

🦉 서술형 시험대비
p.26~27

01 (1) She made him finish his work by the next day.
(2) She doesn't let her children play online games.
(3) I must go to the dry cleaner's to have my suit cleaned.
(4) Mom got me to help my sister with her homework.
(5) I helped him calm[to calm] down before playing the guitar on the stage.

02 (1) me sad   (2) made him healthy

03 Eric had his camera repaired by a repairman.

04 (1) A strange man broke into my house, but he stole nothing and left it clean.
(2) They made Stacy happy by saying white lies.
(3) He found his new smartphone broken.
(4) At first, Samanda thought William honest.
(5) This thick blanket will keep you warm.

05 turn

06 (1) clean   (2) carried   (3) to be   (4) find[to find]
(5) watch

07 Having lots of holidays next year makes her excited.

08 (1) Eve let Adam use her pen.
(2) She made Dan follow her advice.

09 (1) He had his car washed yesterday.
(2) We could make the lamp brighter.

01 (1), (2) 목적어와 목적격보어의 관계가 능동이므로 목적격보어로 원형부정사가 적절하다. (3) 목적어와 목적격보어의 관계가 수동이므로 목적격보어로 과거분사가 적절하다. (4) get이 사역동사의 뜻으로 쓰일 때 목적격보어로 to부정사를 쓴다. (5) help는 목적격보어로 동사원형이나 to부정사가 나온다.

02 (1) 책을 읽으며 슬펐다는 내용을 목적어와 형용사를 목적격보어로 하는 5형식으로 나타낸다. (2) 운동해서 건강하게 되었다는 내용을 목적어와 형용사를 목적격보어로 하는 5형식으로 나타낸다.

03 사역동사의 목적어와 목적격보어의 관계가 수동일 경우 목적격보어로 과거분사를 쓴다.

04 (1) 동사 leave의 목적격보어로 부사가 아닌 형용사가 적절하다. (2) 동사 make의 목적격보어로 명사가 아닌 형용사가 적절하다. (3) 목적어와 목적격보어의 관계가 수동이므로 목적격보어로 과거분사가 적절하다. (4), (5) 동사 think, keep의 목적격보어로 부사가 아닌 형용사가 적절하다. break into: 침입하다 blanket: 담요

05 사역동사 make의 목적어와 목적격보어의 관계가 능동이므로 목적격보어로 원형부정사가 적절하다.

06 (1) 사역동사의 목적어와 목적격보어의 관계가 능동이므로 목적격보어로 원형부정사가 적절하다. (2) 목적어와 목적격보어의 관계가 수동이므로 목적격보어로 과거분사가 적절하다. (3) get은 사역동사의 의미로 쓰일 수 있지만 목적격보어로 to부정사가 나온다. (4) help는 준사역동사로 목적격보어로 원형부정사 또는 to부정사가 나온다. (5) 사역동사의 목적어와 목적격보어의 관계가 능동이므로 목적격보어로 원형부정사가 적절하다.

07 '주어+동사+목적어+목적격보어'의 어순으로 쓰며 동사의 목적격보어로 형용사를 써야 하는 것에 주의한다.

08 get은 have, allow는 let, force는 make와 같은 의미로 쓰인다.

09 (1) 목적어와 목적격보어의 관계가 수동이므로 목적격보어로 과거분사로 쓴다. (2) '주어+동사+목적어+목적격보어'의 어순으로 쓰며 동사의 목적격보어로 형용사를 쓴다. 또한 '더 밝게'이므로 비교급으로 써야 한다.

교과서
Reading

확인문제   p.28

1 T   2 F   3 T   4 F

확인문제   p.29

1 T   2 F   3 F   4 T   5 T   6 T

교과서 확인학습 A   p.30~31

01 One-Dollar   02 in the Philippines
03 has no electricity, all the other houses
04 too, to   05 are packed close together
06 because of   07 light up, without using
08 is called, because, was invented by
09 many blackouts   10 come up with
11 be made for, lasts for
12 very safe   13 never start
14 to make   15 How to make
16 Fill, with   17 Add, to keep, clear
18 push, into   19 a third, remain
20 is bent, spreads   21 are widely used
22 The charity, how to make, install
23 Thanks to, thousands of
24 has, made, such as   25 for many years to come

교과서 확인학습 B   p.32~33

1 One-Dollar Magic Lamps
2 "Wow, I can read a book in my room now!" shouted Marco, a boy in a village in the Philippines.
3 His house has no electricity just like all the other houses in the village.
4 People in the village are too poor to pay for electricity.
5 Even during the daytime, they live in darkness because the houses are packed close together.
6 Now things are changing because of a single plastic bottle.
7 One plastic bottle in the ceiling can light up a whole room without using any electricity.
8 This amazing plastic bottle is called a Moser lamp because it was invented by Alfredo Moser.
9 In 2002, there were many blackouts in his town in Brazil.
10 These blackouts made him come up with a new way to light his house.
11 A Moser lamp can be made for about one dollar and lasts for about 10 years.
12 It is also very safe.
13 It can never start a house fire.
14 Surprisingly, it is very easy to make this magic lamp.
15 How to make a Moser lamp from a bottle

16　1. Fill a clear plastic bottle with water.

17　2. Add some bleach to keep the water clear.

18　3. Make a hole in the roof, and push the bottle into the hole.

19　4. Let a third of the bottle remain above the roof.

20　5. Sunlight is bent by the water in the bottle and spreads around the room.

21　In the Philippines, Moser lamps are widely used by the My Shelter Foundation.

22　The charity also teaches local people how to make and install the lamps.

23　Thanks to the charity, thousands of homes in the Philippines now have Moser lamps.

24　It has also made Moser lamps popular in other countries, such as Argentina, India, and Fiji.

25　Moser lamps will light up the lives of many people for many years to come.

시험대비 실력평가
p.34~37

01 ④　　02 ②　　03 ④　　04 ③

05 ③　　　　06 two-thirds

07 The water in the bottle bends sunlight

08 lasts　　09 ①, ③, ④　10 ③　　11 ④

12 thousands of homes in the Philippines

13 like　　14 ①　　15 ⑤　　16 ②

17 to remain → remain　　18 ①　　19 how to

20 ④　　21 ③　　22 ②

23 A Moser lamp　　24 ⑤

25 (A) for　(B) happy　(C) grows　　26 ⑤

27 (1) CD 케이스의 절반을 흙과 물로 채우고, 잔디 씨앗을 흙 안에 넣는다.
　　(2) 케이스를 닫고 모든 옆면에 테이프를 붙인다.
　　(3) 햇빛이 비치는 곳에 약 10일 동안 놓아둔다.

01 ⓐ pay for: ~의 대금을 지불하다, ⓑ in darkness: 어둠 속에

02 '전기'를 쓰지 않고 방 전체를 밝힐 수 있다고 하는 것이 적절하다. ① (사물의) 원천, 근원, ③ 화학 약품, ⑤ 자원

03 ④번 다음 문장의 One plastic bottle에 주목한다. 주어진 문장의 a single plastic bottle을 가리키므로 ④번이 적절하다.

04 낮 동안에도, 집들이 빽빽하게 들어차 있어서 그들은 어둠 속에 살아간다.

05 ⓒ에는 keep을 쓰는 것이 적절하다. ⓐ Fill, ⓑ Add, ⓓ Make, ⓔ push

06 two-thirds: 3분의 2, 병의 3분의 1은 지붕 위에 남아 있도록 한다. = 병의 '3분의 2'는 지붕 아래에 남아 있도록 한다.

07 'The water in the bottle'을 주어로 해서 고치는 것이 적절하다.

08 last: (기능이) 지속되다, 특정한 시간 동안 계속해서 사용될 수 있다.

09 ⓐ와 ②, ⑤: 형용사적 용법, ① 명사적 용법, ③, ④ 부사적 용법

10 ③ 이 글은 값싸고 매우 안전한 Moser 램프에 관한 글이므로, 제목으로는 '값싸고 안전한 신기한 램프'가 적절하다.

11 이 자선단체 '덕분에', ①, ③: … 대신에, ② … 없이, …이 없다면, ⑤ …와는 달리

12 thousands of+명사: 수천의 ~

13 such as = like: 예를 들어, …와 같은

14 light up: ~을 환하게 밝히다

15 ⓐ fill A with B: A를 B로 채우다, ⓒ push A into B: A를 B에 넣다

16 ⓑ와 ②, ③, ⑤는 부사적 용법, ① 형용사적 용법, ④ 명사적 용법

17 사역동사 let+목적어+목적격보어(동사원형): ~이 …하게 하다

18 투명한 플라스틱병에 물을 채워 넣어야 하므로, 올바르게 이해하지 못한 사람은 성민이다.

19 install은 teaches와 병렬 구문이 아니라, how to make and how to install에서 중복되는 'how to'를 생략한 것이다.

20 ⓑ와 ⑤: 형용사적 용법, ①, ④: 명사적 용법, ②, ③: 부사적 용법

21 이 글은 My Shelter 재단의 여러 활약에 관한 글이므로, 주제로는 'My Shelter 재단의 놀랄 만한 활약들'이 가장 적절하다. remarkable: 놀랄 만한, 놀라운, 주목할 만한, long-lasting: 오래 지속되는

22 ⓐ와 ②번: 약, ~쯤(부사), ①, ③ …에 대한(전치사), ④ 주위에, 근처에, 가까이에(부사 = around), ⑤ …에 종사하여, …에 착수하여(전치사)

23 'Moser 램프'를 가리킨다.

24 Moser lamp를 만드는 데 얼마나 오래 걸리는지는 대답할 수 없다. ① A Moser lamp. ② Because in 2002, there were many blackouts in his town in Brazil. ③ No. ④ For about 10 years.

25 (A) 약 '10일' 동안이라고 해야 하므로 for가 적절하다. during+기간을 나타내는 명사, for+숫자, (B) 'make+목적어+목적격보어'의 형태로 쓰인 5형식 구문으로, 목적격보어의 자리에 형용사 happy를 쓰는 것이 적절하다. (C) 때를 나타내는 부사절에서는 현재시제가 미래시제를 대신하므로, grows가 적절하다.

26 뒤에 복수 명사가 나오므로 much로는 바꿔 쓸 수 없다.

27 First, Second, Finally 다음의 내용을 쓰는 것이 적절하다.

01 so, that, can't

02 because the houses are packed close together.

03 with using some electricity → without using any electricity

04 two thousand (and) two   05 A Moser lamp

06 (1) to make (2) making (3) this magic lamp

07 the My Shelter Foundation widely uses Moser lamps / the My Shelter Foundation uses Moser lamps widely

08 popularly → popular   09 Because of

10 A Moser lamp can be made for about one dollar and lasts for about 10 years.

11 (1) 1달러 정도로 만들 수 있다. (2) 10년 정도 지속된다. (3) 매우 안전하다. (4) 만드는 것이 매우 쉽다.

12 (A) widely (B) how (C) light up

13 to have Moser lamps

01 too+형용사+to부정사 = so+형용사+that+주어+cannot ...: 너무 ~하여 …할 수 없다

02 'are'를 보충하면 된다. be packed: 들어차다

03 천장에 플라스틱병 하나를 설치함으로써 '전기를 쓰지 않고' 방 전체를 밝힐 수 있다고 하는 것이 적절하다.

04 연도는 보통 두 자리씩 끊어서 읽지만, 2000년부터는 보통 'two thousand ~(미국식)', 'two thousand and ~(영국식)'로 읽는다.

05 'Moser 램프'를 가리킨다.

06 to부정사나 동명사를 주어로 해서 고치거나, make의 목적어인 this magic lamp를 주어로 해서 고치는 것이 적절하다.

07 부사 widely는 타동사 앞이나 목적어 뒤에 쓰는 것이 적절하다.

08 make+목적어+목적격보어'의 형태로 쓰인 5형식 구문으로, 목적격보어의 자리에 형용사를 쓰는 것이 적절하다.

09 이 정전들은 그가 집을 밝히는 새로운 방법을 생각해 내도록 만들었다. = 이 정전들 '때문에', 그는 집을 밝히는 새로운 방법을 생각해 냈다. Because of, Due to 등 이유를 나타내는 말을 쓰는 것이 적절하다.

10 'for'를 보충하면 된다.

11 두 번째 단락의 내용을 쓰는 것이 적절하다.

12 (A) 동사를 꾸며주므로 부사 widely가 적절하다. (B) '어떻게' 램프를 만드는지를 가르치는 것이므로 how가 적절하다. (C) 많은 사람들의 삶을 '밝혀 줄' 것이라고 해야 하므로 light up이 적절하다. light up: ~ 를 환하게 밝히다, lighten up: 기운 내다, lighten: (일·부채·걱정 등을) 가볍게 해주다, 밝아[환해]지다

13 가목적어, 진목적어 구문으로 고치는 것이 적절하다.

01 (i)nstall   02 hanger   03 ②   04 ⑤

05 (t)hings   06 ④   07 leftovers : 남은 음식

08 ③   09 ③   10 ③

11 Shake your hands before you use a paper towel.

12 ⑤   13 ⑤   14 plant

15 She thinks television is a waste of time, so she doesn't let her children watch TV.

16 (1) me happy (2) her nervous   17 ③

18 ⑤   19 ④   20 ①   21 ①

22 ②   23 using   24 ①, ⑤

25 Many blackouts   26 ②, ④   27 ⑤

28 bleach   29 (A) clear (B) a third (C) is bent

30 ④   31 ①, ④   32 your book holder

01 유의어 관계다. 외치다 : 설치하다

02 'hang'은 동사로 '걸다'는 뜻이고, 'hanger'는 명사로 '옷걸이'이다..

03 ① volume: 음량 / 음량을 줄여 주시겠어요? ② spread: 퍼뜨리다 / 다른 사람들에 대한 소문을 퍼뜨리지 마라. ③ leftovers: 남은 음식 / 낭비를 막기 위해 남은 음식을 집으로 가져가는 것이 좋다. ④ lamp: 램프, 등 / 어두울 때 등을 켜라. ⑤ forward: 앞으로 / 더 자세히 보기 위해 앞으로 가자.

04 마을 사람들은 너무나 가난해서 전기세를 낼 수가 없다. pay for: ~을 지불하다

05 'thing'은 '상황'이란 의미가 있다. 복수 동사 'are'가 사용이 되었으므로 복수형 'things'를 쓴다.

06 '~할 것을 잊지 마'라는 의미로 'forget to부정사'를 사용한다. 'forget -ing'는 '~한 것을 잊다'는 의미가 된다. ⓔ는 '내일까지'라는 시간의 부사구다.

07 영어 설명: 식사 후에 남은 음식

08 무엇을 할 것인지에 관한 물음에 '놀이동산에 갈 거야'라고 말하고 있으므로 (③)이 적절하다.

09 G의 '온갖 음식을 먹어 볼 거야.'라는 말에 '딤섬을 먹어 보는 걸 잊지 마.'라고 상기시켜 주는 말이 적절하다.

10 A가 '캔과 병을 재활용할 것을 잊지 마.'라고 말할 때 B가 '물론이야. 잊을게'라고 말하는 것은 어색하다. 'I won't.'가 적절하다.

11 질문: 유리는 Jaden에게 무엇을 제안했나요? 종이 수건을 사용하기 전에 손을 털라고 제안하고 있다.

12 유리가 하루에 얼마나 많은 종이 수건을 사용하는지는 대화에 언급되어 있지 않다.

13 목적어와 목적격보어의 관계가 수동이므로 과거분사를 써야 한다. He got his car washed yesterday.

14 사역동사의 목적격보어로 '나무를 심는' 능동의 의미가 필요하므로 원형부정사가 적절하다.

15 사역동사 let의 목적격보어로 목적어와의 관계가 능동일 경우 원형부사사를 쓴다.

16 (1), (2) 딸이 태어나서 행복했고, 사고에 대해 듣고 초조하게 되었으므로 동사 make를 이용하여 행복하게 만들고 초조하게 만들었다고 '주어+동사+목적어+목적격보어'의 형식으로 쓴다. 목적격보어로 형용사를 쓰는 것에 유의한다.

17 문맥에 맞게 형용사를 목적격보어로 받는 동사는 keep이다.

18 ⓒ My parents won't let me go out late at night. ⓓ It will help me (to) improve my English. ⓖ Eating an apple a day can make us healthy.

19 make는 5형식 문장에서 목적격보어로 명사, 형용사, 동사원형을 쓸 수 있다.

20 keep의 목적격보어로 형용사가 적절하다. clean은 동사로도 쓰이지만 형용사로도 쓰인다.

21 사역동사 have의 목적격보어로 목적어와의 관계가 능동이므로 원형부사사가 적절하다.

22 주어진 문장과 ②번의 make는 사역동사로 그 쓰임이 같다.

23 전치사 뒤에 동명사를 쓰는 것이 적절하다.

24 ⓐ와 ①, ⑤번: …와 (똑)같이[마찬가지로], …처럼(전치사), ② 비슷한(형용사), ③, ④: 좋아하다(동사)

25 2002년, 브라질에 있는 그의 마을의 '많은 정전들'이 그가 집을 밝히는 새로운 방법을 생각해 내도록 만들었다.

26 ⓑ와 ①, ③, ⑤: 명사적 용법, ② 형용사적 용법, ④ 부사적 용법

27 이 신기한 램프를 만드는 것은 매우 쉽다.

28 bleach: 표백제, 천을 하얗게 만들기 위해 사용되는 화학 물질

29 (A) keep+목적어+목적격보어(5형식): 목적격보어의 자리에 형용사를 써야 하므로 clear가 적절하다. (B) 분자가 2이상일 때부터 분모에 s를 붙이므로 a third가 적절하다. (C) 뒤에 by가 있고, 햇빛이 병 속의 물에 의해 '굴절된다'고 해야 하므로 수동태 is bent가 적절하다. bend: 구부러지다, 구부리다

30 위 글은 '병으로 Moser 램프를 만드는 법'에 관한 글이다.

31 ① 마지막으로, 끝으로(무엇을 열거하면서 마지막 요소 앞에 붙이는 말), ④ Finally: 마지막으로, 마침내, ②, ③: 마침내, ⑤: 결과적으로

32 '당신의 독서대'를 가리킨다.

단원별 예상문제   p.46~49

01 safe   **02** (A) packed   (B) Thanks to

03 ③   **04** ⑤   **05** ②

06 put my phone in a glass   **07** ①

08 Don't forget to turn off the light when you leave your room.

09 ⑤   **10** ④   **11** ①, ⑤   **12** ③, ④, ⑤

13 (1) This movie made the actors famous.
(2) My parents made me study hard.

14 wash → to wash

15 People in the village are too poor to pay for electricity.

16 (A) during   (B) packed   (C) any

17 ④, for   **18** ①, ③, ④   **19** ⑤

20 to keep the water clear[clean]

21 ④   **22** ②

23 The charity also teaches local people how to make and install the lamps.

24 ④

---

01 둘은 반의어 관계이다. 인기 있는 : 인기 없는 = 위험한 : 안전한

02 (A) packed: 꽉 들어찬 (B) thanks to: ~ 덕분에

03 물건을 청소하거나 사물에서 색을 제거하는 데 사용되는 강한 화학물질

04 '더 넓은 또는 증가하는 영역을 덮거나, 도달하거나, 영향을 미치다'라는 의미로 'spread(퍼지다)'가 적절하다.

05 ②번의 'turn up'은 '동사+부사'로 이루어진 이어동사로 인칭대명사가 목적어일 때는 '동사+대명사+부사'의 어순으로 써야 한다. 'turn up it'을 'turn it up'으로 고쳐야 한다.

06 '지금 해 보자'라는 말은 '휴대폰을 유리 속에 넣어 보자'는 것을 의미한다.

07 유명 여배우가 학교로 온다는 소식에 빨리 만나보고 싶다는 말이 자연스럽다.

08 '~하는 것을 잊지 마'는 'Don't forget to부정사'를 사용한다.

09 위의 대화에서 Yuri는 종이 수건을 한 장만 사용하는 방법에 대해 이야기하고 있다. 종이 수건을 사용하기 전에 손을 털면 '종이 수건 한 장이면 충분할 거야'라는 말이 자연스럽다.

10 손을 말리기 위해 종이 수건 한 장만 사용할 수 있다는 말에 적어도 두세 장의 종이 수건이 필요하다고 했기 때문에 ⓓ는 'impossible'이 적절하다.

11 ② Let him join your club. ③ He made me introduce myself. ④ She had Mike call me.

12 ① We found the window broken. ② I saw him sing[singing] in front of students.

13 (1) '주어+동사+목적어+목적격보어(형용사)'의 어순으로 쓴다.
(2) 사역동사의 목적격보어로 동사원형을 쓴다.

14 get은 목적격보어로 to부정사가 적절하다.

15 too+형용사+to부정사: 너무 ~하여 …할 수 없다

16 (A) during+기간을 나타내는 명사, while+주어+동사, (B) pack은 '(사람, 물건으로) 빽빽히 채우다'는 뜻이므로, 수동태로 써서 '빽빽하게 들어차 있다'고 하는 것이 적절하다. be packed: 들어차다, (C) '전기를 쓰지 않고'라는 부정의 뜻이 되어야 하는데, 빈칸 앞에 without이 있으므로 부정을 나타내는

'no'를 또 쓰는 것은 적절하지 않다.

17 about one dollar는 행위자가 아니라 '1달러 정도'라는 뜻이므로, for로 고치는 것이 적절하다.

18 ⓐ와 ②, ⑤번: 가주어, ① 목적어, ③ 가목적어, ④ 비인칭 주어

19 '제작 방법'은 알 수 없다. ① Moser lamp, ② Alfredo Moser, ③ 2002년, 브라질에 있는 Alfredo Moser의 마을에는 정전이 잦았기 때문에, 그가 집을 밝히는 새로운 방법을 생각해 내게 되었다. ④ 1달러 정도

20 keep+목적어+목적격보어(5형식): 목적격보어의 자리에 형용사를 쓰는 것이 적절하다.

21 Moser lamp를 설치하는 데 얼마나 오래 걸리는지는 대답할 수 없다. ① We need a clear plastic bottle, water, and some bleach. ② To keep the water clear. ③ In the roof. ⑤ Sunlight is bent by the water in the bottle and spreads around the room. operate: 작동되다

22 'ⓐ와 ②번: 재단, ①, ④: (일의 바탕이 되는) 토대[기반/근거], ③, ⑤: 설립, 창립, National Foundation Day: 건국기념일

23 'how'를 보충하면 된다. also는 일반동사 앞에 쓰는 것이 적절하다.

24 필리핀의 '수천' 가구가 이제 Moser 램프를 갖게 해주었다.

서술형 실전문제   p.50~51

01 I've heard that we can save trees by using less paper.

02 Just shake your hands before you use a paper towel.

03 Don't forget to try the fruit there

04 (1) I didn't want to go to my cousin's birthday party, but my mom made me go.

  (2) They had their house painted.

  (3) The present made the children happy all day long.

05 (1) The noise kept me awake.

  (2) He found the exam difficult.

  (3) These blackouts made him come up with a new way to light his house.

  (4) He had his computer repaired yesterday.

  (5) Help me (to) take some pictures of them.

06 People call this amazing plastic bottle a Moser lamp

07 blackouts   08 very safe

09 the My Shelter Foundation

10 thousand → thousands

---

02 just로 동사 shake를 수식하여 just shake로 문장을 시작한다 (명령문). '~ 전에'라는 접속사 before 뒤에 '주어+동사' 어순으로 'you use a paper towel'을 쓴다.

03 '~할 것을 잊지 마'라는 뜻으로 상대방에게 해야 할 일을 상기시켜 줄 때 'Don't forget to부정사'를 사용한다.

04 (1) make의 목적격보어로 목적어와의 관계가 능동이므로 원형부정사를 쓴다. (2) had의 목적격보어는 목적어와의 관계가 수동이므로 과거분사를 쓴다. (3) '주어+동사+목적어+목적격보어(형용사)'의 어순으로 쓴다.

05 (1) 동사 keep의 목적격보어로 동사원형이 아닌 형용사가 적절하다. (2) 동사 find의 목적격보어로 부사가 아닌 형용사가 적절하다. (3) 사역동사 make의 목적격보어로 목적어와의 관계가 능동이므로 원형부정사를 써야 한다. (4) 사역동사 have의 목적격보어로 목적어와의 관계가 수동이므로 과거분사를 써야 한다. (5) help는 목적격보어로 동사원형이나 to부정사가 나오며 뜻의 차이는 없다.

06 People을 주어로 해서 고치는 것이 적절하다.

07 blackout: 정전, 어떤 지역에 대한 전기 공급이 일시적으로 끊기는 기간

08 Moser 램프는 절대 집에 불을 낼 수 없기 때문에, '매우 안전하다'고 말할 수 있다.

09 'My Shelter 재단'을 가리킨다.

10 thousands of+명사: 수천의 ~, cf. hundred, thousand, million 등의 단어가 숫자 뒤에서 단위로 사용될 때는 단수형으로만 사용한다. e.g. two hundred, three million

창의사고력 서술형 문제   p.52

|모범답안|

01 (1) A: I'm going to go to Gyeongju.

    B: Don't forget to visit the National Museum.

    A: O.K., I won't forget.

  (2) A: I'm going to go on a field trip.

    B: Don't forget to take something to eat.

    A: O.K., I won't forget.

02 (1) Mom made me do the dishes this morning.

  (2) The doctor made him stop smoking.

  (3) Miranda made her husband buy some fruit.

03 (A) wire hanger   (B) bend

  (C) both ends   (D) top part   (E) free

단원별 모의고사   p.53~56

01 ⑤   02 (1) hole   (2) wire   03 ②

04 (a)mazing   05 ④   06 ④

07 ⑤   08 ④

목적격보어가 있는 5형식이다.

09 her parents, winter break, amusement park, food, dim sum

10 heard, movie star, favorite actress, played, chief

11 ③

12 shake our hands before we use a paper towel

13 me happy   14 ①

15 (1) tidily → tidy (2) plant → planted

16 ③   17 to have → have   18 ②

19 (A) the Philippines (B) because (C) because of

20 No, it doesn't.

21 because Alfredo Moser invented it

22 to come → come

23 The My Shelter Foundation does.   24 ⑤

01 ⑤번은 'widely'에 관한 설명이다. 'surprisingly'에 대한 영어 설명은 'unexpectedly or in a way that is unusual(예상치 못하거나 특이한 방식으로)'이다.

02 (1) hole: 구멍 (2) wire: 전선

03 병들거나 가난하거나 집이 없기 때문에 어려움에 처한 사람들에게 무료로 돈, 음식 또는 도움을 주는 시스템, 또는 이런 식으로 돈과 도움을 제공할 목적을 가지고 있는 단체

04 '매우 놀라운'의 의미를 가진 'amazing'이 적절하다.

05 그가 누군지 묻는 B의 말에 '말해주지 않을 거야.'라고 말하고 있으므로 빈칸에는 '놀라게 할 거야!'라는 'It's a surprise!'가 적절하다.

06 식사를 마쳤는지 묻는 말에 (C) 정말 맛있었다고 답하고, (B) 남은 음식을 집으로 가져가고 싶은지 묻고 (A) 부탁한다고 말하고 나서 마지막으로 (D) 내일까지 남은 음식 먹으라고 상기시켜주는 말을 하는 것이 자연스럽다.

07 전기를 절약하는 방법에 관한 대화로, 방을 떠날 때 불을 끄는 것을 잊지 마라는 의미가 적절하다. 'enter'를 'leave'로 바꾸어야 한다.

08 다음 달에 체육관이 개장한다는 말에 '그렇게 할게. 고마워.'라고 답하는 것은 어색하다.

11 Jaden이 종이 컵 사용을 줄일 수 있다고 말하고 있으므로 종이를 덜 사용하는 것에 대한 내용이 오는 것이 적절하다.

12 손을 말리기 위해서 어떻게 종이 수건 한 장만 사용할 수 있는가? → 종이 수건을 사용하기 전에 손을 털라고 말하고 있다.

13 make 동사로 '주어+동사+목적어+목적격보어(형용사)'의 형식을 이용한다.

14 사역동사의 목적어와 목적격보어가 수동의 관계에 있을 경우 목적격보어로 과거분사를 쓴다..

15 (1) 동사 keep의 목적격보어로 부사가 아닌 형용사가 적절하다. (2) 사역동사의 목적어와 목적격보어가 수동의 관계에 있을 경우 목적격보어로 과거분사를 쓴다.

16 ③은 4형식으로 쓰였고 주어진 문장과 나머지는 모두 목적어와

17 사역동사의 목적격보어로 동사원형이 적절하다.

18 too+형용사+to부정사: 너무 ~하여 …할 수 없다

19 (A) 나라 이름이 복수형일 때는 the를 붙여야 하므로 the Philippines가 적절하다. (B)와 (C) 'because+주어+동사', 'because of+명사'이므로 (B)는 because가, (C)는 because of가 적절하다.

20 천장에 있는 플라스틱병 하나는 '전기를 쓰지 않고' 방 전체를 밝힐 수 있다.

21 Alfredo Moser를 주어로 해서 고치는 것이 적절하다.

22 사역동사 make+목적어+목적격보어(동사원형)

23 'My Shelter 재단' 덕분에, 필리핀의 수천 가구가 이제 Moser 램프를 갖고 있다. enable+목적어+to부정사: (사람에게) ~할 수 있게 하다

24 '그 단체(My Shelter 재단)'가 아르헨티나, 인도, 피지와 같은 다른 나라들에서도 Moser 램프가 인기가 있도록 만들었다.

Have Fun This Winter!

01 rescue   02 ⑤   03 ②   04 ④

05 ③   06 ⑤   07 ③

08 in the relay

01 둘은 유의어 관계이다. 갈라지다, 구하다

02 매년 3월 초에 알래스카(Alaska)에서는 세계 최대의 개썰매 경주가 열린다(take place).

03 1925년의 어느 추운 겨울날, 놈 마을에서는 끔찍한 일이 일어났다. 몇몇 아이들이 매우 아팠고 병(disease)이 계속 퍼졌다.

04 '위험하거나, 해롭거나, 불쾌한 상황에서 나오도록 누군가나 어떤 것을 돕다'라는 의미로 'rescue(구조하다)'가 적절하다.

05 모든 경쟁자들이 가장 빠르고 먼저 끝내려고 하는 시합

06 'trail'은 '코스, 흔적, 오솔길'의 의미이다.

07 '각 팀은 앵커리지(Anchorage)에서 놈(Nome)까지 약 1,800 km를 달려야 한다.'는 뜻으로 '이동하다'는 'travel'이 적절하다.

08 'be in the relay'는 '릴레이에 참가하다'는 의미다.

01 (1) continue, 계속하다   (2) disease, 질병
   (3) sled, 썰매

02 (1) kept spreading   (2) right away

03 (1) often   (2) memory

04 (1) sled   (2) reach   (3) medicine

05 (1) broadcasts   (2) highlights

01 (1) 계속 일어나거나, 존재하거나, 무언가를 하거나, 혹은 무언가나 누군가가 이런 일을 하게 하다 (2) 사고에 의해서라기보다는 감염이나 건강 쇠약으로 야기되는 사람, 동물, 식물 등이 아픈 것 (3) 길고 좁은 나무 조각이나 금속 조각으로 눈과 얼음 위를 여행하는 데 사용되는 물체

02 (1) keep -ing: 계속해서 ~하다, spread를 동명사로 바꾸어 준다. (2) 'right away'가 '당장'의 뜻이다. 같은 표현으로 'right now', 'at once' 등이 있다.

03 (1) 자주: often (2) 기념, 기억: memory

04 (1) 내 남동생은 썰매 타는 것을 좋아한다. (2) 메인 가에 도착할 때까지 곧장 가세요. (3) 이 약을 먹으면 곧 좋아질 거야.

05 (1) 라디오나 TV에 나오는 프로그램 (2) 어떤 것의 가장 좋거

나 가장 흥미진진하거나, 재미있거나 흥미로운 부분

[해석] 오후 6시에서 11시까지 하는 MBS Sports의 경기 생중계를 꼭 보세요. 또한 매일 밤 11시에, 여러분은 그날 가장 흥미진진했던 경기의 하이라이트를 즐길 수 있습니다.

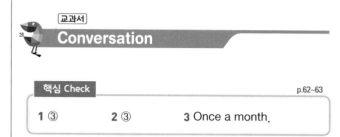

1 ③   2 ③   3 Once a month.

1 T   2 T   3 T   4 F

Listen & Speak 1-A

(1) What, doing / listening to / do you like / I'm not interested in, to sing, favorite / what a nice

(2) Are you interested in watching, be sure to watch, every night, enjoy, highlights, the most interesting

Listen & Speak 2-A

(1) favorite / go swimming / How often, go swimming / Not very often, go swimming once a month

(2) any special plans / to play / How often / Every weekend, How about / like playing, outdoor

Communicate A

special plans, winter break / to go, place, go skating, sledding / Good, favorite / never played, I'm interested in learning, to play / how to play / awesome, the most popular / Everyone, loves, playing / How often, when / at least, three times / I'm sure, good at, can't wait to

Communicate B

What winter sport, interested in / interested in / How often do / once, a month

Progress Check

(1) playing / not interested in, to pass / Good luck

(2) favorite / listen to / How often / Almost

(3) It's, to show, How often, tell, that

시험대비 기본평가
p.68

01 ④ 　　　　02 ②
03 what a nice granddaughter! 　　04 ④

01 B의 마지막 말이 빈도를 나타내는 'Not very often.'이므로 빈 칸의 질문은 빈도를 묻는 말이 적절하다.

02 '오래된 팝송들을 좋아하니?'라는 물음에 'No'로 대답하고 있기 때문에 부정문이 적절하고, old pop songs는 복수 명사로 대명사 'them'으로 나타내는 것이 적절하다.

03 형용사와 명사가 있을 때 What으로 시작하는 감탄문을 사용한다. 'What+a(n)+형용사+명사+주어+동사' 어순으로 영작한다.

04 'How often do you ~?'는 '얼마나 자주 ~을 하니?'라는 빈도를 물을 때 사용한다.

시험대비 실력평가
p.69~70

01 ④
02 Do you have any special plans for this weekend
03 ②　　　04 ③　　　05 ⑤
06 favorite　07 ④　　　08 ⑤
09 Are you interested in watching the Winter
　Olympics?　　　10 ③

01 'A: 얼마나 자주 라디오를 듣니?'라는 물음에 'B: '2시간 동안.' 이라는 대답은 자연스럽지 못하다. 'For two hours.'는 'How long do you listen to the radio?'에 대한 답으로 적절하다.

02 미래 계획을 묻는 표현으로 'Do you have any plans ~?'를 이용한다.

03 G가 '탁구 하는 걸 정말 좋아하거든. 너는 어때?'라는 말에 '축구하는 걸 좋아해.'라고 말하고 있으므로 빈칸에는 '야외 스포츠를 즐겨.'가 적절하다.

04 B의 대답이 '스포츠를 많이 좋아하지는 않지만, 가끔 수영하러 가.'라는 말에서 G의 빈칸은 스포츠를 좋아하는지 묻는 말이 가장 적절하다.

05 감탄문에서 how를 이용할 경우는 'How+형용사(+주어+동사)~!' 어순을 취하고, what은 'What+a(n)+형용사+명사(+주어+동사)~!' 어순을 취한다. how를 what으로 고쳐야 한다.

06 '가장 좋아하거나 가장 즐기는'의 뜻을 가지는 'favorite'가 적절하다.

07 빈칸 다음에 Anna가 '어떻게 하는지 가르쳐 줄 수 있어.'라고 말하고 있으므로 Suho가 아이스하키를 하는 법을 배우는 데에는 관심이 있다는 ④번이 가장 적절하다.

08 대화의 내용에는 한국에서 인기 있는 겨울 스포츠에 대한 것은 없다.

09 '~에 관심이 있다'는 'be interested in' 표현을 쓴다. 전치사 in 뒤에는 동사 watch를 동명사 watching으로 써야 한다.

10 (a)는 형용사 '생방송인, 실황의' 뜻을 가진 'live'가 적절하고, (b)는 그날의 가장 흥미로운 경기의 '하이라이트'가 적절하다. 'spotlight'는 '환한 조명'이란 뜻이다.

서술형 시험대비

p.71

01 She plays table tennis every weekend.
02 How often do you play?
03 I'm interested in learning how to play it
04 Everyone I know loves watching it and playing it.
05 I love them every day

01 질문: 하나는 어떤 스포츠를 하며 얼마나 자주 하는가?

02 'How often do you ~?'는 '얼마나 자주 ~을 하니?'라는 빈도를 물을 때 사용한다.

03 'I'm interested in'을 쓰고, in 뒤에 동명사 learning을 사용한다. learning의 목적어로 how to play it을 쓴다.

04 Everyone이 주어, 'I know'가 'everyone'을 수식하는 관계 대명사절 역할을 한다. everyone이 주어라 단수 동사 loves가 오고 love의 목적어로 동명사 watching과 playing을 쓴다.

05 질문: 당신은 얼마나 자주 가족 모두에게 사랑한다고 말해 주나요?

교과서

Grammar

핵심 Check
p.72~73

1 (1) draw　(2) opening　(3) injured
2 (1) to draw　(2) to open　(3) to listen

시험대비 기본평가
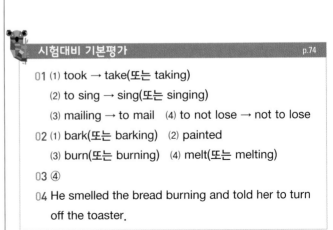
p.74

01 (1) took → take(또는 taking)
　(2) to sing → sing(또는 singing)
　(3) mailing → to mail　(4) to not lose → not to lose
02 (1) bark(또는 barking)　(2) painted
　(3) burn(또는 burning)　(4) melt(또는 melting)
03 ④
04 He smelled the bread burning and told her to turn
　off the toaster.

01 (1), (2) 지각동사의 목적어가 목적격보어의 행위의 주체가 될 경우 목적격보어로 원형부정사나 현재분사를 쓰는 것이 적절하다. (3) ask의 목적격보어로 to부정사가 적절하다. (4) to부정사의 부정형은 'not to 동사원형'으로 쓴다.

02 (1) 지각동사의 목적격보어는 목적어와의 관계가 능동일 경우 원형부정사나 현재분사가 쓰인다. (2) 지각동사의 목적격보어는 목적어와의 관계가 수동일 경우 과거분사가 쓰인다. (3) 그것이 타는 것이므로 burnt가 아닌 burn 또는 burning이 적절하다. (4) 눈이 녹는 것이므로 능동의 의미를 나타내는 melt 또는 melting이 적절하다. melt: 녹다, 용해하다

03 tell의 목적격보어로 to부정사가 적절하다.

04 to를 추가하여 목적격보어로 현재분사를 쓰고 tell의 목적격보어로 to부정사를 쓴다.

시험대비 실력평가   p.75~77

01 ⑤   02 ②, ④   03 ①

04 We heard Kate sing[singing] a lovely song.

05 ③

06 (1) sing (2) meeting (3) popping (4) burning (5) fix (6) to continue (7) to close (8) not to

07 ③   08 reads → to read   09 ③, ④

10 ②   11 ④   12 ③

13 him go[going] out   14 ④

15 (1) to fall → fall(또는 falling)
(2) uploaded → upload(또는 uploading)
(3) to check → check (4) clean → to clean
(5) helped → to help (6) bringing → to bring

16 to search   17 ③

18 (1) Alex often hears birds sing[singing] on his way to school.
(2) I smell something burning.
(3) He asked me to marry him.

01 목적어와의 관계가 능동이므로 지각동사의 목적격보어로 원형부정사 혹은 현재분사가 적절하고 want의 목적격보어로 to부정사가 적절하다.

02 hear는 지각동사이므로 목적격보어로 원형부정사 혹은 현재분사, 과거분사를 받는다. someone이 우는 주체가 되므로 cry 또는 crying이 적절하다.

03 ask의 목적격보어로 to부정사가 적절하다.

04 지각동사 hear의 목적어와 목적격보어의 관계가 능동이므로 목적격보어로 원형부정사 혹은 현재분사를 쓰는 것이 적절하다.

05 advise의 목적격보어로 to부정사가 적절하다. The doctor advised him not to smoke and drink.

06 (1)~(3) 지각동사 hear, see, listen to의 목적격보어로 현재분사나 원형부정사가 적절하다. (4) smell은 목적격보어로 현재분사가 적절하다. (5) make는 사역동사이므로 목적격보어로 원형부정사가 적절하다. (6), (7) tell, ask의 목적격보어로 to부정사가 적절하다. (8) 목적격보어로 쓰인 to부정사의 부정형은 'not to 동사원형'으로 쓴다.

07 지각동사 hear의 목적격보어이므로 현재분사나 원형부정사가 적절하다.

08 want의 목적격보어로 to부정사가 적절하다.

09 목적어와의 관계가 능동이므로 지각동사의 목적격보어로 원형부정사 혹은 현재분사가 적절하다.

10 want의 목적격보어로 to부정사가 적절하다.

11 지각동사 watch의 목적격보어로 원형부정사 혹은 현재분사가 적절하다. I watched him sleep[sleeping] soundly on the sofa. soundly: (수면 상태가) 푹, 깊이

12 (A) 지각동사의 목적어와 목적격보어의 관계가 능동이므로 현재분사가 적절하다. (B) 지각동사의 목적어와 목적격보어의 관계가 능동이므로 원형부정사가 적절하다. (C) 동사 find의 목적어와 목적격보어의 관계가 수동이므로 과거분사가 적절하다.

13 Edan이 나가는 소리를 들었다는 의미이다. 목적어와 목적격보어의 관계가 능동이므로 원형부정사 또는 현재분사로 써야 한다.

14 make는 사역동사이므로 목적격보어로 동사원형이 나와야 하며 나머지는 모두 목적격보어로 to부정사가 나와야 한다.

15 (1), (2) 지각동사의 목적격보어로 원형부정사나 현재분사가 적절하다. (3) 사역동사 have의 목적격보어로 원형부정사가 적절하다. (4) want의 목적격보어로 to부정사가 적절하다. (5) ask의 목적격보어로 to부정사가 적절하다. (6) tell의 목적격보어로 to부정사가 적절하다.

16 ask의 목적격보어로 to부정사가 적절하다.

17 주어진 문장과 ③번은 명사적 용법으로 목적격보어로 쓰였다. ① 부사적 용법(원인) ② 명사적 용법(보어) ④ 명사적 용법(진주어) ⑤ 형용사적 용법

18 (1) 지각동사의 목적격보어로 원형부정사나 현재분사를 이용한다. (2) smell은 목적격보어로 현재분사를 쓴다. (3) ask의 목적격보어로 to부정사를 쓴다.

서술형 시험대비   p.78~79

01 (1) Alex usually gives a hand when he sees someone carry[carrying] something heavy.
(2) A neighbor finally heard the dog bark(barking) and called 911.
(3) Tim just felt the ground shake[shaking].
(4) He heard his name called.
(5) The Greek general ordered a soldier to tell the people of Athens about their victory.
(6) Years of training enabled him to win the match.

(7) I expect you to keep good company when you go abroad.

02 to be careful

03 We watched a man running outside.

04 (1) to come (2) not to forget (3) to clean
   (4) to eat (5) to be

05 listen(또는 listening)

06 (1) to be (2) painted (3) touch[touching]
   (4) carry

07 (1) I heard someone call[calling] my name.
   (2) Kate smelled something burning.
   (3) Jake found his brother using his phone.
   (4) He got very angry when he came back and saw it stolen.
   (5) Our teacher always tells us to come to school on time.
   (6) He will not permit me to take part in it.
   (7) I asked him not to close the door.
   (8) She let me play computer games.

08 allowed him to watch TV

01 (1)~(3) 지각동사의 목적어와 목적격보어의 관계가 능동이므로 목적격보어로 원형부정사 혹은 현재분사가 적절하다 (4) 지각동사의 목적어와 목적격보어의 관계가 수동이므로 과거분사가 적절하다. (5)~(7) order, enable, expect의 목적격보어로 to부정사가 적절하다.

02 ask는 목적격보어로 to부정사를 쓴다.

03 지각동사 watch의 목적어가 목적격보어의 행위의 주체이므로 목적격보어로 원형부정사나 현재분사를 쓸 수 있지만 진행형의 문장이므로 목적격보어로 현재분사가 더 적절하다.

04 want, warn, order, advise, encourage의 목적격보어로 to부정사가 나오며 to부정사의 부정은 'not to 동사원형'이다.

05 지각동사 see의 목적어 a girl과 목적격보어의 관계가 능동이므로 목적격보어로 원형부정사나 현재분사가 적절하다.

06 (1) tell은 to부정사를 목적격보어로 받는다. (2) 지각동사의 목적어와 목적격보어의 관계가 수동일 때 목적격보어로 과거분사가 적절하다. (3) 지각동사의 목적어와 목적격보어의 관계가 능동일 때 목적격보어로 원형부정사나 현재분사가 적절하다. (4) 사역동사 have는 원형부정사를 목적격보어로 받는다.

07 (1) 지각동사의 목적어와 목적격보어의 관계가 능동이므로 원형부정사가 적절하다. (2) smell은 목적격보어로 현재분사가 적절하다. (3) '그의 동생이 전화기를 사용하고 있는 것'이므로 목적격보어로 현재분사가 적절하다. (4) 지각동사의 목적어와 목적격보어의 관계가 수동이므로 과거분사가 적절하다. (5), (6) tell, permit, ask는 목적격보어로 to부정사를 쓴다. (7) to부정사의 부정형은 'not to 동사원형'으로 쓴다. (8) let은 사역동사이므로 목적격보어로 동사원형을 쓴다.

08 allow는 목적격보어로 to부정사를 쓴다.

Reading

확인문제   p.80

1 T   2 F   3 T   4 F

확인문제   p.81

1 T   2 F   3 T   4 F   5 F

교과서 확인학습 A   p.82~83

01 Most   02 takes place
03 It is called   04 take part in
05 has to cover
06 take, race through snowstorms
07 in memory of   08 a terrible thing happened
09 kept spreading
10 right away, did not have any
11 had to get it   12 to get the medicine
13 the race to Nome   14 in the relay
15 the others, at different points
16 of the 20th team   17 made, his lead dog
18 so, that, could not 19 However, stay on the trail
20 frozen   21 cracking
22 was saved, just in time
23 reached   24 to continue on
25 Here's, shouted   26 On, arrived in
27 was saved
28 is now celebrated, the biggest sled dog race

교과서 확인학습 B   p.84~85

1 The Most Heart-Warming Winter Sport
2 In early March every year, the world's biggest sled dog race takes place in Alaska.
3 It is called the Iditarod Trail Sled Dog Race.
4 Around 80 teams of 12 to 16 dogs take part in this race.
5 Each team has to cover about 1,800 km from Anchorage to Nome.
6 The race can take more than two weeks, and the teams often race through snowstorms.
7 The Iditarod Race began in 1973 in memory of the dogs that saved Nome.
8 One cold winter day in 1925, a terrible thing happened in Nome.

9 Some children got very sick, and the disease kept spreading.

10 The people of Nome needed medicine right away, but the town did not have any.

11 Someone had to get it from a hospital in Anchorage.

12 Because of the heavy snow, a dog sled relay was the only way to get the medicine from Anchorage to Nome.

13 Soon, the race to Nome began.

14 Twenty-one dog teams were in the relay.

15 On January 27, the first team left, and the others waited at different points.

16 Gunnar was the driver of the 20th team.

17 The strongest dog on his team was Balto, so he made Balto his lead dog.

18 When Gunnar and Balto finally got the medicine, the snow was so heavy that Gunnar could not see his own hands.

19 However, Balto was able to stay on the trail.

20 When they were crossing a frozen river, Balto suddenly stopped.

21 Then, Gunnar saw the river ice cracking.

22 The whole team was saved because Balto stopped just in time.

23 When Balto and Gunnar reached the final team, they were sleeping.

24 Gunnar told Balto to continue on.

25 "Here's the medicine, Doctor!" shouted Gunnar.

26 On February 2, Gunnar and his team finally arrived in Nome.

27 The town was saved.

28 This heart-warming story is now celebrated every year by the Iditarod Race, the biggest sled dog race in the world.

시험대비 실력평가
p.86~89

01 is taken → takes　　　　02 ④

03 the Iditarod Trail Sled Dog Race　　　　04 ⑤

05 ②　　　　06 to continue

07 Gunnar saw the river ice cracking.

08 saved → was saved　　　　09 spreading

10 ②　　　11 ③　　　12 ①, ④

13 Because he slipped and broke his neck.

14 to rescue him　　　　15 ③

16 Because it snowed heavily

---

17 The strongest dog on his team was Balto, so he made Balto his lead dog.

18 (A) In　(B) km　(C) take

19 People[They] call it the Iditarod Trail Sled Dog Race.

20 ③　　　　21 ⑤

22 It's the biggest sled dog race in the world.

23 ⑤　　　　24 ①　　　　25 ⓐ so　ⓑ that

26 One of the gorillas

27 looked after 또는 cared for

---

01 take place는 자동사로 쓰이므로 수동태는 적절하지 않다. take place: 개최되다[일어나다]

02 ⓑ와 ④번: 약 …, …쯤(부사), ① 사방에(서), 빙 둘러(부사), ②둥글게, 빙돌아(전치사), ③ 이리저리, 여기저기(부사), ⑤ 둘레에, 주위에(전치사)

03 '아이디타로드 개썰매 경주'를 가리킨다.

04 아이디타로드 경주는 '놈'을 구한 개들을 기념하여 1973년에 시작되었다.

05 Gunnar는 자신의 손조차도 볼 수 없었다. '그러나', Balto는 코스를 제대로 따라갈 수 있었다라고 하는 것이 적절하다. ① 게다가, ③ 결과적으로, ④ 예를 들면, ⑤ 이렇게 하여, 그러므로

06 tell+목적어+to부정사

07 지각동사 see는 목적격보어로 동사원형이나 현재분사가 올 수 있으나, 여기서는 진행 중이므로 현재분사가 적절하다.

08 놈 마을 사람들의 목숨이 구해진 것이므로 수동태로 쓰는 것이 적절하다.

09 keep ~ing: 계속해서 ~하다

10 ②번 다음 문장의 it에 주목한다. 주어진 문장의 medicine을 가리키므로 ②번이 적절하다.

11 이 글은 폭설로 인해 '앵커리지에서 놈으로 약을 가져오는 유일한 방법이었던 개썰매 릴레이'에 관한 글이다.

12 ⓐ와 ②, ③, ⑤는 부사적 용법, ① 형용사적 용법, ④ 명사적 용법

13 미끄러져서 목이 부러졌기 때문이다.

14 to his rescue: 그를 구하기 위해

15 ③ 밀접하게, 친밀하게, 나머지는 모두 '즉시, 당장'

16 because of+명사(구), because+절

17 'so'는 접속사로 쓰여 '그래서'의 의미로 결과의 절을 이끈다. make+목적어+목적격보어(명사): 목적어를 ~으로 만들다

18 (A) 월 앞에는 In을 쓰는 것이 적절하다. (B) 약자로 쓸 때는 앞에 복수 숫자가 나오더라도 km으로 쓰고, 풀어 쓰면 kilometers를 쓰는 것이 적절하다. (C) 2주 이상 '걸릴 수' 있다고 해야 하므로 take가 적절하다. spend: (시간을 어떻게·어디서) 보내다, 지내다(주어는 보통 사람), take: (얼마의 시간이) 걸리다

15

19 People이나 They를 주어로 해서 고치는 것이 적절하다.

20 ⓑ와 ③번: <어떤 일정한 거리를> 가다, ① (감추거나 보호하기 위해) 씌우다[가리다], ② 다루다, 포함시키다, ④ (텔레비전, 신문 등을 위해) 취재[방송/보도]하다, ⑤ (비용 등을) 충당하다, (보험을 걸어서) 보호하다

21 ⓐ on the trail: (특정 목적을 위한) 루트[코스]를 따라가는, ⓑ continue on: 계속하다 ⓒ 날짜가 있으면 on을 쓰는 것이 적절하다.

22 '세계에서 가장 큰 개썰매 경주'이다.

23 이 글은 'Gunnar와 그의 팀의 가슴 따뜻한 이야기가 아이디타로드 경주를 통해 오늘날 매년 기념되고 있다.'는 내용의 글이므로, 제목으로는 'Iditarod Race의 기원'이 적절하다.

24 ① 언제 Gunnar와 Balto가 약을 받았는지는 대답할 수 없다. ② Because the snow was so heavy. ③ Because they were sleeping. ④ On February 2. ⑤ Yes.

25 so+형용사+that절: 너무 ~해서 …하다

26 '고릴라들 중의 한 마리'를 가리킨다.

27 take care of = look after = care for: ~을 돌보다

서술형 시험대비   p.90~91

01 is held
02 one thousand (and) eight hundred kilometers
03 too, to   **04** reached   **05** Nome   **06** On
07 nineteen twenty-five   **08** must → had to
09 (A) Because of   (B) the others   (C) so
10 medicine
11 (A) dog sled relay   (B) twenty-one dog teams
12 to crack → cracking
13 The Iditarod Race, the biggest sled dog race in the world, now celebrates this heart-warming story every year.

---

01 take place = be held: 열리다

02 km를 풀어 쓰면 kilometers라고 쓰는 것이 적절하다.

03 so ~that 주어 can't ... = too ~ to ...: 너무나 ~해서 …할 수 없다

04 arrive in = reach: ~에 도착하다

05 'Nome'을 가리킨다.

06 날짜가 있으면 on을 쓰는 것이 적절하다.

07 연도는 보통 두 자리씩 끊어 읽는다. 십 단위와 단 단위 사이에는 보통 하이픈을 쓴다.

08 과거 시제로 써야 하므로 'must'의 과거 'had to'로 고치는 것이 적절하다.

09 (A) 'because of+명사(구)', 'because+절'이므로 Because of가 적절하다. (B) 나머지 전체를 나타낼 때는 'the'를 써야 하므

로 the others가 적절하다. (C) 'as+주어+동사: ~이기 때문에', 'so+주어+동사: 그래서'의 의미로 결과의 절을 이끌므로, so가 적절하다.

10 당장 약이 필요했지만, 마을에는 '약'이 하나도 없었다.

11 놈의 사람들이 당장 약이 필요했을 때, '개썰매 릴레이'가 앵커리지에서 놈으로 약을 가져오는 유일한 방법이었다. 곧, 놈으로 향하는 질주가 시작되었고 '21개의 개 팀'이 릴레이에 참여했다.

12 지각동사 see는 목적격보어로 동사원형이나 현재분사가 올 수 있으나 진행중인 한 시점을 가리킬 때는 현재분사를 써야 한다.

13 The Iditarod Race, the biggest sled dog race in the world를 주어로 해서 고치는 것이 적절하다.

영역별 핵심문제   p.93~97

01 reach   **02** take, snowstorm   **03** ①
04 in memory of   **05** ④   **06** ②
07 I have an interest in ice skating.
08 I go once or twice a month.
09 ③   **10** ④   **11** ①   **12** ⑤
13 ③   **14** ⑤   **15** go(또는 going)
16 ②   **17** ③
18 (1) He looked at the baby sleeping on the bed.
    (2) I heard Amy locking her room.
19 (1) Do you want me to believe that false story?
    (2) Can you ask him to return the book to the library tomorrow?
    (3) I heard somebody cry[crying] while I took a walk to the park.
    (4) I saw Ann wait[waiting] for a bus at the bus stop.
20 ⑤   **21** around   **22** ④
23 ④   **24** ②   **25** ⑤
26 Balto was able to stay on the trail.   **27** ③, ⑤
28 (A) excited   (B) gorillas   (C) falling   **29** caught

---

01 유의어 관계이다. 외치다 : 도착[도달]하다

02 take+시간: 시간이 걸리다, snowstorm: 눈보라

03 ① lead: 선두 / 카 레이서는 선두 차량을 따라잡기 위해 더 빨리 운전하기 시작했다. ② polar: 북극의 / 북극곰은 크고 희다. ③ heart-warming: 가슴 따뜻한 / 그녀는 가슴 따뜻한 이야기를 듣고 울었다. ④ terrible: 끔찍한 / 어젯밤에 끔찍한 꿈을 꾸었다. ⑤ victory: 승리 / 우리의 승리는 영원히 기억될 것이다.

04 in memory of: ~을 기념하여

05 폭설 때문에 개썰매 릴레이가 앵커리지에서 Nome으로 약을 가져오는 유일한 방법이었다. / 명사 'the heavy snow'가 있기 때문에 접속사 because는 적절하지 않다.

06 '가주어(It) ~ 진주어(to부정사) …' 구문으로 ⓑ의 동사

'show'를 'to show'로 바꾸어야 한다. ⓓ는 목적격 관계대명사고, ⓔ는 'everyone in your family'를 가리키는 대명사다.

07 '~에 관심이 있다'는 'have an interest in ~' = 'be interested in ~' 등으로 나타낼 수 있다.

09 A가 '어떤 TV프로그램에 관심이 있니?'라고 묻는 말에 B가 '한국의 역사와 문화에 매료되었어.'라고 말하는 것은 어색하다.

10 James가 '스포츠는 좋아하지 않지만 때대로 수영하러 가.'라고 말하는 것을 보아 (A)에는 무엇에 관심이 있는지를 묻는 말이 적절하다.

11 얼마나 자주 수영을 가는지 묻는 말에 'Not very often(그렇게 자주는 아니야.)'라고 말하고 있으므로 ①번이 적절하다.

12 Anna의 답에서 일주일에 두세 번 경기를 한다고 했으므로 빈칸은 얼마나 자주 무엇을 하는지 묻는 말이 적절하다.

13 수호가 일주일에 두세 번 스케이트를 타러 가는지 대화에 언급되어 있지 않다.

14 첫 문장에는 목적격보어로 현재분사가 나와야 한다. 두 번째 문장에서 want의 목적격보어로 to부정사가 적절하다.

15 지각동사의 목적어가 목적격보어의 행위의 주체가 될 경우 목적격보어로 원형부정사나 현재분사를 쓴다.

16 I watched her talk[talking] on the phone.

17 주어진 문장과 ③번은 목적격보어로 쓰인 현재분사이다. 각각 ① 분사구문, ② 진행형을 만드는 현재분사, ④와 ⑤는 동명사이다.

18 지각동사의 목적어와 목적격보어의 관계가 능동이며, 진행형으로 쓰이고 있으므로 목적격보어로 현재분사를 이용한다.

19 (1), (2) want와 ask는 목적격보어로 to부정사가 나와야 한다. (3), (4) hear, see의 목적어와 목적격보어의 관계가 능동이므로 현재분사나 원형부정사가 적절하다.

20 (A) from A to B: A부터 B까지, (B) through snowstorms: 눈보라를 뚫고

21 about = around: 약 …, …쯤(부사)

22 ④ 경주의 우승팀이 경주를 끝내는 데 얼마나 오래 걸리는지는 대답할 수 없다. ① In early March every year. ② It is called the Iditarod Trail Sled Dog Race. ③ Around 80 teams of 12 to 16 dogs do. ⑤ In 1973.

23 나머지 전체를 나타낼 때는 'the'를 써야 하므로 the others가 적절하다.

24 ⓐ와 ②, ⑤: 형용사적 용법, ①, ④: 부사적 용법, ③: 명사적 용법

25 1월 27일에 첫 번째 팀이 출발했고, 나머지 팀들은 '서로 다른' 지점에서 기다렸다.

26 on the trail: (특정 목적을 위한) 루트[코스]를 따라가는

27 finally = at last = in the end = in the long run: 마침내[드디어] ③ 적어도, ⑤ 실제로, 정말로

28 (A) 감정을 나타내는 동사는 수식받는 명사가 감정을 느끼게 되

는 경우에 과거분사를 써야 하므로 excited가 적절하다. (B) '~ 중의 하나'는 'one of the 복수명사'로 써야 하므로 gorillas가 적절하다. (C) 지각동사 see는 목적격 보어로 동사원형이나 현재분사가 올 수 있으므로 falling이 적절하다.

29 과거시제로 쓰는 것이 적절하다.

단원별 예상문제   p.98~101

01 awesome
02 (A) lead (B) frozen
03 ③
04 ②
05 ③
06 It's important to help these poor people at Christmas.
07 ④
08 old pop songs, grandma's favorite, birthday party
09 ④
10 I'll go skating and sledding there.
11 ②
12 ②
13 ③
14 ③
15 ④
16 I saw Jake play[playing] basketball.
17 ④
18 Around 80 teams of 12 to 16 dogs take part in this race.
19 over
20 ①, ④
21 was happened → happened
22 Gunnar
23 ④
24 His dog
25 ④

01 반의어 관계이다. 인기 있는 : 인기 없는 = 끔찍한 : 멋진, 굉장한

02 (A) lead: 선두 (B) frozen: 얼어붙은

03 '표면에 금이 가게 하거나 조각으로 부수기 위해 무언가를 깨다'의 의미로 'crack(갈라지다)'이 적절하다.

04 '더 넓은 또는 증가하는 영역을 덮거나, 도달하거나, 영향을 미치다'라는 의미로 'spread(퍼지다)'가 적절하다.

05 (C) 어떤 운동에 관심이 있는지 묻는 말에 대한 응답으로 (A) 아이스 스케이팅에 관심이 있다고 답하고, (B) 그것을 얼마나 자주하는지 묻고 그에 대한 응답 (D)가 마지막에 오는 것이 적절하다.

06 '가주어 ~ 진주어' 구문을 이용하여 'It is important to help ~'로 문장을 시작한다.

07 B의 답으로 보아 라디오를 듣는 빈도를 묻는 말이 적절하다.

08 소녀는 다음 주 할머니의 생일 파티에서 할머니가 가장 좋아하는 노래를 불러주기 위해 오래된 팝송을 듣고 있다.

09 everyone은 단수 취급하므로 동사 'love'를 단수 동사인 'loves'로 바꾸어야 한다.

10 '~하러 가다'는 의미로 'go –ing'를 이용한다.

11 첫 번째 문장에서는 지각동사의 목적격보어로 원형부정사나 현재분사가 적절하다. 두 번째 문장에서는 '형용사[부사]+enough+to 동사원형(= so+형용사[부사]+that+주어+can ...)' 구문이 적절하다.

12 지각동사의 목적어와 목적격보어의 관계가 능동일 경우 목적격보어로 원형부정사나 현재분사를 쓴다.

13 encourage의 목적격보어로 to부정사가 적절하다.

14 첫 번째 빈칸은 tell의 목적격보어로 to부정사를 쓴다. 두 번째 빈칸에는 지각동사의 목적격보어로 원형부정사나 현재분사를 쓴다.

15 ⓑ We never allow our children to play with toy guns. ⓓ I want you to come to my birthday party. ⓕ We watched an old man run[running] outside. ⓖ We were so surprised to see the snow falling[fall] from the sky.

17 ask의 목적격보어로 to부정사가 적절하다.

18 'to'를 보충하면 된다. 12 to 16: 12 내지 16, 12~16

19 more than = over: ~ 이상

20 ⓒ와 ①, ④번: 관계대명사, ②, ③, ⑤: 접속사

21 happen은 수동태로 쓸 수 없는 자동사이다.

22 'Gunnar'를 가리킨다.

23 Gunnar가 왜 20번째 팀의 몰이꾼이었는지는 대답할 수 없다. ① One cold winter day in 1925. ② No. ③ Twenty-one dog teams were in it. ⑤ Balto.

24 '그의 개'를 가리킨다.

25 그의 개가 19시간 동안 짖고 또 짖었다.

---

04 ask, tell은 목적격보어로 to부정사를 쓴다.

05 지각동사의 목적어와 목적격보어의 관계가 능동이므로 목적격보어로 원형부정사나 현재분사가 적절하다.

06 keep ~ing: 계속해서 ~하다

07 이유를 나타내는 접속사 as, because, since 등을 쓰는 것이 적절하다.

08 (A) '건너고 있을 때'라고 해야 하므로 crossing이 적절하다. (B) reach는 타동사이므로 전치사 없이 reached로 쓰는 것이 적절하다. (C) '가슴을 따뜻하게 하는' 이야기라는 뜻이므로 heart-warming이 적절하다.

09 just in time: 바로 제때

10 모든 어려움에도 불구하고 Gunnar와 그의 팀은 마침내 놈에 도착해서 놈 마을 사람들의 목숨을 '구할 수' 있었다. 이 가슴 따뜻한 이야기는 세계에서 가장 큰 개썰매 경주인 아이디타로드 경주를 통해 오늘날 매년 '기념되고' 있다.

🐰 창의사고력 서술형 문제   p.104

|모범답안|

01 (1) A: How often do you clean your room?
    B: I clean my room once a week.
  (2) A: How often do you wash your hands?
    B: I wash my hands very often.
  (3) A: How often do you play the piano?
    B: I play the piano three times a day.

02 (1) I saw a lady ride[riding] a bike.
  (2) I watched a girl eat[eating] a piece of pizza.
  (3) I saw a boy take[taking] a picture.
  (4) I looked at a man wait[waiting] for someone.

03 (A) at a zoo   (B) over the wall   (C) falling
  (D) took care of

🐢 서술형 실전문제   p.102~103

01 How often did you play ice hockey when you were in Canada?

02 go skating, sledding, during, ice hockey, learning how to play, how to play

03 (A) What TV programs are you interested in?
  (B) How often do you watch them?

04 (1) her dad to order pizza   (2) to wear suncream

05 (1) Did you hear Julia close[closing] the door?
  (2) Ms. Park saw her son read[reading] a book.

06 Some children got very sick, and the disease kept spreading.

07 As[Because]

08 (A) crossing   (B) reached   (C) heart-warming

09 just in time   **10** (A) saved   (B) celebrated

---

01 '얼마나 자주 ~을 하니?'는 'How often do you ~?' 형태이고, Anna의 대답에서 played라고 과거시제를 사용하고 있으므로 'How often did you play ~?'를 사용한다. when은 접속사로 '주어+동사' 어순으로 쓴다.

03 (A) 의문형용사 'what'이 명사 TV programs를 수식하는 역할을 한다. (B)는 '얼마나 자주 ~을 하니?'는 'How often do you ~?' 형태를 사용한다.

🐇 단원별 모의고사   p.105~108

01 ④   **02** (1) special (2) slipped   **03** ②

04 ⓐ frozen ⓑ cracking   **05** ③   **06** ④

07 ⑤   **08** ②

09 doesn't like, swimming once, month

10 table tennis, this weekend, every weekend

11 He is interested in learning how to play ice hocky.

12 I can't wait to learn from you.

13 ②   **14** ①

15 (1) He felt someone look[looking] at him.
  (2) I told him to bring his passport.

16 (1) to walk → walking[walk]
  (2) cried → cry[crying]   (3) speaking → spoken
  (4) listening → to listen   (5) being not → not to be

17 fix[fixing] / fixed

18 the world's biggest sled dog race　　　19 ②, ⑤

20 ④　　　　　21 ⑤, on

22 (A) terrible　(B) any　(C) 20th

23 was saved

24 the snow was so heavy that Gunnar could not see his own hands

25 ②

---

01 ④번은 'relay'에 관한 설명이다. 'race'에 대한 영어 설명은 'a competition in which all the competitors try to be the fastest and to finish first(모든 경쟁자들이 가장 빠르고 먼저 끝내려고 하는 시합)'이다.

02 (1) special: 특별한 (2) slip: 미끄러지다, 과거형이기 때문에 '단모음+단자음'으로 끝나는 단어는 자음을 한 번 더 쓰고 –ed 를 붙인다.

03 '긴 줄 또는 누군가 혹은 무언가에 의해 남겨진 일련의 표시'란 의미로 '흔적, 코스'를 의미하는 'trail'이 적절하다.

04 ⓐ는 '얼어붙은'의 의미를 가진 'frozen'을 쓰고, ⓑ는 '지각동 사(saw)+목적어+현재분사(cracking)'를 사용한다.

05 '얼마나 자주 탁구를 치니?'라는 말에 빈도를 나타내는 답이 적절 하다.

06 오래된 팝송을 좋아한다는 긍정의 답 다음에 오래된 팝송에 관심 이 있다는 말이 오는 것이 적절하다.

07 빈칸 다음에 '단지 다음 주에 있는 배드민턴 시험에 통과하고 싶 어.'라고 말하고 있으므로 배드민턴에 관심이 없다는 부정의 말이 적절하다.

08 얼마나 자주 패스트푸드를 먹는지 묻는 말에 패스트푸드를 먹는 것은 건강에 좋지 않다고 말하는 것은 자연스럽지 못하다.

11 수호는 아이스하키를 하는 방법을 배우는 데 관심이 있다.

12 '빨리 ~하고 싶다'는 표현은 'I can't wait to부정사'를 사용한 다.

13 advise의 목적격보어로 to부정사가 적절하다.

14 지각동사의 목적어와 목적격보어가 능동의 관계에 있을 경우 목 적격보어로 원형부정사나 현재분사를 쓴다.

15 (1) 지각동사의 목적어와 목적격보어가 능동의 관계에 있을 경 우 목적격보어로 원형부정사나 현재분사를 쓴다. (2) tell의 목 적격보어로 to부정사를 쓴다.

16 (1), (2) 지각동사의 목적어와 목적격보어가 능동의 관계에 있 을 경우 목적격보어로 원형부정사나 현재분사를 쓴다. (3) 지각 동사의 목적어와 목적격보어가 수동의 관계에 있을 경우 목적격 보어로 과거분사를 쓴다. (4), (5) want, tell의 목적격보어로 to부정사가 적절하다. to부정사의 부정형은 'not to 동사원형' 으로 쓴다.

17 그가 내 컴퓨터를 고치는 주체이므로 현재분사나 원형부정사를 쓰고, 내 컴퓨터가 '고쳐진 것'이므로 과거분사 fixed를 쓰는 것

이 적절하다.

18 '세계 최대의 개썰매 경주'를 가리킨다.

19 take part in = participate in = join: ~에 참여〔참가〕하다, ① (특히 미리 준비되거나 계획된 일이) 개최되다[일어나다], ③, ④: (일·과제·의무 등을) 행하다[수행하다/실시하다]

20 개의 품종은 알 수 없다. ① 매년 3월 초, ② 알래스카, ③ 12~16마리 개로 구성된 80여 팀, ⑤ 1973년

21 '소속'을 나타내는 'on'으로 고치는 것이 적절하다.

22 (A) '끔찍한' 일이 일어났다고 해야 하므로 terrible이 적절하 다. terrific: 아주 좋은, 멋진, (B) 부정문이므로 any가 적절하 다. (C) '20번째' 팀이라고 해야 하므로 20th가 적절하다.

23 목숨이 구해진 것이므로 수동태로 쓰는 것이 적절하다.

24 'so'를 보충하면 된다.

25 Balto는 코스를 제대로 따라갈 수 있었다.

교과서 파헤치기

Lesson 7

단어 TEST Step 1   p.02

01 단 하나의	02 주요한; 우두머리, 부장
03 어둠, 암흑	04 퍼지다 05 전기
06 재단	07 놀이공원 08 대규모 정전 사태
09 주거지, 쉼터	10 불가능한 11 천장
12 널리, 폭넓게	13 구부리다, 휘다 14 자선단체
15 설치하다	16 외치다 17 발명하다
18 흔들다, 털다	19 마법의, 신기한 20 남은 음식
21 전체의	22 표백제 23 충분한
24 꽉 들어찬	25 인기 있는 26 놀랍게도
27 남아 있다	28 지붕 29 안전한
30 마을	31 작동하다 32 구하다
33 더 적은	34 놀라운 35 지불하다
36 최소한, 적어도	37 ~을 환하게 밝히다
38 더 이상 ~ 않다	39 ~할 것을 잊다 40 (소리 등을) 높이다
41 ~ 덕분에	42 ~을 생각해 내다, ~을 만들어 내다
43 ~와 꼭 마찬가지로	

단어 TEST Step 2   p.03

01 bend	02 ceiling	03 shake
04 charity	05 darkness	06 difficult
07 whole	08 blackout	09 widely
10 leftover	11 chief	12 less
13 impossible	14 shout	15 electricity
16 single	17 work	18 save
19 amusement park		20 foundation
21 roof	22 magic	23 shelter
24 village	25 popular	26 install
27 remain	28 safe	29 last
30 surprisingly	31 bleach	32 packed
33 enough	34 invent	35 light up
36 thanks to	37 not ~ anymore	
38 dry off	39 pay for	40 forget to부정사
41 come up with	42 turn up	43 fill A with B

단어 TEST Step 3   p.04

1 last, 지속되다   2 village, 마을   3 roof, 지붕
4 leftover, 남은 음식   5 blackout, 정전   6 save, 구하다
7 ceiling, 천장   8 popular, 인기 있는   9 lamp, 램프, 등
10 spread, 퍼지다   11 invent, 발명하다
12 bleach, 표백제   13 install, 설치하다

14 daytime, 낮   15 electricity, 전기
16 charity, 자선, 자선단체

대화문 TEST Step 1   p.05~06

Listen & Speak 1-A

1. turn up / turn it up anymore, highest / Let, put, I've heard, works like / What an interesting idea, Let's
2. I've heard, is coming / right, favorite actress / played, chief scientist / can't wait to see

Listen & Speak 2-A

1. finished, meal / good / want to take, leftovers / please / Don't forget to eat
2. your plan for, winter break / I'm going to, with my parents / sounds exciting, going to do / going to go, amusement / to try all kinds / Don't forget to try

Communicate A

What's wrong / difficult / have to / a way to save / I've heard that, can save, by using less / I've heard that, too, stop using paper cups / can also use, to dry off / impossible, at least / shake, before, more than enough / try, next time / don't forget to shake, at least, times

Communicate B

I've heard, saving electricity, best way to save / heard that, too, save electricity / Why don't, turn off, when / Don't forget, turn off, when, leave

Progress Check

1. I've heard that, is coming / my favorite player / not going to, surprise
2. plan for, winter break / to visit, with / sounds exciting, going / spend, beach, seafood / Don't forget to try / won't forget

대화문 TEST Step 2   p.07~08

Listen & Speak 1-A

1. G: Can you turn up the volume on your phone? I like this song.
   B: I can't turn it up anymore. It's the highest volume.
   G: Let me just put your phone in a glass. I've heard a glass works like a speaker.
   B: What an interesting idea! Let's try it now.
2. B: I've heard that a movie star is coming to our school.

G: That's right. She's my favorite actress.

B: Oh, who is she?

G: Miranda Kim. She played the chief scientist in the movie *Jupiter*.

B: Wow, I can't wait to see her!

1. W: Excuse me, are you finished with your meal?

M: Yes, it was really good.

W: Do you want to take the leftovers home?

M: Yes, please.

W: Don't forget to eat the leftovers by tomorrow.

2. B: What's your plan for this winter break?

G: I'm going to visit Hong Kong with my parents.

B: That sounds exciting. What are you going to do there?

G: I'm going to go to an amusement park. I'm also going to try all kinds of food.

B: Good. Don't forget to try some dim sum.

Yuri: What's wrong, Jaden?

Jaden: My science homework is too difficult.

Yuri: What do you have to do?

Jaden: I need to find a way to save trees.

Yuri: That's easy. I've heard that we can save trees by using less paper.

Jaden: Oh, I think I've heard that, too. Then, I can just stop using paper cups.

Yuri: Yes! You can also use just one paper towel to dry off your hands.

Jaden: That's impossible. I need at least two or three paper towels.

Yuri: Just shake your hands before you use a paper towel. Then, one will be more than enough.

Jaden: Oh, that's a good idea, Yuri! I'll try that next time.

Yuri: Good! Just don't forget to shake your hands at least 10 times.

A: I've heard that saving electricity is the best way to save the Earth.

B: I've heard that, too. What can we do to save electricity?

A: Why don't we turn off the light when we're not using it?

B: That's a good idea. Don't forget to turn off the light when you leave your room.

1. B: I've heard that a famous baseball player is coming to our school.

G: That's right. He's my favorite player.

B: Oh, who is he?

G: I'm not going to tell you. It's a surprise!

2. B: What's your plan for this winter break?

G: I'm going to visit Vietnam with my parents.

B: That sounds exciting. What are you going to do there?

G: I'm going to spend some time on the beach and eat lots of seafood.

B: Good. Don't forget to try the fruit there, too.

G: O.K., I won't forget.

01 One-Dollar, Lamps   02 read, shouted, village

03 electricity, like, other, village

04 too, to pay

05 during, daytime, because, packed

06 things, because of, single

07 light up, without using

08 called, because, invented by

09 there were, blackouts

10 come, with, way, light

11 made for, lasts, about

12 also, safe   13 never start, fire

14 Surprisingly, easy, make

15 How, make, from   16 Fill, clear, with

17 Add, to keep, clear

18 roof, push, into, hole   19 Let, third, remain above

20 is bent, spreads around

21 in, widely used by   22 charity, local, how, install

23 Thanks to, thousands of

24 has, made, other, such

25 light up, for, years

01 One-Dollar Magic

02 shouted, in the Philippines

03 has no electricity, all the other houses

04 too, to pay for electricity

05 during, because, are packed close together

06 are changing because of

07 in the ceiling, light up, without using

08 is called, because, was invented by

09 were many blackouts

10 come up with, way to light

11 be made for, lasts for about

12 very safe　　　　13 never start

14 to make　　　　15 How to make

16 Fill, with

17 Add, bleach to keep, clear

18 push, into　　　19 a third, remain above

20 is bent by, spreads around

21 are widely used

22 The charity, how to make, install

23 Thanks to, thousands of

24 has, made, other countries, such as

25 light up, for many years to come

---

1 1달러짜리 마법의 전구

2 "우와, 이젠 제 방에서 책을 읽을 수 있어요!" 필리핀의 한 마을에 사는 소년인 Marco가 외쳤다.

3 그의 집은 마을의 다른 모든 집들과 마찬가지로 전기가 없다.

4 마을 사람들은 너무나 가난해서 전기세를 낼 수가 없다.

5 심지어 낮 동안에도, 집들이 빽빽하게 들어차 있어서 그들은 어둠 속에 살아간다.

6 이제 플라스틱병 하나 때문에 상황이 바뀌고 있다.

7 천장에 있는 플라스틱병 하나는 전기를 쓰지 않고 방 전체를 밝힐 수 있다.

8 이 놀라운 플라스틱병은 Moser 램프라고 불리는데, 그것이 Alfredo Moser에 의해 발명되었기 때문이다.

9 2002년, 브라질에 있는 그의 마을에는 정전이 잦았다.

10 이 정전들은 그가 집을 밝히는 새로운 방법을 생각해 내도록 만들었다.

11 Moser 램프는 1달러 정도로 만들 수 있고 10년 정도 지속된다.

12 그것은 또한 매우 안전하다.

13 그것은 절대 집에 불을 낼 수 없다.

14 놀랍게도, 이 신기한 램프를 만드는 것은 매우 쉽다.

15 병으로 Moser 램프를 만드는 법

16 1. 투명한 플라스틱병에 물을 채운다.

17 2. 물을 깨끗이 유지하기 위해 표백제를 조금 넣는다.

18 3. 지붕에 구멍을 내고, 병을 구멍 안으로 넣는다.

19 4. 병의 3분의 1은 지붕 위에 남아 있도록 한다.

20 5. 햇빛이 병 속의 물에 의해 굴절되어 방에 퍼진다.

21 필리핀에서 Moser 램프는 My Shelter 재단에 의해 널리 사용된다.

22 또한 그 자선단체는 지역 사람들에게 램프를 만들고 설치하는 법을 가르친다.

23 이 자선단체 덕분에, 필리핀의 수천 가구가 이제 Moser 램프를 갖고 있다.

---

24 그 단체는 아르헨티나, 인도, 피지와 같은 다른 나라들에서도 Moser 램프가 유명해 지도록 만들었다.

25 Moser 램프는 앞으로 오랫동안 많은 사람들의 삶을 밝혀 줄 것이다.

---

1 One-Dollar Magic Lamps

2 "Wow, I can read a book in my room now!" shouted Marco, a boy in a village in the Philippines.

3 His house has no electricity just like all the other houses in the village.

4 People in the village are too poor to pay for electricity.

5 Even during the daytime, they live in darkness because the houses are packed close together.

6 Now things are changing because of a single plastic bottle.

7 One plastic bottle in the ceiling can light up a whole room without using any electricity.

8 This amazing plastic bottle is called a Moser lamp because it was invented by Alfredo Moser.

9 In 2002, there were many blackouts in his town in Brazil.

10 These blackouts made him come up with a new way to light his house.

11 A Moser lamp can be made for about one dollar and lasts for about 10 years.

12 It is also very safe.

13 It can never start a house fire.

14 Surprisingly, it is very easy to make this magic lamp.

15 How to make a Moser lamp from a bottle

16 1. Fill a clear plastic bottle with water.

17 2. Add some bleach to keep the water clear.

18 3. Make a hole in the roof, and push the bottle into the hole.

19 4. Let a third of the bottle remain above the roof.

20 5. Sunlight is bent by the water in the bottle and spreads around the room.

21 In the Philippines, Moser lamps are widely used by the My Shelter Foundation.

22 The charity also teaches local people how to make and install the lamps.

23 Thanks to the charity, thousands of homes in the Philippines now have Moser lamps.

24 It has also made Moser lamps popular in other countries, such as Argentina, India, and Fiji.

25 Moser lamps will light up the lives of many people for many years to come.

구석구석지문 TEST Step 1 p.19

Link-Share
1. make the lamp brighter
2. out of, another lamp
3. All the other steps
4. learned that, brighter than

Write
1. a lot of, with
2. can even make
3. fill half of, put, into
4. close, all of the sides
5. Finally, it, for about
6. is ready
7. make you happ

Culture Project-Share
1. like to talk
2. keeps food fresh
3. It, to make
4. put, inside
5. pour, between
6. let, dry off, cool

Culture Project-Share
1. We'd like to talk about a pot-in-pot cooler.
2. It keeps food fresh without electricity.
3. It 's very easy to make one.
4. First, put a pot inside a larger pot.
5. Then, pour sand and water between these pots.
6. Just let the water dry off, and it'll cool the food.

구석구석지문 TEST Step 2 p.20

Link-Share
1. We thought we could make the lamp brighter with a glass bottle.
2. We made one lamp out of a plastic bottle and another lamp out of a glass bottle.
3. All the other steps were the same.
4. We learned that the glass bottle lamp was brighter than the plastic bottle lamp.

Write
1. You can make a lot of things with a CD case.
2. You can even make a grass container.
3. First, fill half of the CD case with soil and water, and put grass seeds into the soil.
4. Second, close the case and tape all of the sides.
5. Finally, leave it in the sun for about ten days.
6. Now, your grass container is ready.
7. It will make you happy when the grass grows.

Lesson **8**

단어 TEST Step 3

1 snowstorm, 눈보라 2 terrible, 끔찍한
3 spread, 퍼지다 4 take place, 개최되다, 일어나다
5 race, 경주 6 trail, 흔적, 코스 7 continue, 계속하다
8 cage, 우리 9 rescue, 구하다 10 medicine, 약
11 slip, 미끄러지다 12 reach, 도달하다 13 sled, 썰매
14 disease, 질병 15 crack, 금이 가다, 갈라지다
16 relay, 릴레이 경주, 계주

단어 TEST Step 1

01 (개가) 짖다 02 갈라지다, 금이 가다
03 외치다 04 굉장한, 엄청난 05 도달하다, 닿다
06 썰매 07 릴레이 경주, 계주 08 특별한
09 기념하다, 축하하다 10 조부모님 댁
11 구하다 12 가슴 따뜻한 13 눈보라
14 실외의 15 구하다, 구조하다
16 (사람들 사이로) 퍼지다 17 대략
18 얼어붙은 19 인기 있는
20 경주하다, 달리다; 경주, 질주
21 선두 개, 우두머리 개 22 가다, 이동하다
23 손녀, 외손녀 24 미끄러지다 25 코스, 흔적
26 방송 27 하이라이트, 가장 흥미로운 부분
28 언어 29 우리
30 발생하다, 일어나다 31 약
32 질병, 병, 질환 33 폭설 34 끔찍한
35 한 달에 한 번 36 개최되다, 일어나다
37 곧바로, 즉시 38 계속하다
39 ~에 참여[참가]하다
40 ~을 기념[추모]하여 41 계속 ~하다
42 반드시 ~하다 43 ~가 되다

대화문 TEST Step 1

p.24~25

Listen & Speak 1-A
1. What, doing / listening to / do you like / I'm not interested in, to sing, grandma's favorite songs / what a nice
2. Are you interested in watching, be sure to watch, live broadcasts, every night, enjoy, highlights, the most interesting

Listen & Speak 2-A
1. favorite / sometimes go swimming / How often, go swimming / Not very often, go swimming once a month
2. any special plans / going to play table tennis / How often, play / Every weekend, playing, How about / like playing, enjoy outdoor

Communicate A
special plans, winter break / to go, grandparents' place, go skating, sledding, winter sports / Good for, favorite / never played, I'm interested in learning, to play / how to play / awesome, the most popular / Everyone, loves, playing / How often, when / at least, three times / I'm sure, good at, can't wait to learn

Communicate B
What winter sport, interested in / interested in ice skating / How often do / once, twice a month

Progress Check
1. are, doing / practicing badminton / playing / not interested in, to pass, next week / Good luck
2. favorite / listen to / How often, listen to / Almost every day
3. It's, to show, How often, tell, that

단어 TEST Step 2

p.22

01 awesome 02 bark 03 heavy snow
04 crack 05 disease 06 language
07 slip 08 snowstorm 09 terrible
10 neck 11 frozen 12 happen
13 around 14 heart-warming 15 trail
16 race 17 celebrate 18 reach
19 spread 20 rescue 21 broadcast
22 cage 23 sled 24 medicine
25 outdoor 26 popular 27 save
28 shout 29 special 30 climb
31 live 32 go sledding 33 lead dog
34 granddaughter 35 take part in
36 in memory of 37 right away 38 keep -ing
39 take place 40 at least
41 be interested in 42 once a month
43 go on a trip

대화문 TEST Step 2

p.26~27

Listen & Speak 1-A
1. B: What are you doing?

G: I'm listening to old pop songs.

B: Oh, do you like old pop songs?

G: No, I'm not interested in them. I just want to sing my grandma's favorite songs at her birthday party next week.

B: Wow, what a nice granddaughter!

2. M: Are you interested in watching the Winter Olympics? Then, be sure to watch MBS Sports to enjoy our live broadcasts from 6 p.m. to 11 p.m. At 11 p.m. every night , you can also enjoy our highlights of the most interesting games of the day.

Listen & Speak 2-A

1. G: What's your favorite sport, James?

B: I don't like sports much, but I sometimes go swimming.

G: How often do you go swimming?

B: Not very often. I only go swimming once a month.

2. B: Do you have any special plans for this weekend, Hana?

G: Well, I'm going to play table tennis with my dad and brother.

B: How often do you play?

G: Every weekend. I love playing table tennis. How about you?

B: I like playing soccer. I enjoy outdoor sports.

Communicate A

Anna: Do you have any special plans for the winter break?

Suho: I'm going to go to my grandparents' place in Pyeongchang. I'll go skating and sledding there. I love winter sports.

Anna: Good for you! I love winter sports, too. My favorite is ice hockey.

Suho: Oh, I've never played ice hockey, but I'm interested in learning how to play it.

Anna: Really? I can teach you how to play.

Suho: That's awesome. Is ice hockey the most popular sport in Canada?

Anna: Yes, it is. Everyone I know loves watching it and playing it.

Suho: How often did you play ice hockey when you were in Canada?

Anna: I played at least two or three times a week in the winter.

Suho: Wow, I'm sure you're really good at ice hockey. I can't wait to learn from you.

Communicate B

A: What winter sport are you interested in?

B: I'm interested in ice skating.

A: How often do you go ice skating?

B: I go once or twice a month.

Progress Check

1. B: What are you doing?

G: I'm practicing badminton.

B: Do you like playing badminton?

G: No, I'm not interested in it. I just want to pass the badminton test next week.

B: O.K. Good luck!

2. G: What's your favorite TV show, Jason?

B: I don't watch TV, but I listen to the radio.

G: How often do you listen to the radio?

B: Almost every day.

3. M: It's important to show your love for the people around you. How often do you tell everyone in your family that you love them?

본문 TEST Step 1   p.28~29

01 The Most Heart-Warming

02 early, biggest, takes place

03 It is called   04 Around, to, part

05 has, cover, from

06 take, than, through snowstorms

07 in memory, saved   08 cold, terrible, happened

09 got, kept spreading

10 needed, right away, any

11 had to, from

12 Because, heavy, way, medicine

13 race, began   14 Twenty-one, in, relay

15 On, others, at, points

16 of, 20th team   17 strongest, made, lead

18 finally, so, that, own   19 However, stay, trail

20 crossing, frozen, stopped

21 saw, cracking   22 whole, because, just

23 reached, final, sleeping

24 told, continue on

25 Here's, medicine, shouted

26 On, arrived in   27 was saved

28 is, celebrated, biggest sled

본문 TEST Step 2   p.30~31

01 Most Heart-Warming

02 every year, biggest sled dog, takes place

03 It is called   04 Around, take part in

05 has to cover, from. to

06 take more than, race through snowstorms

07 in memory of   08 a terrible thing happened

09 got, sick, kept spreading

10 right away, did not have any

11 had to get it

12 Because of, to get the medicine

13 the race to Nome   14 in the relay

15 the others, at different points

16 of the 20th team

17 strongest dog, made, his lead dog

18 so, that, could not

19 However, able to stay on the trail

20 frozen, suddenly stopped

21 cracking   22 was saved, just in time

23 reached   24 to continue on

25 Here's, medicine, shouted

26 On, arrived in

27 was saved

28 is now celebrated, the biggest sled dog race

본문 TEST Step 3   p.32~33

1 가장 가슴 따뜻한 겨울 스포츠

2 매년 3월 초에 알래스카(Alaska)에서는 세계 최대의 개썰매 경주가 열린다.

3 그것은 아이디타로드 개썰매 경주(Iditarod Trail Sled Dog Race)라고 불린다.

4 12~16마리 개로 구성된 80여 팀이 이 경주에 참여한다.

5 각 팀은 앵커리지(Anchorage)에서 놈(Nome)까지 약 1,800 km를 달려야 한다.

6 이 경주는 2주 이상 걸릴 수 있으며, 팀들은 종종 눈보라를 뚫고 경주한다.

7 아이디타로드 경주는 놈을 구한 개들을 기념하여 1973년에 시작되었다.

8 1925년의 어느 추운 겨울날, 놈 마을에서는 끔찍한 일이 일어났다.

9 몇몇 아이들이 매우 아팠고 병이 계속 퍼졌다.

10 놈의 사람들은 당장 약이 필요했지만 마을에는 약이 하나도 없었다.

11 누군가는 앵커리지에 있는 병원에서 약을 가져와야 했다.

12 폭설 때문에 개썰매 릴레이가 앵커리지에서 놈으로 약을 가져오는 유일한 방법이었다.

13 곧, 놈으로 향하는 질주가 시작되었다.

14 21개의 개 팀이 릴레이에 참여했다.

15 1월 27일에 첫 번째 팀이 출발했고, 나머지 팀들은 서로 다른 지점에서 기다렸다.

16 Gunnar는 20번째 팀의 몰이꾼이었다.

17 그의 팀에서 가장 강한 개는 Balto였기 때문에, 그는 Balto를 그의 선두 개로 삼았다.

18 Gunnar와 Balto가 마침내 약을 받았을 때, 눈발이 너무 거세서 Gunnar는 자신의 손조차도 볼 수 없었다.

19 그러나, Balto는 코스를 제대로 따라갈 수 있었다.

20 그들이 얼어붙은 강을 건너고 있을 때 Balto는 갑자기 멈췄다.

21 그때, Gunnar는 강의 얼음이 갈라지는 것을 보았다.

22 Balto가 바로 제때 멈췄기 때문에 팀 전체가 목숨을 구할 수 있었다.

23 Balto와 Gunnar가 마지막 팀에 다다랐을 때, 그들은 자고 있었다.

24 Gunnar는 Balto에게 계속 가라고 말했다.

25 "여기 약이 있습니다, 의사 선생님!"이라고 Gunnar가 소리쳤다.

26 2월 2일에 Gunnar와 그의 팀은 마침내 놈에 도착했다.

27 놈 마을 사람들은 목숨을 구할 수 있었다.

28 이 가슴 따뜻한 이야기는 세계에서 가장 큰 개썰매 경주인 아이디타로드 경주를 통해 오늘날 매년 기념되고 있다.

본문 TEST Step 4 - Step 5   p.34~37

1 The Most Heart-Warming Winter Sport

2 In early March every year, the world's biggest sled dog race takes place in Alaska.

3 It is called the Iditarod Trail Sled Dog Race.

4 Around 80 teams of 12 to 16 dogs take part in this race.

5 Each team has to cover about 1,800 km from Anchorage to Nome.

6 The race can take more than two weeks, and the teams often race through snowstorms.

7 The Iditarod Race began in 1973 in memory of the dogs that saved Nome.

8 One cold winter day in 1925, a terrible thing happened in Nome.

9 Some children got very sick, and the disease kept spreading.

10 The people of Nome needed medicine right away, but the town did not have any.

11 Someone had to get it from a hospital in Anchorage.

12 Because of the heavy snow, a dog sled relay was the only way to get the medicine from Anchorage to Nome.

13 Soon, the race to Nome began.

14 Twenty-one dog teams were in the relay.

15 On January 27, the first team left, and the others waited at different points.

16 Gunnar was the driver of the 20th team.

17 The strongest dog on his team was Balto, so he made Balto his lead dog.

18 When Gunnar and Balto finally got the medicine, the snow was so heavy that Gunnar could not see his own hands.

19 However, Balto was able to stay on the trail.

20 When they were crossing a frozen river, Balto suddenly stopped.

21 Then, Gunnar saw the river ice cracking.

22 The whole team was saved because Balto stopped just in time.

23 When Balto and Gunnar reached the final team, they were sleeping.

24 Gunnar told Balto to continue on.

25 "Here's the medicine, Doctor!" shouted Gunnar.

26 On February 2, Gunnar and his team finally arrived in Nome.

27 The town was saved.

28 This heart-warming story is now celebrated every year by the Iditarod Race, the biggest sled dog race in the world.

구석구석지문 TEST Step 2　　　　　　　p.39

Link-Share

1. Are you interested in learning the history of the marathon?

2. The first marathon was run by Pheidippides in 490 B.C.

3. The Greek army in Marathon ordered him to tell the people of Athens about their victory.

4. He ran 40 km from Marathon to Athens.

Write

1. One cold winter day, a man left home to get wood for a fire.

2. He slipped and broke his neck.

3. He could not move, but no one was near him.

4. His dog came to his rescue.

5. She barked and barked for 19 hours.

6. A neighbor finally heard the dog barking and called 911.

Culture Project-Share

1. Every winter, you can see many people jumping into the sea at Haeundae Beach.

2. It's a way of wishing for good health in the New Year.

구석구석지문 TEST Step 1　　　　　　　p.38

Link-Share

1. Are, interested in learning

2. was run by, B.C

3. ordered him to tell

4. ran, from, to

Write

1. left, to get wood

2. slipped, broke his neck

3. not move, no one, near

4. came to his rescue

5. barked and barked for

6. heard the dog barking, called

Culture Project-Share

1. Every winter, see many people jumping

2. a way of wishing

MEMO

적중100

영어 기출 문제집

정답 및 해설

미래 | 최연희